New Feminist Library

*Dedicated to the memory of Sarah Eisenstein, 1946–1978,
activist, scholar, friend*

Editorial Board

Sheila Rowbotham

Friends of
ALICE WHEELDON

Introduction by
by Sandi Cooper and Blanche Wiesen Cook

Monthly Review Press
New York

First published in Great Britain 1986 by Pluto Press

Copyright © 1987 by Sheila Rowbotham

Library of Congress Cataloging-in-Publication Data

Rowbotham, Sheila.
  Friends of Alice Wheeldon/Sheila Rowbotham.
    p. cm.
  Bibliography: p.
  Includes index.
  ISBN 0-85345-729-8 : $26.00. ISBN 0-85345-728-X (pbk.) : $10.00
  1. Wheeldon, Alice. 2. Feminists—Great Britain—Biography.
3. Socialists—Great Britain—Biography. 4. Wheeldon, Alice—Drama.
5. World War, 1914–1918—Drama. 6. Feminism—Great Britain—
History. I. Title.
HQ1593.W46R68   1987
305.4′2′0941—dc 19   87-31261
                                                 CIP

Monthly Review Press
122 West 27th Street
New York, N.Y. 10001

Printed in U.S.A.

10 9 8 7 6 5 4 3 2 1

Contents

Preface and Acknowledgments

Alice Wheeldon and her daughter Hettie lived in the Midlands railway town of Derby. They had both been suffragettes in the Women's Social and Political Union (WSPU) and were socialists. During the First World War they opposed conscription; their home in London Road and Alice's second-hand clothes business in Pear Tree Road became safe havens for conscientious objectors on the run.

They were friendly with William (or Willie) Paul, a member of the Socialist Labour Party, a small Marxist group linked to the American socialist Daniel de Leon. Willie lived in nearby Littleover, and Alice had helped him to start a clothes stall in Derby market.

Hettie, who taught Scripture in Ilkeston, was courting Willie's friend, Arthur MacManus. He was one of the Clydeside shop stewards (rank-and-file delegates) who had been deported from Glasgow by the government, and was working at Cunard's in Liverpool. Arthur, also a member of the SLP, was helping the Wheeldons to smuggle conscientious objectors across the sea to Ireland and America.

In December 1916, a man who called himself Alex Gordon sought shelter with Alice. He claimed to be a conscientious objector on the run and he introduced her to Comrade Bert, who said he was a member of the revolutionary syndicalist group, the Industrial Workers of the World (the British group of the Wobblies).

'Alex Gordon' was, in fact, F. Vivian and 'Comrade Bert', Herbert Booth. They were both spies employed by an intelligence unit in the Ministry of Munitions, whose activities were soon to become centralized in MI5 and the Special Branch. Alex Gordon maintained that Alice Wheeldon was conspiring to kill both Lloyd George and Arthur Henderson, a Labour Party supporter of the war in the government. Alice Wheeldon's reason was that he had promised to help the men on the run escape if she obtained poison to kill dogs which he told her were guarding conscientious objectors (COs) in detention centres.

She obtained some poison, curare, from her son-in-law, Alf Mason, a laboratory attendant at Hartley University College in Southampton, thus drawing him and her daughter Winnie into the plot. The prosecution case rested on the poison intercepted in the post, on letters in which Alice, Hettie and Winnie vehemently cursed Lloyd George, and on the evidence of Alex Gordon and Herbert Booth – though Gordon never testified in court. When the Wheeldons Alice and Hettie were brought to trial early in 1917, the political climate meant that the word of an absent agent provocateur was more respectable than the testimony of socialist feminist opponents of the war.

Alice, her daughter Winnie, and her son Alf received sentences of ten, five and seven years respectively. There was nothing to implicate her other daughter Hettie, who was found not guilty.

The three served two years of their sentences and were released after the Home Office, at the request of Lloyd George, reviewed their case. Weakened by her time in prison, Alice Wheeldon caught influenza and died in her early fifties shortly after her release in 1919.[1]

The case of Alice Wheeldon aroused strong emotions in 1917, and is still capable of stirring recognition, indignation and sorrow after all these years, perhaps all the more so because Alice Wheeldon was without the usual heroic accoutrements. There she was, living in Derby, known to her friends as a kind woman, holding her radical views with passion, selling papers, speaking in the market place, going to meetings, looking after her shop.[2] Then she is suddenly cast in the role of conspirator, plotting assassination, morally deranged, and outside the pale of reasonable political motivation. She is projected beyond the ordinary, she becomes distanced from everyday concerns, and is framed as part of the sensational.[3]

But the combination of circumstances that brought about Alice Wheeldon's trial and death have more than an emotional and dramatic pull. There is an intellectual fascination, historically and politically, in understanding the forces which converged upon her to fracture her existence.

The Wheeldons were rank-and-file rebels. They were the kind of people who usually leave only chance or scattered reference, of whom nothing much is remembered except in scraps of local and kinship memories. In this case, however, the brilliant spotlight of public affairs trapped the family tragically and remorselessly. Ironically, their fate illuminated, for the curiosity of posterity, a lower-middle-class Midlands milieu in which socialism, feminism and pacifism combined. This was not the stuff of which memoirs and autobiographies are customarily made. Instead, we have to read through the lines of local newspaper crime reports and look through Alice's, Hettie's and Winnie's intercepted letters to reconstruct their story.

I originally reconstructed the story in the play *Friends of Alice Wheeldon* in 1980; here I have also reworked the historical background material, drawing on new sources. I have presented the story so that both the play and the historical essay stand on their own separately, and may be read independently. There is thus some repetition in the outline of the story. I hope readers will find the two accounts complementary rather than cumbersome.

Five years have passed since I wrote *Friends of Alice Wheeldon*. The play's preoccupations grew from the dilemmas of the 1970s. The reflections in 'Rebel Networks in the First World War', written in 1985, are informed by the political circumstances of the 1980s. In the long term, I believe these issues have a wider political relevance for what kind of socialism we can make and the forces which oppose its making.

The problems that the friends of Alice Wheeldon faced found apparent – but only partial – resolutions. Versions of their dilemmas lurk in contemporary left politics, and the state continues to use its powers of surveillance and the legal cover of the conspiracy charge for political reasons. The story, its setting and the concerns of its characters thus speak, at many levels, to the present.

I am grateful to the Warden and fellows of New College, Oxford, for permission to quote from the 'Notes on the Strike Movement' in the Milner Papers, and to the staff of the Bodleian Library for their help when I consulted the papers. Similarly, thanks to the staff of the Marx Memorial Library, the British Museum and the Public Record Office, and to the Public Record Office for permission to quote from the papers that relate to the Wheeldon trial.

Thanks to Lord Addison for permission to quote from the Addison papers, and to Norah Romer for sending me the manuscript letters of her father, Reuben Farrow. For information about the characters I am obliged to Albert Chapman, Trevor Eames, Harry Young, Doris Alison and Lord Brockway, and to Radio Derby for enabling me to contact people.

Thanks to Tony Bunyan, Charles Foster, E.P. Thompson, Guff Putovsky, Sean Damer and Doug Gill for references, and to Mike Seifert for casting a legal eye over Herbert Booth's statement in the trial. I am greatly indebted to Ray Challinor for references and suggestions and to Ken Weller and the late Gloden Dallas for long discussions over the years about the links between syndicalism, feminism and the socialism of the ILP.

A grant from the Arts Council made it possible for me to work on the play. Ron Rose and DAC Theatre Company showed great faith in enabling me to write it. Their knowledge and skills along with the director Penny Chern's, structured my initially rambling version. Bobby Campbell checked my Glaswegian dialogue. Tim Myers researched and arranged the songs which are all from the period. Paul Atkinson did extra child care which meant I could learn from the process of the play's production. *Friends of Alice Wheeldon* is published basically as it was performed in 1980, with a few scenes restored. Thanks to Trevor Griffiths, Claire Venables, Max Stafford-Clark and Adam Ganz for reading it and for their observations and criticisms.

The title itself has a double meaning. The play is about Alice Wheeldon's milieu, her friends. It also echoes the 'Friends of Astrid Proll', a defence group that tried to prevent the extradition from Britain in 1978-9 of a German feminist for her part in anti-state activity in Western Germany some years earlier.

The Introduction to this book and the extended historical essay 'Rebel Networks in the First World War' were written in 1985. It was the indefatigable enthusiasm and insistence of Ros Baxandall, Jean McCrindle and Ellen Ross that the play should be published that finally compelled me to get down to them. At several points when I despaired, Conor McAvinchey's encouragement and promises of orange juice when it was finished prevented me from being smothered in footnotes. I am grateful to him and to Hilary Wainwright and Debbie Burnett for their comments and interest.

Introduction
by Sandi Cooper
and Blanche Wiesen Cook

During the First World War, to be a socialist, a Wobbly, a dissenter, or a pacifist was to court censure, imprisonment, deportation, or death. The apparatus of surveillance and repression did not single out those who were notably brave or even particularly active in public affairs; it was sufficient to speak out, to write a newspaper column, to join a march. Even a personal letter might suffice, for as mail covers and censorship intensified, the concept of private correspondence lost its meaning. Basic human rights and civil liberties were suspended not only in the mililtaristic, autocratic monarchies of central and eastern Europe, but also in the most self-congratulatory democracies—the United States and the United Kingdom. As Jane Addams noted in 1915: "War itself destroys democracy. Not only in Russia and Germany, but in the more demŏcratic countries as well."

In Britain, Bertrand Russell warned that the democracies were being conquered from within, by government orchestration of a patriotic consensus that rivaled those of the Prussian and Austro-Hungarian empires. Indeed, so sophisticated did the British government become at "creating" and "managing" information—about events at home as well as overseas—that the methods developed during the First World War in Britain served as an inspiration for the Nazi propaganda apparatus established by Joseph Goebbels in the next generation.

Yet some—antiwar feminists, socialists, peace activists—dared to face the modern state and risk their security, their livelihoods, and ultimately their lives for their convictions. Who were these people? Sheila Rowbotham's stirring play, *Friends of Alice Wheeldon*, and her introductory essay, "Rebel Networks in the First World War," treat us to a remarkable recreation of the social and political world of that earlier era—in the life and struggles of British activist Alice Wheeldon, her family, her political friends, and her intimate associates.

Notwithstanding the dramatic changes in technology and weaponry, the issues confronted during the First World War by radicals such as Alice Wheeldon have not been resolved by the passage of time. None of the themes are old, weary, or unfamiliar: women's rights, workers' rights, civil liberties, human rights, war and peace, revolution and counterrevolution, terrorism and state terrorism—are issues that are again and again distorted and trivialized by propaganda or officially imposed silence.

Like the Wheeldons, Rowbotham's "rank-and-file rebels," thousands of U.S. citizens organized and opposed growing American militarism, war-preparedness, and actual entry into the war. They too were arrested, deported, imprisoned, and harassed. Their mail and journals were confiscated and censored. In the United States, as well as in Britain, conscientious objectors found safe havens. There was defiance and resistance, despair and suicide. Still, communities of support and survival emerged and the struggle went on throughout the Red Scare and the blacklists that followed the war.

The publication of *Friends of Alice Wheeldon* invites us to reexamine the ways the two Atlantic democracies reacted when suffragists, civil libertarians, and pacifists challenged their decisions to make war and to impose a national prowar consensus. Antiwar forces maintained that their rights to free speech and to organize dissent were sacred. They believed that the public had a fundamental right to know, to debate, and to participate in foreign policy decisions. Indeed, they proudly hailed the democratic control of foreign policy. Such organizations as England's Union for Democratic Control lobbied for full disclosure, an end to secret treaties, secret alliances, and secret ordinances—the bulwarks of international tyranny.

In the emerging twentieth-century Leviathan states such convictions were met by repression, imprisonment, and violence. Protesters were beaten by police and soldiers; dissident writings were mocked, distorted, and banned; homes and offices were raided, ransacked, and burned. In the war-making democracies, government officials in charge of "public opinion" went well beyond the traditional practices of lying about lost battles and minimizing casualty figures. A new breed of professional propagandist, masters of the twisted word, joined the state bureaucracy. To oppose the war meant to support the enemy. Dissent was deemed treason. Political warfare, including disinformation and destabilization, flourished during the First World War.

Even before the United States actually entered the war in 1917, Woodrow Wilson attacked U.S. pacifists as "tools" of the "masters of Germany." He referred to a "new intrigue, the intrigue for peace." By 1917, the president of the United States was using the same language that the German and Austro-Hungarian emperors had routinely used to belittle prewar peace advocates. Wilhelm II, for instance, had denounced "pacifists, socialists, women peace activists and anarchists" in one sweeping note in 1898 as enemies of German freedom. In Wilson's view, pacifists were not only un-American dupes of Germany, they were sinister and disloyal. However, Wilson promised on June 14, 1917, "they will make no headway." "This is a People's War," he asserted, "a war for freedom and justice and self-government amongst all the nations of the world, a war to make the world safe for the people who live upon it and make it their own."

Wilson's Flag Day speech was followed the very next day by congressional passage of the Espionage Act. On June 15, 1917, it became un-American to speak, write, or organize against war or in favor of peace, neutrality, or freedom of information regarding the international situation. To do so courted twenty years in jail combined with fines up to $10,000.

As a result of the Espionage Act thousands of Alice Wheeldon's American counterparts were imprisoned. The incarcerated included anarchists, such as Emma Goldman and Alexander Berkman, who were later deported; scores of socialists, such as Eugene Debs, Victor Berger, Kate Richards O'Hare, Rose Pastor Stokes, and Scott Nearing, and hundreds of Wobblies, led by "Big Bill" Haywood; civil libertarians such as Roger Baldwin, who demanded only the right to free speech in wartime, were also arrested and imprisoned. U.S. antiwar protesters included social reform women who organized the Woman's Peace Party and the American Union Against Militarism: Jane Addams, Crystal Eastman, and Lillian Wald, and their male allies including Norman Thomas, Oswald Garrison Villard, Max Eastman, and Amos Pinchot.

U.S. antiwar protesters, like the English radicals whom

Rowbotham depicts, held out an alternate vision; democratic control of foreign policy; a decent socialist economy that guaranteed work, economic security, health, housing, and education for all; international peace based on fair trade practices; national sovereignty and the liberation of oppressed nationalities; an end to race domination and imperial rule.

Thus the lines were drawn during the First World War. As the war progressed to its end, leaving 10,000,000 dead, 20,000,000 more wounded and maimed, four European empires toppled, and the nineteenth century obliterated, the domestic and international agenda of the war critics seemed more and more realistic to increasing numbers of war-weary citizens and subjects. With the Russian Revolution of 1917, it looked to many that the alternate vision had a chance to be realized.

But in 1914, that vision was still very distant. In many ways August 1, 1914 was the first day of the twentieth century. The war realized the worst fears of the peace advocates who had struggled for twenty-five years to organize international institutions to prevent the disaster that finally occurred. Peace advocates had held twenty-three international congresses; an unknown number of national and regional peace congresses (from 1902 to 1913, for instance, there were at least eight national peace congresses in France and ten in Italy); published dozens of peace newspapers; lobbied prominent politicians in every country on behalf of implementing the conventions signed at the two Hague Conferences (1899 and 1907); and helped to bring about the negotiation of over 100 bilateral treaties guaranteeing the use of arbitration between two signatories. During this endless struggle, peace activists had watched armaments increase annually—always, of course, in the name of preserving peace and the balance of power.

As German troops entered Belgium and France, Belgian and French pacifists no longer stood apart as critics of their states. Reluctantly, French pacifists silenced their presses and some reactivated their military commissions. Gaston Moch rejoined the army and Charles Richet served in the medical corps. The Belgian senator Henri LaFontaine fled to England and then the United States. Alfred Fried left Vienna for a Swiss exile, realizing that antiwar criticism would be of no avail. He spent his last few years writing assessments of the prewar movement.

Other prewar activists became prowar enthusiasts. Curiously,

Italy's only Nobel Peace Prize laureate, E. T. Moneta, urged Italian intervention in the war as early as October 1914, when his nation was officially still neutral. Rather than arguing that Italy use its neutrality to negotiate a peace, Moneta insisted that peace would have no chance unless the Entente prevailed over German militarism. From 1914 to 1915, when Rome finally joined on the Franco-British side, Moneta—echoed by Rosalia Gwis Adami, Italy's leading women pacifist—called for entry. In Moneta's view—much as in Wilson's later view—peace required a world constructed of parliamentary democracies in the American or British model.

Those who would not collaborate were hounded into silence. German peace activists spent the war under surveillance, kept from speaking, organizing, and publishing. Germany's most famous antiwar voices, Rosa Luxemburg and Karl Liebknecht, spent the war in jail. In France, Séverine (Carolyn Rémy) challenged official French papers on the origins of the war. For her pains, her columns were silenced. In Britain, the friends of Alice Wheeldon were supported by such groups as the Union of Democratic Control and the No Conscription Fellowship, led by peace activists such as Helena Swanwick and Bertrand Russell. But in the end, they too were silenced. And in the United States the IWW, as well as socialist and anarchist groups, continued to protest the war and U.S. participation in it; their protests were met with violent repression during and after the war.

As the prewar movement disintegrated with the outbreak of war, a new generation of activists filled the antiwar protest ranks. They were joined by those members of older movements—among them a number of suffragists—who refused to give in to war patriotism. In October 1914, the British suffrage leader Emmeline Pethick-Lawrence and the Hungarian feminist Rosika Schwimmer sailed to the United States, hoping to engage U.S. women in an international women's crusade to stop the war. They trusted Woodrow Wilson's affirmations about neutrality and asked him to call a conference of neutral nations to arrange a ceasefire and begin negotiations. That objective denied, the two visitors prevailed upon peace activists to help organize an international women's meeting at The Hague that would urge negotiations and mediation upon the world's embattled leaders.

Encouraged by demonstrations, especially a New York parade

of over 1,500 women who marched down Fifth Avenue on August 29, 1914, to the sound of muffled drums—a sombre procession to mourn the death of peace in the world—antiwar women met in Washington in January 1915 to form the Woman's Peace Party (renamed the Women's International League for Peace and Freedom in 1919). A broad-based organization, its membership came from the Daughters of the American Revolution, from conservative prewar activists such as Lucia Ames Mead as well as unionists such as Rose Schneiderman. Jane Addams was elected its first president. One of the first WPP acts was to plan for an international conference of women from belligerent and neutral nations.

That conference, attended by over 1,100 women from twelve nations—neutrals and belligerents—met at The Hague from April 28 through May 1, 1915. Despite the dangers of wartime travel—and despite the barriers to travel erected by governments opposed to their efforts—British, Belgian, German, U.S., and several French women arrived. (The vast majority of French and Serbian women refused to discuss a ceasefire and a negotiated peace while their national territories were still occupied.)

Although the meeting was ridiculed and Jane Addams was attacked by a New York newspaper as "a silly, vain, impertinent old maid who may have done good charity work at Hull House, but is now meddling with matters far beyond her capacity," those who attended articulated an enduring program. Many of the unanimous resolutions voted by the women at The Hague later found expression in Woodrow Wilson's Fourteen Points, but the spirit and content of these resolutions went much further than Wilson's, or any diplomat's. They envisioned democratic control of foreign policy; education for peace; complete freedom of the seas and of trade routes; mediation to end the war; a continuing conference of neutrals and a permanent council of mediation and arbitration. And unlike the "peacemakers" of 1918, the women at The Hague demanded political equality for the sexes and women's representation at the peace table as the bases upon which permanent, durable peace might be constructed. Women at The Hague accepted the position once argued by socialists and left-wing pacifists: that the arms race was fueled largely by industrialists' profits. They sought investigations and analyses of the connections between profiteering and militarization.

These demands continue to engage us, as feminists and activists. Sheila Rowbotham has given us not a panegyric to the past but a celebration of long-neglected and very real heroes who went beyond grit and courage, onward to bold imagination. They understood that "thought is revolutionary," and were willing to step off that intellectual cliff into the imaginary unknown.

Sheila Rowbotham writes: "We keep talking on the Left as if we *already know* what the content and future of socialism is. We talk of socialism as if it were an already completed agenda." When we return, as she did, to the early antimilitarist, socialist, and feminist agendas, and the visions of Alice Wheeldon, Alexandra Kollontai, Sylvia Pankhurst, and Crystal Eastman, we see only too well what was often neglected by the movement's forefathers, but remains so earnestly and quite simply to be done. To live our lives with determination is to fight fearlessly against whatever fills the world with poverty and war, slavery, misogyny, repression, and mindless cruelty; to fight ever more fearlessly, in the words of Alice Wheeldon, "so as to obtain that glorious time when peace and joyousness shall fill all life."

Rebel Networks in the First World War

Radical Politics in Derby before the First World War

Alice Wheeldon left no political statement, no autobiographical notes. She made no individual testimony to history. The lives and opinions of Alice Wheeldon and her family can only be pieced together from diverse snippets and fragments of information.

Alice and Hettie, her daughter, we know to have been members of the Women's Social and Political Union (WSPU) from Sylvia Pankhurst's account in 1920.[1] Alice Wheeldon was remembered by a local socialist, Lester Hutchinson, as a kind-hearted, generous, emotional woman, capable of bursts of indignation. On one occasion when she was speaking in the market, she tapped one of her hecklers on the head with an umbrella.[2] Sylvia Pankhurst described her as 'a hard-working kindly widow'.[3] She was a WSPU activist, selling *The Suffragette* and other literature. Copies of the paper were still there when the police raided her house at 12 Peartree Road in 1917.[4] Though Sylvia Pankhurst did not know Alice before the war, she described her in 1920 as the 'kind of zealous, energetic voluntary worker who is the backbone of any movement'. She was not, however, involved in any 'serious militancy'. Alice Wheeldon and Sylvia Pankhurst met only after the Gordon affair, when both attended a Derby Labour Party Conference. Hettie Wheeldon was evidently offered a post as organizer in the Women's Social and Political Union. But she did not take up the offer, working instead as a Scripture teacher in nearby Ilkeston.[5]

It is not clear how Alice, Hettie and Alice's other daughter, Winnie Mason, who lived in Southampton, felt about the arguments and divisions within the suffrage movement on the kind of tactics best suited to gain the franchise, on whether the aim should be women's suffrage or adult suffrage – for some men still did not have the vote – and on the democratic structure of the organization.

Though the great body of suffrage supporters believed in using constitutional methods, and some sought an alliance with Labour, the Women's Social and Political Union used militant direct action. By 1914, this had escalated into outbreaks of decentralized attacks on property which left the militant hard core an isolated grouping, operating as a kind of underground. In June 1914, a church at Breadsall near Derby was burned down, apparently by suffragettes. There was much consternation in the local press, and panics when women were observed loitering near churches. There was a bomb scare at Aston-on-Trent and much concern that suffrage supporters were indoctrinating young girls at school.[7] A letter to the *Derby Daily Express* on 8 June 1914 illustrated the depth and ferocity of the hostility aroused by the direct action campaign for the vote. 'I would commence by shearing off the tresses and shaving the heads of every militant suffragette justly convicted of any and every offence against law and order; if that failed to subdue them I would give such cats – the cat o' nine tails.'[8]

Another writer was worried that

> so many single women with extreme notions of female emancipation have been in charge of our daughters at school during the past 20 years, and the atmosphere has not always fostered the best attitude towards men, home, marriage and motherhood. Probably at the root of the matter, the suffragette frenzy is largely a sex question and springs from the fact that unmarried and childless women must have some outlet for their free energies.[9]

Opponents of feminism did not distinguish between the political views and tactics of the various suffrage bodies. So whatever Alice and Hettie's opinions, as known suffragettes they would encounter hostility. Presumably the public discussion of suffragette indoctrination in schools would have put pressure on Hettie. Thus even before the war, both women would have experienced the hardening of attitudes which comes from finding yourself in a disliked minority. Whether or not they were themselves involved in militancy directly, they were part of a movement in which it was used. This meant they were up against direct state coercion as an everyday event. Such experiences bred an intransigence and an antagonism to the state which was also developing in the Irish agitation and in the waves of industrial unrest which erupted before the First World War.

In 1913-14, the militant wing of the suffrage movement was faced with a fundamental clash of political views among the Pankhursts, which resulted in the expulsion of Sylvia's East London Federation of the Suffragettes from the WSPU. The immediate issues were Sylvia's links with socialism and the labour movement.[10] When the Dublin workers were locked out, their leader, Jim Larkin – described by Sylvia as 'a tall, red-haired young man who had learnt in America the methods and phraseology of the Industrial Workers of the World (IWW)[11] – was imprisoned. Sylvia Pankhurst came to his defence. On 1 November 1913, to Christabel's fury, Sylvia spoke to a meeting of ten thousand with James Connolly and George Lansbury to demand Larkin's release. Christabel believed that the suffrage agitation must be kept apart from socialism and syndicalism. Sylvia was equally resolved 'to keep our working women's movement in touch with the main body of the working class movement'.[12] There is no record to show what Alice and Hettie, as rank-and-file activists in the WSPU, thought of these conflicts. But because they were also involved in the Independent Labour Party in Derby and part of the left-wing current which was growing more and more rebellious just before the war, it is likely they inclined towards Sylvia's position.

The Labour Party still lacked a local organizational base in these early days. (Until 1918 there were no individual members, merely affiliated organizations.) But there were Socialist Societies affiliated through the Independent Labour Party, and one of these existed in Derby.[13] A member of the Derby Socialist Society, Reuben Farrow, has preserved his memories of the group in a series of manuscript letters, providing valuable glimpses of everyday activities and the political divisions. Reuben was a railway clerk and Christian Socialist, active in the Adult Schools and in the Pleasant Sunday Afternoons organized through the church. He was moved by an ethical concern about poverty and injustice. His wife, Florence Farrow, was also active, and a practical commitment shows in Reuben's concern that women should be involved in the educational, religious and political movements in which he was engaged; 'an ample reservoir of baby sitters' is thus noted in his reminiscences as being of some importance.

The Farrows knew several of those in the labour movement who were becoming national figures, including Ramsay Macdonald, Phillip Snowden, Margaret Bondfield and Jim Thomas. Indeed the baby sitters were needed, because by 1912 Reuben and Florence were intensively involved in establishing a local Independent Labour Party branch which invited Jim Thomas to be its parliamentary candidate. Derby was moving from Liberal to Labour. Reuben Farrow, as one of the first three socialist town councillors, was at the centre of this historical shift. He represented Pear Tree Ward, where the Wheeldons lived.

But, the development from local Socialist Society into a section of a national party seeking office was not a smooth affair. Reuben Farrow was aware of losses as well as gains. Though a political colleague of Jim Thomas's, his approach to socialist politics was fundamentally different. Reuben disapproved of what he saw as Jim Thomas's 'opportunism', and Jim Thomas was impatient with Reuben's ethical pacifism. Reuben wrote:

> the expression 'close colleagues' only applied to public affairs. I found 'personal friendship' very difficult. I had become a 'Christian Pacifist' – it was evident that he considered this a hindrance in political 'fights' – something to be hidden away. All my political activities stemmed from my Christian principles; it seemed to me that he was an 'opportunist' whose prevailing endeavours were based upon the idea 'how can we score a victory?' Ethics seemed to take second place.[14]

The extent of the influence of the ethical socialism Reuben Farrow describes has been underestimated. The development of the Labour Party and the rise of the Communist Party marginalized this ethical concern with socialism as a way of life, and its supporters were increasingly dismissed, on the left as well as the right, as cranks or hypocrites. The ramifications of ethical socialism, however, enabled socialists to envisage a wider transformation of social relationships than was possible simply by voting for a party or by changing economic ownership. It was a means of imagining a freer, happier way of living in a co-operative commonwealth, at peace with the natural world. While the immediate task was parliamentary manoeuvring, the utopian glimpse of William Morris persisted, even though its revolutionary intensity was diminished. In

Sheffield, the socialist writer and lecturer Edward Carpenter described ethical socialism as the 'broader socialism'. It could embrace vegetarianism, nudism, the emancipation of women, sexual liberation, anti-pollution campaigns, the design of furniture and dress, magnetism, spiritualism and progressive schooling.[15]

Reuben's ethical socialism was mild and moderate, but nonetheless deeply felt. His unease with leaders like Jim Thomas was submerged in a more clear-cut battle which split the Derby Socialist Party. The membership, he recalled,

> fell into two distinct camps. One was frankly atheistic and Marxist, the other was sincerely 'socialist', but based upon Christian ethics. The latter were numerically a majority – but were not so regular in attendance as the others, because we were busy with other activities, such as our Trade Union branches and Ward Election Committees. In our absence, the extremists would pass resolutions in favour of disaffiliating from the Independent Labour Party (ILP). We insisted that, as the resolutions had not been announced to all members beforehand, they were invalid. So, at a subsequent meeting we reasserted our loyalty to the ILP. This happened several times. We got tired of this – so it was privately agreed that we ILPers should simply hand in our separate resignations; leave the others 'in possession' and meet on other premises. There, we formed a new branch of the ILP, the National headquarters accepted us as the continuation of the previous Socialist Society, and that trouble was settled.[16]

The neat organizational manoeuvre worked, but it did not quell the rumbling dissatisfaction among many people like Alice and Hettie Wheeldon with Labour's political policies. The problem extended beyond Derby. The Osborne Judgement in the House of Lords in 1909 prevented trades unions putting forward candidates and giving funds to political parties. It struck effectively at the financial basis of the new Labour Party and left the parliamentary party tied to the coat-tails of the Liberals. Outside, left opposition grew. G.H.D. Cote comments:

> Rising prices, with wages lagging behind, were leading to a growth of industrial militancy and to a preaching of 'direct action' doctrines which denied the effectiveness of parliamen-

tary proceedings and denounced the Labour parliamentarians as 'collaborationists' whose compromising tactics blurred the realities of the class war. Syndicalism and Industrial Unionism were in the air, and owed their vogue not only to the lag in real wages but also to the catchingness of the militancy of the women suffragists and of the Ulster diehards and their English conservative allies.[17]

Sylvia Pankhurst has presented this conflict as a clear-cut contest between 'revolutionary Marxism . . . against the old trade unionism, and the opportunist political Labourism of Macdonald'.[18] But this was a retrospective view, and from a particular vantage point. At a local level, stances and assumptions did not fall neatly on one side or another. While this split was real in Derby, there were also other divisions – for example, the unease Reuben Farrow felt towards the smoother political operator, Jim Thomas. The ethical aspirations towards a new life were also found across divisions of right and left. Bert Parker, for instance, another Christian Socialist who, according to Farrow, was a great believer in the 'thorough mastication of simple foods',[19] was to become a conscientious objector in the war.

Alice Wheeldon and one of her sons, William, were both spiritualists.[20] The connection between spiritualism, feminism and radicalism has only recently been noted in Europe. In America, it is better known; the new continent gave more encouragement to the dream of perfecting all human relationships – even beyond the grave. So, while Alice and Hettie were to express their contempt for Reuben's 'milk-and-water Jesus Christ manner'[21] a few years later and were clearly to the left of Christian socialism, their own socialism might well have made Karl Marx raise an eyebrow.

The 'rebel' milieu, then, was eclectic, open to ideas, in favour of women's suffrage, welcome to socialists of all kinds and suspicious of parliament – without dismissing it completely.[22] The social and recreational worlds of the Herald League and the Clarion Clubs (organized around the socialist newspapers, the *Herald* and the *Clarion*) created a network in which an alternative politics to that of the parliamentary Labour Party flourished. We can glimpse Alice and Hettie as part of such a milieu in Derby. They lived among working-class and lower-middle-class women and men, lacking formal higher education but identifying with a radical culture, eagerly debating ideas and deeply estranged from upper-class London politics and values.

This world was given a rude shock by the outbreak of war in 1914. As we shall see, old alliances were shaken up and new ones forged in the struggle to maintain and develop an opposition to the war.

The Socialist Labour Party and Marxism

Quite when Hettie Wheeldon met Arthur MacManus, the man she was to marry, is unclear. Tom Bell recalls that his friend Arthur 'had been frequenting Derby in connection with the shop stewards' movement'.[1] In January 1916, Arthur addressed several meetings in Derby on the principles of the Clyde Workers' Committee's organization and policy (see p.30 below).[2] By this time, Derby was the centre of the clandestine opposition to the war of the Socialist Labour Party (SLP), the small Marxist group to which Arthur MacManus belonged. Two other members who were war resisters and part of the 'flying corps' were in the area. John S. Clarke was working on the Turner's farm at Arleston and Willie Paul came to stay at nearby Littleover. Together, they kept the SLP paper *The Socialist* going.[3] Paul set up a clothing stall in the market, with help from an eccentric SLP businessman, W.R. Stoker of Wigan. Through Lester Hutchinson, he consulted Alice Wheeldon because she was in the second-hand clothes business.[4] Alice might well have found Paul and Clarke places to stay. She was part of the network which concealed war resisters and which kept in touch with conscientious objectors in prison. As Tom Bell remarked, 'Many of these comrades kept an open door for men on the run. In Derby, the house of Mrs Wheeldon was a haven for anyone who was opposed to the war.'[5] Arthur MacManus was a 'welcome visitor at the Wheeldons' house'.[6] Some time in 1916, he and Hettie got engaged.

Tom Bell has left an affectionate portrait of his friend Arthur in his autobiography *Pioneering Days*. He tells how Arthur's Irish parents had intended him for the priesthood and how he 'fled' to the factory instead. His father was a Fenian. His mother idolized her younger son, a small, wiry boy, but he 'was at the same time the despair of her heart on account of his waywardness'. She 'had known what it was like to harbour men "on the run" from the police, in the midst of a grinding struggle to get ends to meet'.[7]

Arthur's first job was at the Singer sewing machine factory at Kilbowie, Clydebank, which was run on American lines according to Frederick W. Taylor's 'Principles of Scientific Management'. Taylor was enthused by a crusading spirit against 'autonomous and inefficient' work groups. The techniques of time and motion study which he developed were used to analyse the craft skills in the production process. Once grasped by management, these were broken up into simpler, less skilled operations – thus polarizing mental and manual labour as well as undermining the trade union organization of the craftworkers. Rebellion to this 'dilution' of skilled work came in the form of individual resistance, going slow, sabotage and absenteeism. It also produced a new form of political organizing, associated with the varied experience of workers from many countries through the Industrial Workers of the World (IWW) in the United States – the 'committee from the base'.[8] In 1905-6, among the Singer employees at Newark and Elizabeth, New Jersey, was the Irish Republican Socialist, James Connolly. He argued with the leader of the Socialist Labour Party, Daniel de Leon, over whether or not workers should struggle for higher wages. De Leon saw the IWW as an educative, revolutionary union whose sole aim was to hasten the socialist revolution in line with SLP policy. Connolly's opposing view was that it should be an organization which would struggle militantly to raise living standards and bring unorganized people into mass unions.[9] Ideas about these new forms of organizing, along with the sectarian disputes between the SLP and the IWW, travelled over the Atlantic even before Connolly returned to Ireland in 1910.[10] Singers in Scotland employed 10,000 people in 1910, Tom Bell recalls. The firm adamantly refused to recognize a union:

> It was typical of the new machine age – the sub-division of labour was carried to a fine art, and young boys and girls were brought into the factory to operate the simple processes on ridiculously low wages. I remember Arthur MacManus describing a job he was on, pointing needles. As fast as he reduced the

mountain of needles, a fresh load was dumped. Day in, day out, it never grew less. One morning he came in and found the table empty. He couldn't understand it. He began telling everyone excitedly that there were no needles on the table. It suddenly flashed on him how absurdly stupid it was to be spending his life like this. Without taking his jacket off, he turned on his heel and went out, to go for a ramble over the hills to Balloch.[11]

In January 1910, 18 people attended the Sewing Machine Workers' Industrial Union Group. It was the result of four years of propaganda work in the factory. Copies of *The Socialist* were sold and Willie Paul held factory-gate meetings. In a year, 150 people became members of the Sewing Machine Group of the Industrial Workers of Great Britain (IWGB). In every department where it had members, the IWGB set up a 'shop committee', to which every grievance was reported. Above this, there was a General Committee of representatives. When a woman was sacked early in 1911 for not working hard enough, the resentment of the workers exploded in a spontaneous strike, catching even the IWGB off guard. They proposed a strike committee be set up with five representatives from each department and Arthur MacManus became one of the strike leaders.

The mass demonstrations and meetings of men and women new to trades unions were remarkable. Department after department accompanied by bands marched through the cheering streets of Clydebank. Astutely, management organized a ballot which voted to end the strike. They contrived not to re-employ the strike militants by increasing production in the United States and keeping trade slack in Scotland. Four hundred were sacked. It was defeat.[12] Tom Bell, however, after the strike told a large meeting in the Co-operative Hall in Glasgow that Singer's management were wrong to think they would stop the growth of the shop stewards' movement in this way. He said, 'Every man dismissed would become the nucleus of a group of industrial unionists that would spring up all over the Clyde.'[13] And he was to be proved correct. For, when the Clyde Workers' Committee was formed during the war, many of the men who became active in the shop stewards' movement had earlier been at Singer. But women had also been involved in the Singer strike. Mysteriously, they are absent from recollections of the period. It would be interesting to know what they made of their experiences.

The strike certainly affected the young members of the Socialist Labour Party in Glasgow: MacManus, Paul and Bell. Along with the strike wave and syndicalist agitation which followed, it challenged a few sectarian certainties. The Socialist Labour Party had originated in a left break-off from the Social Democratic Federation (the first Marxist organization in Britain, which was later to become the British Socialist Party). Tom Bell and James Connolly had been involved in this split and had been influenced by the American leader of the Socialist Labour Party, Daniel de Leon, to form the British group. They set about building up a small, tightly disciplined group of professional revolutionaries.[14] The cynics suggested they had the attitude of Calvinists.

> We are the pure, selected few,
> and all the rest are damned,
> There's room enough in Hell for you,
> We don't want Heaven crammed.[15]

However, members of the Socialist Labour Party did not heed the sneers. They were not concerned to be liked but to be correct. They set about distributing Marxist literature and studying earnestly. They read *Capital* and numerous works of economic and social history in the economics classes which they organized in Glasgow. They also trained themselves to be speakers and exercised at meetings of the Independent Labour Party, sneering at the ILPers' concern for municipal trams and their ignorance of Marx.

These zealous young men reduced the opposition to silence. But as Tom Bell rather ruefully reflected, they usually failed to recruit members. And even when people joined, there was a high turnover. He worked out that over a period of 13 years, they lost as many members as they gained.[16]

The formation of the Industrial Workers of the World in the United States, Connolly's opposition to the dogmatism of Daniel de Leon, the strike wave in Britain in 1910-11, and the beginnings of shop steward organization, had an important impact on Willie Paul, John S. Clarke, Tom Bell and Arthur MacManus. William Gallacher, who was in the rival British Socialist Party at the time, remembered their struggle to break through the 'paralysing influence of De Leonism'.[17] They were searching, in their different ways, for a revolutionary socialism which was neither confined to a sectarian ghetto and which did not simply emphasize spontaneous action at work.

Willie Paul was the lecturer and theorist among them. He was an imposing, classically handsome man and an impressive speaker. He also possessed a good baritone voice and was consequently in demand at socials, where he would sing 'England Arise' by Edward Carpenter and old Chartist songs. Harry Young met Paul after the war when he was a young man, and remembers the older lecturer as 'personable'.[18] Willie Paul was certainly capable of giving Marx's ideas a dramatic turn of phrase:

> Why is it, we ask, that those who by their efforts and energy manipulate and work up raw materials, and by embodying labour in the raw materials, give them value; why is it that this useful, necessary labouring class is the only section of the community that owns nothing except its mental and physical labour which it is compelled to sell for the means of life? Why is it, on the other hand, that the other class called the master class, that toils not neither does it spin, owns and controls the wealth of society?[19]

Speaking in Nottingham in 1912 against conscription, he dangled the chairman's gold watch before his audience and detailed the labour, intelligence and social organization not only of the watch-makers but of many others – miners, railroad workers, farmers – who had contributed to its making. His Marxism stressed the inevitable working out of forces in conflict on an international stage.

> All that we wicked Socialists demand is that the socially produced wealth shall be socially owned and controlled. We declare that until the contradiction between social production and individual appropriation is destroyed, all attempts at peace at home or abroad will fail.[20]

Conscription and the production of arms were not the way to peace. 'Neither a million Dreadnoughts nor twenty lines of defence will save you from the curse of militarism nor the plague of international war',[21] he told his audience amidst applause.

Despite their much-vaunted patriotism the capitalists operated internationally. Paul reminded his listeners that in the recent miners' strike coal was brought in from Germany; that in the Singer strike, the American factory was used against the Scots. The only answer was international organization of the working class. Revolution was not synonymous with bloodshed. It was only the capitalist class who interpreted 'every assault upon its privileges as an assault on law and order'.[22] Socialists were not moved by a wish to produce social chaos or to see the sun rise some morning on a blood-stained world.[23] Revolution was not to 'jump from society into chaos'; it was an act of transition from one social system into another. 'Such a step means that the revolutionary movement shall have the structure of the new system built up and developed within the old one, ready to replace the old system when it is destroyed.'[24]

Even the written text of Paul's speech gives the lie to the accusation that SLP propaganda was dry. The Marxism that Paul propounded certainly had a prophetic fatalism, but it was also enthused by a passion for class justice which echoes Marx's writing, and a generous radical internationalism which took inspiration from Tom Paine. In later lectures during the First World War, this dramatic, didactic sense of the inevitability of historical forces enabled Paul to take the long view in bleak times:

> Modern socialism is a scientific movement based upon the historic evolution of the past and the economic conditions of the present. It is not therefore something that has been hatched in the brain of a poet or in the imagination of some idealistic philosopher.[25]

It was some consolation amidst the slaughter of so many to believe that 'Capitalism is only a passing phase in the development of humanity.'[26] William Paul then turned to a study of the state during the First World War. The state's functions were extending into new areas of industry and welfare through the war effort. These developments were accepted with approval by those in the Labour Party who backed the war. Paul's *Origin of Private Property and the State* was adamantly opposed to this view of the state as a neutral force. He argued that the state in capitalism preserved and enforced the aims of the property-holding class. Consequently, he maintained there was no possibility of patching up the system or working along with the state as the Labour Party had done with its 'treacherous acceptance of the Munitions Acts'.[27] Paul thus expressed theoretically the conflict which existed in practice between the left influenced by direct action before the war, many of whom passed into anti-militaristic opposition during the First World War, and those in the labour movement who tried to negotiate and manoeuvre from within parliament and from within the new state machinery which was created in wartime.

John S. Clarke presented similar views through the rather different medium of racy, satirical verse. He came from a gypsy family, and had had an extraordinary career as a seaman, lion-tamer, zoo-keeper, arms smuggler for Russian revolutionaries, editor of a monthly journal, and secretary to an 80-year-old feminist, Jane Clapperton, whom he described as 'one of the most wonderful women I have ever met'. She influenced him a great deal and her life was a link with much earlier, romantic and radical traditions.

> As a young woman, she had escorted the semi-blind Thomas De Quincy through the Edinburgh streets . . . taken tea with Edward John Trelawney who burned the body of the drowned Shelley in company with Lord Byron, and in the '80s of the last century had been lionized for her philosophical writings by Herbert Spencer, Frederick Harrison, Elizabeth Linton, George Henry Lewes and George Eliot.[28]

John S. Clarke's Marxism incorporated a pantheistic union with nature and stress on the spiritual as well as the material emancipation which revolution would bring about. In the secularist journal he edited, he also took up his cudgels against religion and sexual puritanism. When he joined the Socialist Labour Party, he worked enthusiastically on the education of children. He wrote about socialism in a popular style. He had been involved in a local Socialist Society in Newcastle and edited their paper, *The Keel*, in 1906. An early verse expresses his views of capitalist economic relations in a typical manner:

> The landlord calls it rent and he winks the other eye,
> The merchant calls it profit and he sighs a heavy sigh,
> The banker calls it interest and puts it in the bag,
> But our honest friend the burglar simply calls it swag.[29]

Education and propaganda were all-important. The task was to raise socialist consciousness. Reforms were a false option. He dismissed 'Keir Hardie's Legislative Skin Ointment, Ramsay MacDonald's Parliamentary Pills, and many other capitalistic quack remedies'.[30] Though he was a history lecturer with the extensive sweep and learning which characterized the working-class, radical, autodidactic tradition, he believed revolutionary socialist propaganda should be lively and seek the widest possible audience.

In 1914, Clarke became editor of the SLP newspaper, *The Socialist*. Producing it was a collective responsibility he shared with his friends Tom Bell, William Paul and Arthur MacManus. It was a difficult task to oppose the war that was initially greeted with patriotic enthusiasm by many workers. John S. Clarke plugged away, arguing in *The Socialist* that war was the result of the capitalist search for colonies and overseas markets.[31] The editorial of the *The Socialist* after the outbreak of war declared: 'Our attitude is neither pro-German nor pro-British, but anti-capitalist and all that it stands for in every country of the world.'[32] In an article headed 'War against Capitalism', the newspaper exhorted workers to reply to the capitalists, 'You gave us war, we in return give you revolution.'[33]

These abstract, principled declarations were remote from any practical possibilities of action, and initially the authorities disregarded *The Socialist*. But as dissatisfaction with wartime conditions grew, as a shop stewards' movement emerged to threaten the production of munitions and *The Socialist* steadily built up its circulation, they became concerned to stop it. They dismantled the printing press and tried to arrest its main contributors. Despite this harassment from the government, John S. Clarke and his staunch cohorts kept it going for four difficult years on the run, living underground in the Derby area, raising its circulation from around 3,000 in 1914 to an impressive 20,000 by 1918.

Its distribution was patchy but in some places, like Glasgow, it was extensively read, passed from hand to hand, articles from it were pinned on factory notice-boards.[34] As well as theoretical articles and news reports, it included John S. Clarke's verses. His parody of Kipling's 'If' about the exploitation of workers and soldiers in the war became extremely popular on the Clyde. It was an 'If' about 'vile war bread smeared with oily margarine', 'microbey shoddy cloth', and 'snob contempt', about being 'combed out' like lice and the passivity of leaving it all to 'God and Parliament'.[35] Through irony, his writing asserted class dignity.

In 1912, John S. Clarke married. His wife Sarah Clarke's political views and personal character go unrecorded, but she must have been a woman of humour and resourcefulness to live in the eccentric Clarke ménage where pet monkeys pulled her hair and the mouse population flourished, where objects from ancient times gathered dust with stuffed animals, and there were sudden visits from socialists who were up against the law or seeking discussion amidst the livestock and antiquarian trophies.[36]

Immediately before the war, this little network of people was bound together not only by politics in a formal public sense, but by a heady and invigorating radical culture which did not confine itself to issues of industry or the state. Tom Bell describes how he read Dr Foote's *Plain Home Talk*, MacFadden's *Physical Culture*, the German socialist Bebel's *Woman under Socialism*, Engels' *Origin of the Family*, and Havelock Ellis's *Man and Woman*.[37]

Tom Bell had assumed he would not marry, but he modified his position when he fell in love with Lizzie Aitken, a socialist dressmaker, the daughter of a free thinker, who like himself rebelled against bourgeois convention.[38] When they set up home in a one-roomed house in Glasgow, Lizzie did not wear a wedding ring. They were 'ardent physical culturists and vegetarians'.[39] Baby Oliver was born in March 1911 and Tom carried him off for six months to his Marxist economics class. When Oliver was older, there was the Socialist Sunday School which had flourishing branches in Glasgow in this period, reflecting every tendency on the left.[40] Young children learned socialist precepts and listened to distinguished speakers like the Marxist lecturer John Maclean.[41] A few years later, Oliver was being taken to his father's meetings.[42]

John S. Clarke and Arthur MacManus were frequent visitors.[43] Tom Bell remembered their friendship and the shared intellectual comradeship vividly many years later, when he came to write his memoirs. The revolutionary group provided the framework for their rebellious quest for understanding.

We had dabbled in the dialectical philosophy of Josef Dietzgen, in Bergson's philosophy, and Sorel's application of Bergson to syndicalism, and the deification of intuition as opposed to reason. Nietzsche, Bernard Shaw, Ibsen, Hauptmann and Strindberg added their weight to our intellectual challenge to all existing social standards and conventionalities. We read feverishly and discussed fiercely, and walked the streets, often after midnight, in an effort to sort out for ourselves the problem of man and the universe. We experimented psychologically on everything and everybody and eagerly watched for the results.[44]

Tom Bell felt a special closeness to Arthur MacManus.

While I had the advantage of Arthur in economics and the sciences, being ten years older, he was ahead of me in modern literature and especially in poetry. His Irish ancestry fired his blood with imagination and romance. He was in that blissful stage when youth refuses to accept traditional standards and conventional views. His Irish temperament ran riot at the slightest suggestion of fixity and permanence in social institutions. He challenged everything and everybody.[45]

They both liked and admired James Connolly who had been first national organizer of the SLP in Scotland and involved later with the SLP and the Wobblies while in America. In the arguments between Connolly and Daniel de Leon over whether workers should struggle to raise wages Bell and MacManus inclined towards Connolly. But Connolly also got into dispute with the American socialist leader on the question of religion, marriage and the family. Connolly said socialism should stick to political and economic change, leaving sexual morality, religion and personal life open to individual judgement. Socialists could not know everything. But the American SLP had played an important role in publishing Marxist classics on women and the family. De Leon maintained that a socialist party should have a position on all aspects of life.[46] Tom Bell, a sceptic, agreed with de Leon on religion, but continued to respect Connolly's intellectual contribution. MacManus especially was deeply influenced by James Connolly, identifying both with the struggle in Ireland and with the women's suffrage movement, which Connolly supported.

In 1915 Connolly's paper, *The Irish Worker*, was banned. MacManus organized for it to be printed illegally on the SLP printing machine and smuggled it to Dublin as 'glass'. One day, he fell off Tom Bell's bicycle and broke his collarbone but he nonetheless insisted on taking the paper over a rough Irish sea to Dublin.

He returned from these trips early in 1916 with descriptions of drilling and the arming of Irish rebels. Bell and MacManus were troubled by these rumours and uncertain of the chances of a successful uprising. They were also confused by the change in Connolly whom they knew as a propagandist writer and teacher, not as a man of action. They wondered about their own political situation. 'Was the time ripe?' And how did you know when and how to act?[47] Arthur MacManus put this query to Connolly himself. 'The time is never ripe,' said Connolly, 'until you try. If you fail, then it is not ripe. If you succeed, then it is ripe.'[48]

The Easter-week rising in Ireland and Connolly's execution by the British government gave his comment a sombre meaning. But in its narrower context, it expressed a vision of a socialist movement 'born of struggle', which would gather 'to it every element of rebellion and progress, solidifying amidst storm and stress' into 'a real revolutionary force'.[49] Workplace organization and control was part of a process of building an alternative within the shell of the capitalist state. The nationalism of a subject people did not negate internationalism. Connolly's approach appealed to the philosophical rejection of a narrow dogmatic version of Marxism which influenced the theoretical quest of the Glasgow comrades, even if they disagreed with some of the details.[50]

Interestingly, Connolly's critique of an omniscient party allowed for much greater autonomy for rank-and-file workers' groups and for social movements. The Wobblies, nationalist rebellion and women's emancipation could be supported as rebellion against oppression without insisting that they were consistent with an all-embracing SLP line. This acceptance of autonomous action involved a challenge to the de Leonite concept of knowledge. As Connolly put it 'we . . . are not the repositories of all truth'.[51] Socialists had to learn from the struggle of oppressed people around specific grievances.

While in the United States, Connolly worked for the Wobblies and helped start the Irish Socialist Federation. Among the members were the Flynn family, and Elizabeth Gurley Flynn, the famous Wobbly speaker and organizer, recalls that it caused great protest among the other existing federations. They insisted that the Irish did not need a federation because they were not foreign-speaking.

But undaunted and supported by a Jewish friend, Sam Stodel, they held their street meetings with a large green and white banner with the slogan Faugh-a-Balach (Clear the Way). Elizabeth's mother, Annie Gurley, was an early advocate of equal rights for women. She continued to work in tailoring after she had children and was enthusiastic about Irish literature, a socialist and opposed to racial prejudice. Her daughter's first speech in 1906, aged 16, was on women and socialism, based on Daniel de Leon's translation of Bebel's *Women and Socialism*.[52]

When Connolly returned to Ireland, he campaigned with women's organizations for Irish children to be included in an Act of Parliament for feeding poor children.[53] He was prepared to back not only the industrial organization of women, which was consistent with SLP politics in Britain, but also women's suffrage. He spoke on suffrage platforms while the SLP was laboriously showing the vote to be an insubstantial reform,[54] and the whole Connolly family marched on suffragette demonstrations. In his impressive essay on 'Woman' in 1915, he summed up his commitment to autonomous movements in the phrase: 'None so fitted to break the chains as they who wear them, none so well equipped to decide what is a fetter.'[55]

He was convinced that only by building a strong, autonomous movement would women force politicians to meet their demands. He saw the cross-class women's movement as playing a different role in undermining capitalism from that played by the workers' rebellion. While 'the women's army forges ahead of labour in its passion for freedom, it was to take the outworks of the citadel of oppression, the working class alone can raze it to the ground.'[56]

There are echoes of Connolly in Arthur MacManus's socialism. 'In matters of politics,' said Tom Bell, 'Arthur put everything to the test of action in the service of the workers' movement.'[57] The emphasis on militant action made him sympathetic to struggles which were neither socialist nor revolutionary. 'He was fired with enthusiasm for Women's Suffrage when it flared up.'[58]

Tom Bell, who had digested the theories of the anti-feminist socialist Belfort Bax in his youth, was more suspicious. He believed that middle-class women were merely using working women to get the franchise for their own class – repeating the historical role of the middle-class men in the Reform Bill agitation of 1831. But when the government banned the paper of the WSPU, Bell supported MacManus's readiness to print *The Suffragette* on the SLP press.[59]

Tom Bell indicates that in the personal discussions between comrades there was considerable interest in 'the woman question' among women in the SLP and many comrades were full of socialist ideas of equality between the sexes. He admits his admiration of Belfort Bax 'must have been exasperating at times'.[60]

But the public arguments about women's suffrage in the SLP did not occur with a clear-cut division of women for and men against. For instance, Lily Gair Wilkinson argued around 1910, in her *Revolutionary Socialism and the Women's Movement*, that her objection to the suffrage movement was not their use of militant tactics but the suffragette insistence that women's oppression was caused by men rather than the class system. She was enthusiastic about the part women could play in industrial unionism and critical of an extension of the franchise on the existing terms to women as this would primarily benefit propertied women. The significance of the vote even for working-class women was that it could 'extend the possibilities for political action'. It would be useless unless backed by 'an organized economic power, sufficient to ensure the introduction of socialism'.[61] Perhaps the necessity of making a critique of feminism was partly stimulated by interest in the issues the suffragettes raised within the SLP itself.

The arguments continued. A letter from Tom Anderson, who was involved in the SLP's children's schools, appeared in *The Socialist* in 1914. It indicates that openness to the suffrage movement could be linked with impatience with the 'hide-bound' dogmas of the old-style SLP.[62]

> It is no argument to say that the mass of women are indifferent to the vote; or that until we settle the economic question we need not trouble about it; or that we would be better to organize the women industrially, and then we could let the women settle the question for themselves. This is an evasion of the issue. The problem presents itself Now. What is our answer? We have none. We are afraid. We are shufflers on this question. . . In

some circles it is considered extremely revolutionary to oppose votes for women as a useless reform; and loud fireworks are metaphorically exploded in some small obscure back shop in a dimly lighted alley to the satisfaction of all present. These simple and well-meaning yet dangerous people are a menace to every step upward the disinherited make.[63]

Just as the pre-war strike wave and the new forms of organizing at Singer impressed those SLPers who were seeking a revolutionary political organization which could develop in relation to mass action, the militant suffrage movement meant that 'The Woman Question' ceased to be an academic debate and became a practical and immediate demand for political solidarity.

The Women's Social and Political Union could mount large meetings in Glasgow. They had links with the Independent Labour Party. Helen Crawfurd was involved in both the ILP and the suffrage struggle. Nor did all suffrage supporters fit Lily Gair Wilkinson's stereotype of middle-class women who ignored class oppression. There was a working-class socialist feminist tradition with close links to the labour movement.[64] Jessie Stephen was active in both the WSPU and class politics in Glasgow in this period. She stressed the connection between the demand for the vote and the economic and social changes working-class women needed in employment, housing, domestic life, maternity benefits, matrimonial law. 'The vote was only the means to an end, to a new state of society where women could be treated as human beings, not as second-class citizens.'[65]

There was also an anarchist-feminist current in Glasgow in this period with syndicalist links. Dismissive of the vote, they were interested in co-operative living, free love, birth control and sexual liberation.[66]

Individuals were influenced by a mixture of all these ideas and there was personal contact through families, cultural groupings and in the working-class community. So the WSPU recruited dockers to be Emmeline Pankhurst's bodyguard at a suffragette meeting. Jessie Stephen moved between feminism and labour causes; the father of an anarchist feminist, Annie Gordon, set up John Maclean's meetings for him.[67] Lizzie Bell wore no wedding ring and Arthur MacManus enthused about the suffrage movement.

It was not possible for the SLP to remain above the daily hum-
drum of politics or to exist outside the informal political network-
ing which created such a vigorous socialist culture in Glasgow. If
the pure sectarians turned up their noses at the reformism of the
suffrage movement and of the ILP, this absolute dismissal created
a drift of the more pragmatic away from revolutionary socialism.
John Wheatley, the ILP MP for Shettleston, was keen to poach
members and had some success.[68] The ILP's brand of municipal
socialism in Glasgow stressed democratic control and it seemed
realizable. A weakness of the SLP was that in the grand sweep of
theory they tended to miss out on specific policies and the tedious
nitty-gritty of local municipal matters. So there would be earnest
characters of a practical cast who wanted to get something done and
reformed in the here and now who would get steamed up about
taxation, temperance, municipal trams, and drift into the ILP in
exasperation. Suffrage, with its close links with the ILP, could
become one such issue. How to be at once more flexible and less
sectarian without becoming absorbed in 'reformism' troubled both
Bell and MacManus in different ways.

Industrial Rebellion in the First World War

Even while they tussled with this problem – one of the classic 'in-
solubles' in an absolute sense, which presents itself with innumber-
able historical faces in different eras – the known world of politics
was transformed by the First World War.

Some of the socialists in Glasgow were initially overwhelmed by
the popular enthusiasm for the war. Harry McShane, a young
socialist engineer in Glasgow at the time, recalls a music-hall song
which was being sung everywhere immediately before war broke
out.

> Little man, little man,
> You want to be a soldier, little man,
> You are mother's only son –
> Never mind about the gun,
> Stay at home,
> Fight for her all you can.

But the day war was declared, the song died. . .

Nobody was whistling it. Instead another music-hall song, *It's a long way to Tipperary*, was being whistled and sung everywhere . . .

A terrible war fever developed. Men rushed to join the army hoping that the war wouldn't be all over by the time they got to the front; they had to march in civilian clothes because there weren't enough uniforms to go round. Many young people, particularly those who were unemployed, were caught up in the adventure of the thing.[1]

It took time to adjust to the enormity of the war.

As well as believing the war would be short, everyone, including the socialists, thought it would be fought by professional armies and volunteers. But even though we didn't suspect how terrible the war was going to be, we knew that it was a political disaster. Our hopes for an international general strike to stop the war were unfounded.[2]

The failure of the Second International to resist the war was a tragic betrayal for left ILPers, a betrayal felt all the more acutely when Arthur Henderson, who was secretary and now leader of the Parliamentary Labour Party, actually joined a Coalition Government in 1915. For the SLP there were ironic complications. They had refused to join the International in case their views were confused with those of the ILP and their Marxist rivals in the Social Democratic Federation (now the British Socialist Party).[3] Tom Bell recalls:

Arthur and I sat late into the night discussing the situation in all its pros and cons. We walked the streets, excited and restless. One thing was clear as crystal, academic discussions and sectarianism must end. The International is dead, we must make sure in the new International that arises Henderson and his bunch find no place.[4]

Three initial lines emerged on the war in the SLP. There was open hostility; justification of defence in the event of an invasion, and a view of the war as an event which would hasten the inevitable collapse of capitalism.[5]

John S. Clarke, as editor of *The Socialist*, was against the war.[6]

Tom Bell claims that this was also the position he and Arthur Mac-Manus took.[7] But Sylvia Pankhurst says that MacManus 'supported the war during the first eight months of its duration'.[8] It may have been that he saw his industrial organizing as the priority and did not propagandize so actively in the factories against the war. This was a criticism made by John Maclean and endorsed by Harry McShane of the shop stewards. It would be understandable if MacManus feared losing the personal loyalty he inspired. Tom Bell says workers who knew Arthur MacManus 'as one of their crowd' would turn up to defend the SLP anti-war meetings which were in danger of attack from patriotic crowds, not because they knew about the politics but because 'they were always ready for a fight, especially when one of their own was involved'.[9] However, MacManus, Bell, Clarke and Paul were under considerable pressure as a small central group keeping *The Socialist* going and holding the SLP branches together in the early months of the war. They regularly faced attack and arrest when they sold the paper. In 1915 MacManus was also helping Connolly produce *The Irish Worker* and in Glasgow he had become chair of the Clyde Workers' Committees.[10]

There were no indications of the hoped-for mass, working-class movement against the war. But the pressures of war production resulted in a wage demand which greatly alarmed the officials of the skilled engineers' union, the Amalgamated Society of Engineers (ASE). As factory after factory went on strike, rank-and-file exasperation with the lack of support from officials intensified. An effective rank-and-file organization between factories was created.[11] Arthur MacManus played a key role in this and remembered: 'The one fact that struck home was the necessity of the workers doing for themselves what the officials were too cowardly to attempt.'[12]

Developments in Glasgow seemed to be confirming in practice the ideas the SLPers had discussed so fervently in small meetings, in the economics classes, and in Tom Bell's home. Rising prices and appalling housing conditions led to a series of rent strikes in which working-class housewives organized in large numbers. In Glasgow, by October 1915 there were 25,000 tenants on strike and they gained support from shipyard workers and even big employers. The women involved had political links with the ILP.

Mary Barbour, Agnes Dollan and Helen Crawfurd were all ILP women and all active in the rent strike.[13] Though not directly connected with the SLP and the shop stewards' movement, they contributed to a climate of rebellion in Glasgow which already in 1915 was contesting the patriotic conformity of the early months of the 'Great War'.

In June, the Munitions Act became law and when the trade union leaders failed to oppose it, the Clyde Workers' Committee (CWC) was set up to resist the restrictions it put on the right to strike and other customary trade union rights.[14]

Wartime reorganization encouraged the dilution of skilled operations which the Singer management had attempted earlier. An important element in the CWC and the industrial militancy which it co-ordinated and sustained was resistance to the introduction of dilution on the employers' terms. The effort to exercise workers' control had a two-dimensional element in this context. It challenged the employers' encroachment on the practices of the workshop, and it also defended the relative privileges of the male craft workers, respectable and acutely conscious of status, with their blue suits, bowler hats and umbrellas.[15]

James Hinton points out that for the revolutionary socialists, the CWC 'represented a dramatic breakthrough from propagandist policies to leadership in a genuine mass movement. Leadership, however, raised unfamiliar problems; problems which long immersion in the clarities of propaganda had not equipped these revolutionaries to solve.'[16]

The SLP had for years denounced craft privileges. Now it was the craft sectional grievances of the militant engineers which formed the power base of the movement. The defence of craft unionism was thus in constant danger of submerging the long-term aim of broad-based all-grades industrial organization. The concept of workers' control turned against other workers – the unskilled, women, people from outside the immediate area who would not be susceptible to pressure to give up their jobs after the war. Though spasmodic attempts to include and organize women workers in Glasgow were made, these were only partially successful.[17] By spring 1916 unity disintegrated.

Moreover, while the SLP opposed the war, the CWC had no policy. It was concerned with the more limited aim of defending the workers against the threats to their organization brought about by the war. Socialists like John Maclean, enthusiastic about the concept of the political strike, were scornful of this division of political and industrial work. Theoretically, Arthur MacManus might have agreed with him. In practice he found that it was not possible to organize in ideally favourable conditions. So, while MacManus and his SLP friends welcomed the opportunity for mass action as a release from the sterility of the dogmatic sect, they found that coherent principles were hard to maintain in a ferment.

The government launched a determined and intelligent offensive against the CWC. The objective was clear. 'To obtain a reasonably smooth working of the Munitions Act, this committee should be smashed.'[18] But the labour officer responsible for the Clyde area, Paterson, wrote to the Ministry of Munitions on 17 January that the Clyde militants – including MacManus – were too popular to harass directly. Nor was there a decisive case against them. Instead, the authorities should manoeuvre a situation in which they could force their opponents' hand on grounds where the militant base would narrow. There had to be an issue where the Clyde workers would appear in an unpopular light. A strike by skilled men against dilution would mean they could be presented as unpatriotic defenders of privilege.[19]

The government thus pushed through dilution strenuously with the support of some hard-line employers. They were able, when the rebellion came, to drive a wedge between skilled and unskilled, men and women. This was probably all the more important from the authorities' point of view because 1915 had seen the most determined organization among women munitions workers.[20]

A curious feature of the government's intervention was the direct and personal element in the relationship between the state and the shop stewards' movement. In December, Lloyd George went to Glasgow. Though he had told the press that under no circumstances would he have anything to do with the CWC, he and Arthur Henderson nonetheless met with Gallacher, MacManus, Davy Kirkwood and some of the other stewards including two women workers – who are characteristically anonymous.

The stewards put their case against the employers' using dilution to reduce costs, increase profits and extend control over the workforce. They were not opposed to all changes in production

methods, but wanted these to be on the workers' terms and controlled by factory committees.[21] Lloyd George, Gallacher records,
'brushed his moustache, pawed his hair' and whispered to Arthur
Henderson, until an indignant Gallacher threatened to walk out.[22]
Arthur MacManus took up the issue of the war which he said, in
true SLP style, was a 'war for trade and territory . . . for the purposes of imperialism'.[23]

Not surprisingly, the meeting ended in impasse, but Lloyd
George retained his charm and composure and called Gallacher
back as the others left. He put his arm round his shoulder and con-
gratulated him on his relations with the other stewards. Then he
personally appealed to Gallacher to share the platform with him at
the meeting he was to speak at in St Andrew's Hall. Gallacher said
only on condition that the platform was shared with a CWC man,
Johnny Muir. Lloyd George lost his temper: '"I can't talk to you –
you're impossible," he barked and went barging out of the room.'[24]

The meeting on Christmas day 1915 was a fiasco from Lloyd
George's point of view. He and Arthur Henderson were howled
down.[25] This personal humiliation no doubt intensified his determination to break the CWC.

The Clydesiders' efforts to broaden resistance by linking up with
the Tyneside engineers, miners and railwaymen were unsuccessful. But they made considerable efforts to explain their case and
gain support – which explains Arthur MacManus's appearance in
Derby, a railway and specialized munitions town, early in 1916.[26]
Despite their efforts, the government's strategy proved effective.
Within three months of the labour officer's report, Arthur Mac-
Manus and the other shop stewards, including Willie Gallacher,
were all imprisoned or deported from the area.[27] There was no
mass protest. The *Herald* remarked tersely: 'the great mass of
Clyde workers are more interested in wages than freedom.'[28]

The final bitter twist was that a group of Industrial Unionists of
the Detroit faction of the IWW who had played no part in the Clyde
Workers' Committee, because they maintained the building of a
new revolutionary union was more important, took over the Committee and used it as a vehicle for 'educational' work on syndicalist
lines.[29] Gallacher claims this consisted of 'doctrinaire recitation
ready for the day in the future when we'd take and hold'.[30]

Such a day must have appeared particularly far in the future to

Arthur MacManus when he was unceremoniously dragged from his bed, taken to the station and put on a train to Edinburgh with David Kirkwood and two other stewards, Wainwright and Bridges. Arriving in Edinburgh and at a loss where to go, they went to the home of John S. Clarke. He was away lecturing in Glasgow when they arrived, but they were greeted by Sarah and her elderly mother. They settled down as best they could amidst the dust, the books, the stuffed birds and antiquarian specimens.[31] It must have been very crowded with John, Sarah, their small son, four stewards and an old lady, with other men like Gallacher visiting. There was no doubt about their welcome. Sarah enthusiastically baked a caraway seed cake in their honour. Unfortunately she put in canary seed by mistake, as Gallacher remembered years later when he wrote his *Last Memoirs*.[32]

Even John S. Clarke's lecture had not escaped the attention of the authorities who apparently decided his 'Glorious Episodes of British History' were damaging the war effort. In November 1915 his talks on the execution of Charles I, the struggle against the Combination Acts and other popular movements were banned.[33]

He was wily as well as a scholar and poet. On one occasion, according to David Kirkwood, he evaded arrest by simply removing his hat: This transformed his appearance, for 'When John S. Clarke wears a hat, he is like a douce Glasgow business man, but he is so bald that when he wears no hat he looks like Grock the clown.'[34]

Apart from the overcrowding, the deportees became restless when confined to Edinburgh with no money and nothing to do. The authorities kept pumping them for information. 'They had somehow got it into their heads that there was a great treasonable or seditious organization on the Clyde,'[35] David Kirkwood recalled, concluding that the government spies concocted a story of a rebellion to earn their wages.

Apart from discomfort and restless boredom, they were psychologically shaken by the unprecedented ruthlessness of the government's action – and by its effectiveness. Willie Gallacher described how difficult it was to realize that the state did not play by its own rules. 'When the shock measures of the government came, we were quite unprepared. We were "legal" revolutionaries.'[36]

Gallacher went down to London and with the help of Ramsay Macdonald and a radical MP for Leicester, Pringle, sought an interview with Dr Addison who was in charge of the Ministry of Munitions while Lloyd George was away in France. Addison was one of the Liberals who still remained loyal to Lloyd George despite his new right-wing associates and coercive measures. According to Gallacher, Addison was, under pressure, going to withdraw the deportation order.

Meanwhile Sir Edward Carson from the extreme right was demanding that the authorities charge the Clyde shop stewards with high treason. As Carson had been involved in blatantly treasonable armed rebellion against Home Rule proposals for Ireland in 1914, his self-righteousness had a certain irony. On Lloyd George's return from France, the efforts to get the men back to Glasgow were firmly stopped.[37]

There was the practical worry of how to care for dependants and the pressure of conscription. Thousands of pounds were raised to maintain the deportees and their families. However, depressing political tensions appeared in the defence committee. John Wheatley, an Independent Labour Party MP, was one of the trustees. Gallacher felt he cut out the SLP men in favour of Kirkwood, who was his protegé.

In 1916 conscription was in full swing and the deportees were faced with the necessity of getting employment or of being conscripted. They weren't allowed to work in Edinburgh, but they were in a position where they could leave Edinburgh to seek for work, provided they travelled further away from Glasgow.[38]

They considered what to do and decided to go to Liverpool. But Wheatley persuaded Kirkwood to stay in Edinburgh. 'In Liverpool, MacManus, Messer and the others encountered every kind of difficulty. They had to pawn everything they had to keep going, but they could get nothing from the fund. They were no longer deportees, so Wheatley decided.'[39]

Tom Bell was already working in Liverpool and welcomed his old friend. He testified to the remarkable resilience of Arthur's spirits. For when Arthur finally got a job through the Ministry of Munitions at the Cunard Company, he was shunned by the workers.

When Mac presented himself one morning to start work, the other workers downed tools and refused to work with him, on patriotic grounds. Mac encouraged them; told them he didn't want to work either; that he was sent there against his will, and proposed they should have a meeting together. Soon the workers came to look on him as one of their own, and he became very popular with all the workers in the shop.[40]

He would not be confined by the Ministry of Munitions any more than by Singer's management. Officially restricted to Liverpool and Cunards, 'Mac' took off, wandering the country. The 'waywardness' which had distressed his mother now vexed the Liverpool police and the shady government spies whose job it was to keep track of his movements.

Rebelling against the compulsion of working, Mac often stayed off work for days. On these occasions he visited Manchester, Barrow, Coventry, Birmingham and Derby, meeting the shop stewards for conversation and organization.[41]

And of course courting Hettie Wheeldon and seeing his old friends, Willie Paul and John S. Clarke, who were forced into hiding near Derby. All three men were moving around the country in a semi-legal existence, keeping *The Socialist* going. Willie Paul somehow also managed to spend time in the British Museum writing his book on the state.[42]

Anti-war networks

The extraordinary circumstances of the war turned over all the old allegiances, and divided both socialist and feminist organizations.

Christabel and Emmeline Pankhurst in the Women's Social and Political Union, along with their old opponent, Mrs Fawcett, leader of the constitutional suffragists, supported the war. With little idea of the realities of trench warfare, Christabel declared dramatically: 'I want men to go to battle like the knight of old who knelt upon the altar and vowed that he would keep his sword stainless and with absolute honour to his nation.'[1]

Sylvia, of course, was anti-war and by mid 1915 found herself working uneasily with her old opponents from the constitutional wing like Catherine Marshall and Helena Swanwick, who were against the war.[2] Charlotte Despard's Women's Freedom League was also campaigning for peace. It was from the feminists that the early anti-war organizations developed. In the spring of 1915, the International Congress of Women, presided over by Jane Addams, the American social feminist, was held in The Hague in defiance of the war. In Autumn 1915, the British section of the Women's International League was formed and vehemently opposed military conscription.[3]

Diverse labour movements and local socialist groups mobilized when an SLP member, William Holliday, was sentenced to three months' hard labour under the Defence of the Realm Act in May 1915 for saying: 'Freedom's battle has not to be fought on the blood-drenched soil of France but nearer home – our enemy is within the gates.'

Trades councils, teachers' trade union branches, Socialist Sunday Schools, Herald League groups, ILP, SLP and BSP branches supported the William Holliday Defence Fund which Willie Paul organized. The money raised was used to appeal, and he was acquitted. But he was arrested again at another meeting and died in prison. Rowdies tried to break up a memorial meeting addressed by Willie Paul in the Bull Ring in May 1916. 'Some of them were disguised as men,' commented *The Socialist*.[4]

With the formation of the 'No Conscription Fellowship' (NCF) there was an organization which could bring together socialists, feminists, pacifists, radical liberals and Christian opponents to military conscription and defend the young men who had to go before military tribunals if they refused to fight. The idea was Lilla Brockway's. Recently married, she and Fenner Brockway had moved from a London collective household, in which they had met, to a cottage in Derbyshire. The cottage became the headquarters of the new organization which included Bertrand Russell, the feminist Catherine Marshall, the Quaker Barrett Brown and the ILPer Clifford Allen. There was a strong moral and spiritual impetus in the Fellowship's resistance to war.[5]

Clifford Allen said, for example: 'I am a socialist, and so hold in all sincerity that the life and personality of every man is sacred and that there is something of divinity in every human being.'[6] Despite this high ethical tone, they proved an ingenious bunch, putting intellectual scholarship to effective use in debating with the public prosecutor, drawing on the experience of pre-war politics and finding themselves with surprising new allies.[7]

The feminist-pacifists converted the non-violent tactics of resistance of the suffrage movement to new ends. For instance, Catherine Marshall arranged for children to carry white kites to give a sign to prisoners while Miss Lydia Smith sat up a tree watching for the signal.[8]

Against Christabel's sacrificial knights, some feminists argued that women as nurturers were essentially pacifist, while Sylvia argued opposition to the capitalist war. Interestingly, the male conscientious objectors were portrayed by patriots as effeminate. Basil Thomson, the police chief, reports a correspondent who worked in Dartmoor regretting the demise of the 'good old convicts' with the arrival of the conchies who were lowering the prison's tone: 'longhaired, idle young men wandering about a respectable village with their arms around each other's necks. It makes me sick to look at them.'[9]

Meanwhile, Fenner Brockway in prison received a note.

Dear Brockway,

Just heard you are here. What can we do for you? De Valera, Milroy and sixteen other Irish rebels are interned. We are Irishmen and can do anything you want – except get you out. Have your reply ready for 'Trusty' when he calls tomorrow. Cheerio![10]

Brockway got out a letter to Lilla and received a regular copy of the *Manchester Guardian*, courtesy of 'Trusty' and Sinn Fein.

As well as ingenuity and new allies, there was a grimmer aspect to being a war resister.[11] Catherine Marshall kept a careful record of the sufferings of the men who went to prison and the NCF publicized these in their newspaper, *The Tribunal*.[12] Conscientious objectors were sent to camps where accommodation and sanitation could be primitive and were forced to do heavy manual work despite ill health.[13] They suffered physical abuse. On 7 May 1917, Jack Grey was dragged round a field by a rope and immersed in sewage several times with a sack over his head and dragged out by the rope.[14] In May 1916, a man in handcuffs and fetters was attached to a wheel and left hanging in agony.[15]

At Cardiff early in 1916, NCF members were threatened with the death penalty.[16] Seventy-three conscientious objectors died as a direct result of their treatment by the authorities.[17] The health of many others must have been permanently impaired. Three Durham miners were executed by the army in France in 1916. Attempts to find out the circumstances from the army were unsuccessful.[18]

It must have been a strange role reversal for the veterans of suffrage militancy – the women were no longer at the centre of the resistance to physical coercion from the state but instead a vital back-up for the men.

Less dramatically, the women outside the prison and camps, who were left virtually holding the NCF together, had a hard time. As Fenner Brockway says: 'They had to live in the middle of a war-mad world and to undergo the contumely which opposition to the war and relationship to an imprisoned "conchy" involved.'[19] They could be poor, bringing up children alone, desperate for news, without hope that opposition to the war would bring it to an end. The NCF network was invaluable to them too.

The anarchists round the newspaper *Freedom* had their own anti-war organization. Lilian Woolf, an ex-suffragette who became an anarchist, was imprisoned for giving out anti-war leaflets to troops. Pregnant and unmarried on principle, she remained a vegetarian in prison and was forced to drink cabbage water to provide herself with some nutrition.[20]

Hettie Wheeldon became the secretary of the Derby No Conscription Fellowship. On a local level, she did similar work to Catherine Marshall in keeping the records of what was happening to the COs.[21] In Derby, as elsewhere, opponents of the war made different choices. Hettie's brother, William, as an anarchist was an 'absolutist'. He refused to do any work that served the war effort.[22] Bert Parker, Reuben Farrow's Christian Socialist friend, also took this position.[23] Reuben Farrow was a pacifist but continued to work on the railways.[24] He took over as secretary of the NCF when Hettie gave it up.[25] The Socialist Labour Party men tried to keep out of prison as long as they could. John S. Clarke was lying low at Ben Turner's farm at Arleston near Derby, working as a labourer and writing articles.[26] Towards the end of 1916, William Paul was in the area, living at Littleover,[27] where Arthur MacManus's letters to him from Liverpool were being intercepted by the authorities. Arthur told him the police had been round again and that his mother was getting worried about the pressure to join up – hardly dramatic revelations to the police spies.[28]

They were also keeping track of Willie Paul's lectures for the Derby NCF and his growing prosperity as a businessman. Major William Melville Lee, an investigator for the Ministry of Munitions, noted that Paul had 'establishments' in Manchester, Birmingham, Sheffield, Rotherham, Chesterfield and other places. These contributed funds and served as bases for the distribution of 'propaganda'.[29]

If there were pressures which brought together a wide range of political views in the NCF and also incipient links between the anti-war movement and the revolutionary socialists in the shop stewards' movement, there were also contrary forces which made for suspicion and division.

There was an uneasy alliance between absolutists and moderate pacifists, between ethical socialists and revolutionaries, between women who had been militant suffragettes and the constitutional suffragists, anarchists and socialists. The exigencies of the time demanded unity and sometimes it worked. But old sectarian battles continued to pull those on the far left into intransigent isolation. Alice Wheeldon continued to dislike Reuben Farrow's 'milk-and-water Jesus Christ manner'.[30] Hettie, early in 1917, was becoming more and more exasperated with the No Conscription Fellowship. 'The NCF has failed and is dying a natural death,'[31] she told her sister, Winnie Mason, in January 1917.

The Wheeldon women were all undoubtedly worried about William, who had been imprisoned and left naked in his cold cell.[32] Winnie feared that her husband Alf, a chemist, would be called up. There was a widespread belief that industrial conscription in collaboration with the employers would be the next government move. When Lloyd George moved from the Ministry of Munitions to become Prime Minister, hopes sank further. The virulent bitterness which appears in the letters intercepted by the police is comprehensible only in the light of the enormity of the carnage of the war, the unprecedented state powers and the apparent hopelessness of resistance. It expresses the estranged isolation of the revolutionary minority, both within the society at large and within the anti-war movement.

Winnie wrote to Hettie, on 31 December 1916, that there was 'no chance of an exemption' for Alf,

> now that damned buggering Welsh sod's got into power. . .
> Ain't the whole Caboodle lousy, eh? We can't have Peace yet
> else there'd be no need for this Industrial Conscription, so they
> must wait about six months or so while they get it fastened on
> our necks a bit firmer and then we've got it in the neck a treat –
> then I s'pose [sic] they'll talk peace.[33]

Apart from their work in the NCF, Hettie and her mother were part of a more shadowy network which sprang up in an ad hoc response to the needs of men on the run. This appears to have been based on former contacts, political and personal, and word-of-mouth recommendation. Both politics and William's refusal to fight drew the Wheeldons into helping men escape the authorities. Theirs was one of the places which would put up resisters. It was not exactly an underground, but 'that there was a sanctuary for fugitives in Derby was common knowledge to most people'.[34]

Theirs was by no means an isolated or unique refuge. There were places to go in other Midlands and northern towns: Leicester, Sheffield, Liverpool, for example. Hettie and Alice Wheeldon were involved also in helping men escape from Liverpool to America. There had long been a two-way traffic of radical seamen across the Atlantic and the Wobbly links were strong. Arthur Mac-Manus, working as a fitter at Cunards in Liverpool, thanks to the Ministry of Munitions, was strategically placed.

Networks of contacts coexisted alongside the formal organization of the NCF. It was not so much a case of men joining the NCF and then resisting, but of members of the Fellowship doggedly tracking them down and bringing them into the organization.

A letter to Hettie from an 'absolutist' in a camp indicates how information was collected and how personal contact fused with an organization. He mentions by name several men from the Midlands area, explains which camp they are in and describes contacts made with men who are objecting to doing Home Office work. He also asks about the response of women to the war, sending his regards to Mrs Wheeldon and two women friends of hers, Mrs Land and Mrs Fern. He reminisces about his time in the Derby area when contact was easy to make with the NCF. He describes the struggle he and Parker (presumably Bert Parker) had to prevent their hair and beards being cut, adding that he believed if every resister had refused Home Office work and taken the absolutist position, the authorities would have had to set them free.[35]

The humorous bravado of his letter is in contrast to the paranoia, despair, hardship and hatred which was the everyday reality of resistance. The hunted desperation of men on the run was clearly preying on Hettie. She wrote to Winnie in January 1917, 'Mac is terrified. Sticks in all day and only emerges at night.' ('Mac' was undoubtedly Macdonald, a young socialist the Wheeldons were concealing at the time.) 'Sutton is still workless, and living on his sister who has 3 children and an income of 30s a week besides helping to pay off money by that brother of Sutton's who drowned himself 3 years ago, so she's lively isn't she and all the NCF can allow is 3s some weeks, 4s others.' 'Frank Burton' was 'waiting to be seized by the clutching hand'. 'Pail' was turned down by the tribunal. 'Williams' had still heard nothing. 'Moss, whose brother died in the Asylum, is waiting to be killed, for they'll kill him and Leslie, Birch, Thomas, Crispin are still at liberty.'

For this local network of resisters without economic backing or the political links of leading members of the NCF, local supporters like Hettie were of vital significance, providing an alternative emotionally and practically. Families and lovers were divided. 'Jack Vernon is in Notts Hospital, shell shock [*sic*] and Lily won't go to see him. Doesn't want to see him again alive or dead.'[36]

With their roots in a local network of resistance to the war, Alice and Hettie Wheeldon were carrying not only a political but a psychological responsibility. They were committed to helping men against whom the odds were stacked. The state, it appeared, could assume any power it wished for the extraordinary circumstances of the war. Thus the legal support work of the NCF merged obviously with the semi-legal sheltering of men on the run.

Because the Wheeldons' story emerged in a sensational way, it is easy to spotlight their activities as exceptional. They weren't. The combination of opposition to the war and practical help which extended into illegality existed in many parts of the country. What was unusual about Alice and Hettie were personal links they took for granted, with Willie Paul and Arthur MacManus, which connected them to the SLP and to the rank-and-file movement Mac-Manus was involved in creating in the factories. This gave them a much greater significance in the eyes of the authorities than local anti-war work would merit. For the government was most con-cerned to prevent any connection developing between industrial militancy and opposition to the war.

In retrospect, Fenner Brockway reflected in his autobiography, *Inside the Left*, on how the failure to develop this alliance had made the anti-war movement less effective: 'In England we failed to unite the anti-war struggle with the class struggle sufficiently, with the result that we became isolated from the mass of the workers and too often tended to become bourgeois pacifists rather than working-class socialists.'[37]

For Hettie and Alice it was not a matter of political choice. The friendship with Arthur and their work together meant the indust-rial and anti-militarist rebellions intertwined.

Spies and the Shop Stewards' Movement

In October 1916 in nearby Sheffield, a fitter at Vickers, Leonard Hargreaves, was conscripted into the army. The firm withheld papers which would have secured his discharge and he sub-sequently missed his chance to appeal. This seemed to confirm fears that employers would go along with the military authorities and that industrial conscription would be introduced.[1]

There already existed a shop stewards' movement in Sheffield, though of a rather different political and economic character from that on the Clyde.[2] Histories of the rank-and-file industrial move-ments which show the detailed interrelationship with local political and specific radical traditions and inequalities of skill and gender have yet to be written. But we do know that Sheffield presents an interesting contrast to the Clyde in several ways. Most important, there were closer links with less skilled engineering workers.[3] Dilution was not such an issue. The less skilled were much better organized and the women were more easily assimilated into the general union.[4] It is not clear the extent to which the women in Sheffield played an equal role in determining the political direction of resistance. A certain degree of labour movement support, though, is obvious. One of the women's leaders, Mrs Wilkinson, was to be elected to the trades council executive in 1918.[5]

Jack T. Murphy, one of the key figures in the Sheffield move-ment, was the son of a blacksmith, who went to work at Vickers, Brightside, aged 13. As a young man he was a teetotaller, a non-conformist and of a studious disposition, interested in philosophy and politics. He read Marx, Connolly and other left-wing theor-ists while throwing propellor shafts at the Brightside works. He was an active trade unionist and in the Herald League in Sheffield.[6]

A lesser known figure is Walter Hill, involved in the Sheffield shop stewards' movement and influenced by the ideas of Edward Carpenter. Carpenter had been active in the local socialist move-ment since the 1880s, combining the aesthetic revulsion against capitalism of romantic socialism with the links to earlier communi-tarian experiments and a commitment to ecology, mysticism and sexual liberation. Carpenter's opposition to mechanistic forms of Marxism and bureaucratic labourism inclined him to syndicalism in which he saw the possibility of an awakening of self-determining associations federated into a whole.[7] Like many people, Carpenter had been confused at the outset of the war but came to oppose it, which had brought him to the attention of the government spies.

In November 1916 'Alex Gordon', a police spy, posing as a man on the run, arrived in Sheffield after contacting Arthur MacManus in Liverpool. He stayed the night with Walter Hill and reported to the Ministry of Munitions that Hill was 'a follower of the prophet Edward Carpenter, a socialist "head-light". [He] is an advocate of the Homogenic or Comrade Love preached by Carpenter.'[8]

Hargreaves's arrest brought industrial militants and socialist opposition to the war together. It met with a rapid and determined response. On 8 November 1916, the district committee of the ASE and the shop stewards called a meeting. An all-out strike was threatened unless the government returned Hargreaves in a week. This resolution was telegraphed to the ASE executive and to the Prime Minister, Asquith. Two hundred shop stewards waited keyed up for action in the Engineers Institute, waiting to see if the government would respond before 4 p.m.

> Standing outside the Institute was a fleet of motor cycles with their cyclist shop stewards ready to be despatched to the engineering centres, visited the previous weekend.

It was arranged that several should go southwards by different routes to cover Lincoln, Gainsborough, Nottingham, Leicester, Rugby, Bedford, London. Others were to go to Derby, Coventry, Birmingham, Rugby, London. Whilst these were to go southwards, others were to go to Manchester, Liverpool, Bolton, St Helens, Barrow. Another group were to go to Leeds, Huddersfield, Halifax, Bradford, Keighley. And yet others were to go straight to Newcastle and the East Wash towns, northward to Edinburgh and Glasgow.[9]

They were reinforced by further delegates going by train to stay in the big centres in order to off set the 'contradictory reports' which the press would undoubtedly issue about the strike. 'Four o'clock came. The government had not replied. The strike was called. The shop stewards rushed to the factories. The cyclists were off at once. At five o'clock the strike was complete.'[10]

Murphy says ten thousand skilled workers came out. James Hinton puts it at twelve thousand. The government conceded and allowed Leonard Hargreaves to come back. It was an inspiring victory. Though the local official in the Ministry of Munitions wanted a repeat of the Clyde, on this occasion the authorities decided to avoid a confrontation.[11]

It was an impressive show of strength but there was a weakness in the Sheffield movement's solidarity. The skilled men were to be exempt from conscription. But what about the rest? As James Hinton points out, 'the issue of conscription which precipitated the rank-and-file movement centred on craft privilege just as much as the issue of dilution'.[12] This was to leave the Sheffield shop stewards' movement exposed and isolated in the spring of the following year. A bitter parody circulated among the wounded soldiers and unskilled engineers:

Don't send me in the Army, George,
I'm in the ASE.
Take all the bloody labourers,
But for God's sake don't take me.
You want me for a soldier?
Well, that can never be –
A man of my ability
And in the ASE.[13]

However, after the Hargreaves victory, there was a mood of invincibility and high hopes that the rank-and-file movement would develop in a wide network of towns.

The informants of the Ministry of Munitions for their part were preoccupied with preventing three strategic dangers: an alliance between the skilled and unskilled, the creation of a national rank-and-file movement, and a link-up between industrial unrest in munitions and other industries essential to the war effort and the No Conscription Fellowship.

Not surprisingly, employers whose businesses were booming with wartime orders and war production discipline welcomed the spies cordially. Lieutenant de Valda, a Buchan-like adventurer who had joined the army and been moved into an intelligence unit connected to the Ministry of Munitions, which also employed, at a lower echelon, the wretched Alex Gordon, clearly enjoyed himself in Sheffield. While 'safeguarding munitions from "foreign agitators", "sabotage" and other interference by enemy agitators or agents', he was received most hospitably by big business. He was gratified by the 'great kindness and goodwill' shown to him by the heads of firms like Douglas Vickers and Archie Dixon.[14]

Early in December 1916, another Ministry of Munitions spy, 'D.M.S.', who was trying to keep track of Arthur MacManus's sprightly moves, reported that the rank-and-file movement (also called the New Organization or NO) had issued a circular 'addressed to both sexes and all grades, craftsmen, semi-skilled and unskilled workmen *and women* [sic]'. He saw this as a new manoeuvre on the part of the NO to enlist the sympathies of the women workers.[15] Alex Gordon also reported in December from Sheffield that several trustworthy women were acting as despatch bearers carrying messages between the various militant branches as it was unsafe to use the post.[16]

Another spy,' H.B.' (Herbert Booth), attended a New Organization meeting at the ASE Hall, Stanley Street, Sheffield. It consisted of semi-skilled labourers and women meeting 'to see if they could act in unison with skilled men'. Some of the men argued for the need to organize the women and raise their wages. Miss Pearson repeatedly said at the meeting that: ' "The women were only too ready to act with them as their hours and pay were shameful and the only remedy was organization with the skilled men." '[17] Murphy said the skilled men in the New Organization wanted this and suggested a committee should be formed. A woman called Mrs Robinson was among those chosen for the committee.[18]

Despite these impressive efforts to overcome divisions of sex and skill, one of the speakers from the floor gave vent to the racist fear that 'black and yellow labour' would be brought in and kept in compounds as cheap labour. He was apparently afraid that future generations would be 'entirely changed in colour'.[19]

Still, it is clear that significant efforts were made in Sheffield to develop a unified rank-and-file movement. Booth, the agent, saw Murphy as 'quite the hero of the day'.[20] It is characteristic that he should sum up the meeting in terms of an individual. A basic problem in the approach of the informants to the Ministry of Munitions intelligence unit was that they did not pay much attention to the specific industrial circumstances which caused discontent, nor did they have any understanding of local labour traditions. They saw strikes as basically engineered by individuals. Their own lives and political backgrounds inclined them to an institutional and hierarchical approach to organization in which commands came from on top. This was not at all like the organic connection between leading political activists and the base in rank-and-file upsurge. Their leadership involved ascertaining when workers were ready for action and then steering a strategic course.

As Murphy reflected afterwards,

> It is a false and stupid idea to think that strikes are the result of the machinations of agitators. At the heart of every strike is a deep-seated grievance of the workers involved. Workers don't just throw up their jobs and face loss of wages without strike pay just for fun. Only the stupid and ignorant think they do. But the stupid and ignorant are in high places as well as low.[21]

The Ministry of Munitions intelligence agents regarded Arthur MacManus, Jack Murphy, Willie Paul and an SLPer from Leicester, David Ramsay, as 'the Inner Circle' who decided the fate of the munitions industry.[22] They were prepared to go to considerable lengths to get information, not only intercepting letters and telephone conversations but in general hounding their quarry.[23] On one occasion in December 1916, they lost track of MacManus and negotiated with the local police for a house-to-house search to track him down under the guise of searching for 'eligible' men for the services.[24] Though the shop stewards were wary of spies, they were able to infiltrate not only as observers at conferences but gaining the stewards' personal trust. Alex Gordon not only stayed the night with Walter Hill in Sheffield, he arrived with a reference Arthur MacManus had given him around 7 December 1916. He was en route for Glasgow with his 'letter of introduction to McLaine'.[25] (This could have been John Maclean, or Neil Maclean, who had helped Connolly form the SLP, or William McLaine, a shop steward.) The letter was given to 'V', perhaps Vivian, which was Alex Gordon's real name. It is not clear which name MacManus knew him by nor what the letter to Glasgow contained. However, it is interesting that he saw MacManus early in December and a few weeks later arrived at the Wheeldons' house in Derby.

Alex Gordon had been a member of the British Socialist Party before the war. This would have enabled him to approach socialists more naturally than the military agents might. But the experience of a sectarian party was quite different from that of the shop stewards' movement with its emphasis on grass-roots democracy and distrust of leaders. The syndicalist movement shared with anarchism a critique of hierarchy within the movements against oppression. *The Miners Next Step* in 1912, which came out of the syndicalist strike waves before the war, assessed the advantages and disadvantages of leaders thoughtfully. Like Connolly and the Wobblies, their approach influenced the shop stewards' movement. Leaders were needed in specific circumstances but they were not to be enshrined in a permanent hierarchy of power because this took away from others the capacity for conscious union. 'Solidarity' was not an unthinking herding together but a chosen association which carried elements of new democratic relations between human beings.[26]

While MacManus, Murphy and the rest did clearly influence the course of events, their power was born and rooted in action. It was carried as a trust from their connection to and understanding of the people who gave them respect. It was quite different from the automatic authority of the officer in command in which the capacity to control was permanently alienated from the men.[27]

This element in the shop stewards' movement of 'power from the bottom'[28] bemused and troubled the Ministry of Munitions agents.

It was incomprehensible and consequently feared and distrusted by men who were trained as army officers or NCOs or who had known only the life of individualistic adventurers taking the white man's spoil in the Empire. They concluded that wariness against leadership and a conscious attempt to overcome a built-in tension between the visible figures and the rank and file was merely hypocrisy, even going so far as to say that Murphy often 'apes humility' by sitting amongst the audience rather than on the platform at meetings![29]

Alex Gordon informed his employers that 'the Directorate' was made up of fanatical, unbalanced and generally dubious agitators.[30] Doggedly sniffing out an inevitably shifting 'directorate', 'inner circle' or 'revolutionary ring'[31] whom they saw as controlling an insurgent scenario of unthinking masses, the pursuers created the pursued in their own image. While it was true that the individual activists were under sustained pressures, were trying to bring form to a fragmented rebellion on the shop-floor, there was always sustained grievance and the varied circumstances which gave rise to discontent among large numbers of workers. Failure to grasp this flawed the whole approach of the spies.

There was thus a built-in pressure to accentuate the desperate melodrama. The spies had a professional interest in hamming up their reports with the dangerous character of their prey. The more perilous the game, the more significant the hunter after all. The more sinister the plot, the greater chance of a bonus – all-important for the indigent lower echelons like Gordon.

Apart from concentrating their researches on prominent figures, they also set great store on the providers of funds for anti-war organizations, reporting in autumn 1916 that £10,000 had been received by the NCF in three months.[32]

So William Paul's business was of interest and middle-class sympathizers like Edward Carpenter were watched because he gave money to the NCF. Alex Gordon roused himself to a pitch of self-righteous patriotism to describe the elderly homosexual writer as 'a menace to morality and recruiting'.[33]

The Ministry of Munitions cast its net wide. It spied on the wealthy anarchist J.M. Davison, the constitutional suffragist and pacifist Helena Swanwick, G.D.H. Cole, Fenner Brockway, the ILP MP for Sheffield W.C. Anderson, as well as an SLP doctor in

Sheffield, Dr Chandler.[34] It decided Ramsay MacDonald was in league with Arthur MacManus to undermine the influence of the trade union leaders and organize opposition to the Military Service and Munitions of War Acts.[35] It was suspicious of the Union of Democratic Control (UDC) which opposed the secret diplomacy of wartime and was keeping track of Arthur Ponsonby, a liberal aristocrat who was involved.[36]

The assumption was that if people were involved in one kind of protest they were automatically infected with others. While contact existed between individuals in a wide range of movements, it did not follow that every participant in a strike was anti-war or every protester against the war wanted fundamental social change. The police spies found it extremely difficult to grasp the extent and limits of interaction – which depended greatly on past networks, regional variations, personal factors. All these, of course, could change as well.

There are flashes of panic. The Military Service Act unified the opposition: 'All the disintegrating and reactionary elements in the State such as the Pacifists, the SLP, the Syndicalists, the IWW, the Sinn Feiners, the UDC and the militant section of the ILP, flock to serve under the same banner.'[37]

William Melville Lee, in his report, added to this list 'the BSP, the Women's Social and Political Union, the Clyde Workers' Committee, the Central Labour College, the Plebians, the Social Science Classes (Karl Marx)'. While each individual organization was not a great threat, he thought they were 'perilous to the State' as an 'entity'; the exception was the 'Rank and File movement' which he saw as extremely dangerous. He recognized that these disparate groupings were not yet a coherent force but understood that the war had been instrumental in bringing them together.[38]

The capacity to threaten the war effort was potential rather than actual. The spies saw part of the truth – that the war brought people together on the left who had previously been in quite separate worlds – but they failed to note with sufficient attention the different aims and purposes which continued to distinguish them. While individuals overlapped in allegiances there were still broadly nuanced differences between the Wobblies, the shop stewards, the syndicalists, the left ILPers, the Christian Socialists, socialist feminists, pacifist feminists, the No Conscription Fellowship and the Union for Democratic Control. The spies culled from the investigation of the Wobblies that a general strike accompanied by anarchical acts of violence was being discussed. From this they assumed these were actually threatened. They consequently sought conspiracies. The political climate and the peculiar circumstances of these wandering spies induced a framework of assumption in which it was considered to be quite proper to tilt the balance towards encouraging the surveyed to take the action which their surveyors predicted to be their intention. Spying could become provocation.

The 'Poison Plot'

It was in this context and within this framework of conceptions that the agent Alex Gordon arrived at the Wheeldons' house in Derby. He was employed by Herbert Booth who reported to Major Melville Lee at the Ministry of Munitions.[1] Gordon had been, as we have seen, moving around the country, gaining the trust of Arthur MacManus in Liverpool, with Herbert Booth's agreement seeing what he could find out in Manchester and London,[2] visiting Sheffield and staying with Walter Hill. He gleaned some comments from Hill on assassination which echoed those he heard from the Wheeldons. He reported Hill as saying that 'King George will be the last English Monarch . . . that Asquith was breaking down and that Lloyd George would probably be shot at the first opportunity.'[3] It is impossible to know whether Gordon invented these statements or whether such comments expressed the disorientation of socialists in the face of a state which assumed extraordinary powers of coercion and a helpless rage against individuals whom they were unable to control. It is conceivable that dreams of violence grew out of bemused impotence. However, regardless of whether they are fact or fiction they are not proof of a plot. Serious and strategic conspirators would not chatter so.

The relative openness of the networks Alex Gordon was able to penetrate is described by a Sheffield engineering worker, Bill Ward, who remembers a government spy, clearly Alex Gordon, arriving.

He posed as a conscientious objector on the run and was

received as such by the lads. He was working his way up to Glasgow and asked for help. There was the signature of Arthur Mac-Manus on the note but it couldn't be checked of course. There was a shop stewards' meeting at the time and Walter Hill asked him if he'd care to be present. The man heard the full story of what we were doing that evening. Walt Hill even took him home and later gave him money before he finally went to Glasgow.[4]

Safely out of the country, Gordon wrote about it later in *John Bull* – presumably because he needed the money but also because these itinerant investigators seem to have had a need to give voice to and dramatize their seedy duplicity.

After visiting Glasgow, Alex Gordon came down to Derby where he visited the Wheeldons. Exactly why remains unclear. Herbert Booth was clearly being facetious when he told the court at the trial, 'I thought it would be a nice place.'[5] But in his 'Notes on the Wheeldon case', Melville Lee said, 'It must be remembered that what is commonly called the Poison Plot was chanced upon quite accidently in the course of other enquiries, it was not the sequel of any preconceived line of investigation.'[6]

This could simply mean that Gordon was sent to Derby as he was sent to Manchester by Booth, to collect information of a general kind. De Valda, the spy who enjoyed the Sheffield employers' hospitality, says the agent arrived in Derby posing as a 'conchie' on 'the underground railway'.[7] The NCF association would have made Hettie of some interest to the authorities. But undoubtedly the connection to Willie Paul and Arthur MacManus added to the interest in the Wheeldons. Melville Lee replied that Hettie Wheeldon was the organizing secretary of the conscientious objectors at Derby and that MacManus helped her to get those who wanted to go over to America.[8]

One of them so assisted was the German F.L. Kerran, alias Kerhahn, of the Hackney British Socialist Party. He was eventually arrested in the United States, having escaped from the Cornwallis Road internment camp in Holloway, and been helped on his way by the IWW in North London as well as by Alice, Hettie and Arthur.[9] Ferdy Kerran's case illustrates the overlapping networks; a member of the BSP is assisted by members of the IWW, who are in turn intertwined with the North London Herald

League, who presumably have links with Derby and thus with Hettie in the NCF, who is friendly with Arthur in the SLP. This network must have seemed a nightmarish riddle to army spies used to ranks, NCOs and officers – more disturbing even than orderly party structures. F. de Valda, who had so enjoyed his investigation in Sheffield, maintains that when they heard of the 'plot', they had been 'for some time' accumulating 'evidence that some kind of organization had been formed amongst the "conchies" '. He noted that there was 'an elaborate system of getting about the conchies' and 'sympathisers' who were 'ready to harbour' them. [10]

This need not have been an organization in the No Conscription Fellowship sense but a series of interlinked circles. We can assume the Ministry of Munitions intelligence unit observed that something was going on and had several clues pointing in various directions, one of which was to Derby. It seems they knew of the connection to MacManus. Besides MacManus though, there is another possible link between the Wheeldons and Gordon. It appears Walter Hill had indirect connections to the family. His brother had courted Winnie Mason before she married Alf. [11]

How far fear of industrial unrest spreading to Derby also motivated Gordon's arrival is not clear. Melville Lee said during the trial that there were important munitions works in Derby and that he had to guard against sabotage, but he had not known of the Wheeldons before (nor was it he who sent Gordon to Derby).

Derby was one among the many places contacted in the Hargreaves strike in autumn 1916. It was not a major munitions centre but the Midlands Railway Company had reorganized to produce a range of goods for the Ministry of Munitions including hospital trains and fuses. A high-quality aero-engine was also being manufactured in the town. Things were not going too well in 1916. Shell production had that year been held back by steel shortages. The Derby factory had no sooner overcome this problem when they were instructed to change over to producing aero-engine cylinders. Drawing on local skills, Derby appears to have specialized in quality work. Presumably the craftsmen were less threatened than in other centres. Still, the government had had to invest a lot of capital in adapting the factory for war production. [12] This might have given them cause for a certain degree of nervousness about the odd visit by a bevy of SLPers, anti-war women and Arthur MacManus.

Herbert Booth said in his statement in court that he sent Alex Gordon to Derby 'about the 23rd December'.[13] Alice Wheeldon said she put him up on the 27th.[14] Perhaps he took a Christmas break – he had once lived in nearby Leicester. Gordon introduced himself as a conscientious objector to Alice Wheeldon who received him hospitably and gave him lodgings for the night. She was already taking a risk harbouring an absentee.[15] On 28 December he telegraphed Booth who then informed Melville Lee. On 29 December Gordon introduced Booth as 'Comrade Bert' to Alice Wheeldon, who was standing behind the counter in her shop at 12 Pear Tree Road. He told her Comrade Bert was a fugitive from the army and a member of the IWW. Alice Wheeldon confirmed she knew of the Wobblies.[16] Alice Wheeldon wrote to her daughter, Winnie Mason, and the letter was sent in a parcel by rail. She asked Gordon to write to MacManus on behalf of Will Wheeldon and a man she was sheltering, Macdonald.[17]

· On 4 January, Winnie sent four phials of poison with instructions for use. The authorities continued opening mail.[18] 'I haunted Derby GPO as the mail came in, and the Postmaster handed to me all the letters the moment they arrived,'[19] reminisced de Valda. Towards the end of January, someone in the post office hinted to Alfred Mason that their letters were being examined.[20] Winnie Mason wrote to her mother on 29 January telling her to change the code she was using.[21] (Correspondence in code had earlier been used in the suffrage movement.) But it was too late. The authorities were already busy decoding, as De Valda describes with a characteristic flourish:

> At that time there existed in London a very hush-hush department who specialized in decoding; accordingly the coded letters were copied and sent there. In an amazingly short time they had unravelled the puzzle: the code was given as the chess-board code and the key words: 'We will hang Lloyd George on a sour apple tree.'[22]

They were unsure whether the 'plot' they discovered was 'a hoax' until the poison, curare, was found in a St Bruno tobacco tin in a fish-basket, and two guinea pigs they tested with it died.[23] Melville Lee was convinced that Booth's inauspicious employee had indeed uncovered a conspiracy. F.E. Smith, the well-known right-wing politician, happened to be a friend of his brother, Arthur Lee, who was Lloyd George's ally. He also happened to be Attorney-General, thanks to Lloyd George. He advised a prosecution.

On 30 January, Mrs Wheeldon and Alf were arrested in Derby, along with the conscientious objector Macdonald – already terrified out of his wits. Hettie was arrested at the school where she taught in Ilkeston and Winnie at her school in Southampton. William Wheeldon was picked up at the Masons' house but escaped (somewhat mysteriously) from custody and disappeared.[24]

Booth's statement describes Alice Wheeldon saying, ' "The poison has not arrived but I have no doubt it will," . . . she then turned the conversation on to Lloyd George and Arthur Henderson. She said, "I hope the buggers will soon be dead." ' Later in his statement he claims she said:

'Lloyd George had been the cause of millions of innocent lives being sacrificed, the bugger shall be killed to stop it. And as for that other bugger Henderson, he is a traitor to his people but Asquith is the bloody brains of the business. He has not gone so [crossed out and replaced with 'as'] far as Lloyd George he [Lloyd George] is neither fit for heaven nor bloody hell. Another bugger that ought to be done in is George at Buckingham Palace, he has always ponced on the people and is no bloody good.' I said to Mrs Wheeldon, 'What in your opinion is the best way to kill [crossed out replaced with 'poison'] Lloyd George?'

She then told him that 'we' – the suffragettes – spent £300 trying to poison him, planning to get into his hotel and to drive a nail dipped in poison through his boot, 'but he went to France, the bugger'. 'Later on in the evening she said to Gordon, "You know what you are doing you will rid the world of a bloody murderer and be a Saviour to the country." '[25] She gave instructions about the use of the poison and when asked how much the phial contained replied: 'Enough to kill 500.'[26]

Booth's account reads like an odd mixture of truth and falsehood. In a back room in Derby after a few drinks, the generalized hostility to politicians and the king is comprehensible. Similar remarks were being heard about the land at the time. The suffragette story seems unlikely as attack on property, not life, was the code of the militants. But stories of extreme escapades go around in

the self-mythologizing of radical movements, especially in periods
when the left feels powerless. The boundaries between imagination
and action can become blurred in the telling and retelling.

Most of Alice Wheeldon's remarks are those of a woman under
considerable stress, relieved at the conviviality she shares with her
visitors and vying with them to tell a yarn, no doubt. Booth's statement juxtaposes her comments for the most sinister effect. They
are probably embellished with additions. The text is peppered with
small changes of detail – these might be simply typing corrections
but they tend towards cumulative tightening up of his statement.
They suggest that a legal mind could well have been at work behind
the scenes with knowledge of what will convince a court, concerned
to ensure that in the absence of Gordon, Booth would put up a good
show.

Alice Wheeldon did not deny sending for the poison, receiving it
or giving it to Booth with instructions, but the instructions she
insisted were for killing guard-dogs in the concentration camps.
She also admitted 'she had been active in helping men to escape
from military duties ever since conscription was introduced'. She
claimed that Gordon had told her he had been helping conscientious objectors to escape from concentration camps. She was
interested because William Wheeldon was on the run. According
to the report of her testimony:

> Gordon said that in consequence of several escapes, dogs were
> being employed at the camps, and that poison was wanted for
> them. The witness then told him that her son-in-law was liable
> to military service and shared their views, although he had some
> objections to going as far as they did. She put Gordon up for the
> night on December 27th as he said he had nowhere to go. They
> talked on various subjects, one of them being the emigration of
> COs. She was anxious to get her boys across to America. He said
> it was quite easy to do this if they put themselves in his hands,
> and she, being a business woman, made a bargain with him that
> if he rendered this assistance she would procure poison for the
> dogs.
> Gordon promised to help her son, Mason and Alexander
> McDonald, who she had been sheltering from the police, to get
> to America. Gordon told her some of his own experiences as a

fugitive – that he had passed in London under the disguise of an Indian for months; that he had pretended to be deaf and dumb and also a hunchback.[27]

Alice Wheeldon was perhaps naive and too trusting of Gordon, but no more so than Arthur MacManus, Walter Hill and the rest who had accepted him. She was indiscreet in what she was prepared to say to a stranger – again no more so than other socialists he met. These characteristics are those of someone forced by extraordinary events into illegal forms of resistance rather than of someone who self-consciously embarks on underground struggle. Her fatal error was to consent to get the poison.

F.E. Smith, the Attorney-General and a brilliant prosecuting lawyer, made mince-meat of her.

> Pressed by the Attorney-General, Mrs Wheeldon said if a man came to her with the sure statement that he was on the run to escape being taken for the army, she was 'afraid' she would help him.
>
> 'Have you a strong feeling against those specially responsible for introducing this iniquitous Act of Parliament?' 'Yes.' 'And you regard Mr Henderson as a traitor to the working classes?' 'I have said so.' 'And your feeling towards Mr Lloyd George is one of the strongest possible antagonism – would it be true for instance to say that you hate Mr Lloyd George?' 'I do.' (The answer was given with energy.) 'You would like to do him a mischief?' 'He's not worth it.' 'But if he was, you would?' 'Yes.'
>
> She admitted under further cross-examination that she had said, 'George of Buckingham Palace had sponged on the people' and that she had frequently said Lloyd George ought to be dead. She did deny being part of a suffragette plot to poison Lloyd George, but her frank admission of political antagonisms fed the prosecution's portrayal of her as a wild extremist, making her legal defence more difficult.[28]

Against the biting eloquence of F.E. Smith, her lawyer, Dr Riza, was half-hearted. He was treated with patronizing derision by the judge. Although money had been collected for the defence of the four people accused in the case, no barrister could be found who was willing to defend them until Dr Riza, a Persian, who possibly had difficulty getting cases, took it on. This appeared to many people on the left to indicate that pressure had been brought to bear on the legal establishment.[29]

Whatever the reasons, the defence was weak. The trial lasted five days. Alice Wheeldon was cross-examined by the Attorney-General and other leading lawyers. Her voice failed several times as she gave her evidence. She also felt faint but after drinking some water refused to sit down. When F.E. Smith asked her about her son, William, and she said he had been committed to prison for eighteen months, 'she shed tears'.[30]

Alice Wheeldon was found guilty of conspiring to kill with the poison 'curare'; in an atmosphere of war panic, she was condemned by the work of an agent provocateur who was not present and by her own readiness to express her political responses.

The judge and jury ignored obvious inconsistencies in the prosecution's case which were not exposed clearly by the defence. For instance, Booth's statement includes the phrase 'as long as you have a chance get at the dog, I pity it' which he said he copied from Alice's instructions. But later he claimed that the first he had heard about dogs was in court that day.[31]

The references to King George and Arthur Henderson were played down, presumably because the prosecution thought the accusation of plotting widespread slaughter would make the whole case ridiculous. The code phrase 'We'll hang Lloyd George on a sour apple tree' was accepted without question as proof of intention. But it is no more evidence of a conspiracy to attack him with a poisoned dart on the golf course than contemporary songs about building bonfires and putting Tories on them imply a late twentieth-century Guy Fawkes plot.

The case rested, then, on the poison, on Alex Gordon's words and on the politics of Alice Wheeldon. Winnie's and Hettie's letters, alluded to in court though not read out in full, fuelled the prosecution's case. It is quite true they were scattered with uncomplimentary comments about the English. Winnie wrote to her mother:

> Keep mum and trust *absolutely nobody*. I'm not thinking of anyone in particular but you know what slimy cowards the pious christian english are if their dirty shins are in danger. The only

ones to trust are ourselves. I don't want you to involve yourself in any useless risk of anything. I should not tell even Mac or Paul or Robbs or any of them about *anything* which they don't already know.[32]

Then Hettie asked Winnie, 'Who can blame the Germans now for taking their revenge on rhinoceros-skinned, perfidious, canting Britain.'[33] Hettie also referred to a mutiny at Darlington.

5 officers have been killed. Cannot get to know any more naturally. Wish it would spread. The Clyde Engineers are once again fighting the soldiers at the gate who were there to keep them in, with crowbars. Oh missus some stuff.

What about Lloyd George visiting the Holy See or God's Vicar. He might be seeing His Majesty himself soon. Pray without ceasing.[34]

Of course the context – the meaningless slaughter of the war, the fugitive paranoid existence of those who resisted war, the poverty, and political and psychological isolation – counted for nothing at the trial. The sentiments in the letters contributed to the prosecution's presentation of the accused as beyond the bounds of decency.

The connection with the Breadsall church burning was made but not pursued. It contributed to the characterization of a desperate virago plotting arson and assassination from a second-hand clothes shop – though later F.E. Smith said it was doubtful if the church had been deliberately burned down by the suffragettes![35]

F.E. Smith dwelt for some time on Alice Wheeldon's moral character, informing the jury that:

Mrs Wheeldon . . . was in the habit of using language of the most obscene and disgusting character . . . her disgusting form of speech had spread to the two younger women, both of whom were engaged as teachers in the instruction of the young. Each of these young women was possessed of very considerable capacity, and yet in their correspondence they were in the habit of employing language which would be disgusting and obscene in the mouth of the lowest class of criminal.[36]

In 1936, Dr Chandler commented ironically that there was no law against 'cuss words' and that 'it must have been pretty bad if it shocked F.E. Smith'.[37] What was shocking to the male upper-class establishment was not only the dissident, unpatriotic leftism but the raucous vulgarity of lower-middle-class women who were not at all socially deferential.

There was a flutter of anxiety that perhaps there were serried ranks of Wheeldon-type women. The *Derby Mercury* was disturbed about the language but assured its readers that Harriet Wheeldon did not use it before her pupils. Still, it was worrying that she could teach 'morals and religion publicly', while being 'privately a rationalist and a non-Christian'. If this could occur in Ilkeston, perhaps it was to be found elsewhere. Somebody should put a stop to it once for all: 'It certainly ought not to be possible for non-Christians to teach Christianity, and it ought not to be possible for revolutionists and anarchists to be employed in the education of the young at all.' However, the *Derbyshire Mercury* batted off queries by *The Times* into the Derbyshire education system, reassuring its readers: 'There is no reason to despair of elementary education or anything else because of the Wheeldon revelations. They are abnormalities. . .'[38]

This became the stance of the authorities and set the tone of the right-wing historical interpretation of the Wheeldon case. They had to be abnormalities – for they contravened the established way of the world not only by their left-wing political views but because their social existence was at variance with ruling-class masculine assumptions about lower-middle-class women. A variety of extraordinary murder methods – strychnine in bread, a rusty nail tipped with curare pressed into boots, or a poisoned arrow shot from an air-gun – were assembled, not to suggest that the Attorney-General was skating on thin ice but as evidence of the psychological and political wickedness of the accused.

There was a series of contradictory stereotypes in the prosecution's attitudes. The accused were both abnormal and yet significant enough not to be dismissed as cranks, responsible for their actions yet governed by emotion, principled yet of doubtful morality. Educated Hettie and Winnie and Alf might be – but this, in the eyes of their prosecutors, was a cover for their profound folly. They might object to war, yet possessed the 'will to murder'. They might teach morals and religion at school, 'whilst in the privacy of their home they swore like blackguards'. The explanation was to be found, said the *Derby Mercury*, 'in the process by which they evolved themselves from a state of ordinary respectable citizenship into revolutionists and anarchists'.[39]

F.E. Smith declared to the court that the four prisoners 'were a gang of desperate persons poisoned by revolutionary doctrines and obsessed with an insensate and vile hatred of their own country... He had not the slightest fear that in such a case the Jury would not fail to do their duty.'[40]

Ironically, the letters, intercepted by the authorities, give a rare glimpse into the personal world of radical, lower-middle-class women. Along with a sense of isolation from neighbours, impatience with moderate pacifism and the camaraderies of the pure oppositionists, there are more everyday concerns.

'It was sales last week,' writes Winnie to 'Dear Mum', 'and I bort [*sic*] a lovely velvet dress... I also bort a blouse length for school as all my old ones are getting shabby.' She was worried because she was '3 days late coming on... is that a cold do you think or don't you settle down regular straight away.'[41]

The Ministry of Munitions opened a fish-basket lined with cretonne, sent by Alice to Winnie, to discover

> 4 mince pies
> slab of cake
> 2 prs mens socks
> 1 pale blue toilet table cover
> 1 tin golden syrup
> 2 calenders
> 1 chicken stuffed
> 1 tin Raspberry Jam[42]

The chicken was subsequently eaten by Winnie Mason and declared to be 'ecky'... 'but you didn't ort to spend yer money so. I keep saying I appreciate the things alrite but I'd sooner you'd buy yerself summat and keep orl rite.'[43]

This was not the milieu F.E. Smith inhabited but it was not abnormal. This was the England created by the Board School, state education and University Extension classes. The Wheeldons were its left political wing with their pamphlets on socialism and labour matters, their newspaper cuttings and eclectic reading of radical papers, the *Herald*, *The Daily Herald*, *The Socialist*, *The Worker*,

The Suffragette, The Tribunal.[44] There it all was: Herald League, syndicalism, Marxism, the shop stewards' movement, feminism, the anti-war movement and a radical cultural defiance, Winnie telling Hettie to read Shaw's *Mrs Warren's Profession, The Gadfly* by Voynick and the International Friendship.[45]

The growing powers of the centralized state in the wartime atmosphere of paranoia and panic constituted the real abnormality. As the definition of conspiracy and subversion was stretched, attitudes, opinions and connections assumed a sinister guise which justified further stringency and fewer scruples. This was sufficiently new to require explicit legitimation.

The *Derby Mercury* hastens to justify the employment of police spies as a regrettable but unpleasant necessity. It was justified 'by the discovery which the trial has disclosed'. There is an evident uneasiness about surveillance and the extending tentacles of intelligence work. It is still not seen as a legitimate aspect of state activity. The circumstances require it as an exceptional protection for law and order: 'however much we may dislike the secret service system, conditions did exist in Derby in December last which called for and justified examination.'[46]

In this climate of fear and repression three of the defendants were found guilty of conspiracy. Winnie Mason was given five years penal servitude, Alf seven and Alice Wheeldon ten. Hettie was found not guilty.

Divisions in the State

It is too easy to present Alice Wheeldon and the Masons as tragic victims of an inevitable process. When the political forces which converged upon the two families are examined in some detail it becomes clear that a range of interests in the state sparred and clashed. Even in the atmosphere of war panic they were only momentarily united in their efforts and the decision to prosecute the Wheeldons has to be recognized as a gamble which F.E. Smith took and won.

By early 1915 it was becoming clear that the war would last longer than people had assumed. 'With multiplying reports flowing in from abroad of mismanagement, lack of planning and postponed decisions, criticism of the national leadership began to mount.'[1]

In May 1915, the last independent Liberal administration in British history was replaced by a coalition headed by Asquith but including more conservatives – including the extreme right. Sir Edward Carson was made Attorney-General, F.E. Smith Solicitor-General and Lloyd George Minister of Munitions.[2]

Sylvia Pankhurst remarked caustically: 'As usual the Tories are proving themselves the only Marxists on the political stage. To them the economic class war was an ever-present reality. They were striving whole-heartedly to maintain the advantage of their class.'[3]

The integration of big business directly with the administration of the war was the predominant means of increasing production. Inevitably it appeared to be the war of the armaments manufacturers who were able to restructure production methods in their interests and at the expense of the men and women they employed. The exigencies of war strengthened the employers' position. Apart from an anti-war position, the labour movement adopted a variety of strategies against the encroachment of state and employers. There were the rank-and-file rebellions which preoccupied the authorities. But these faced a continuing problem of co-ordinated action – despite the efforts of Arthur MacManus and the rest. Another approach appeared from some of the Clydeside stewards: accepting the war as a given, they tried to gain more control for labour over restructuring. The demand for nationalization under workers' control for labour was in effect a demand upon the state to co-operate with labour rather than capital in the attempt to increase production for the war. This approach was dismissed out of hand by Lloyd George, whose interests were better served by an alliance with employers. From a different source, Mary MacArthur and Margaret Bondfield, in the National Federation of Women Workers, put this strategy into practice in attempting to defend the wages and conditions of women in industry.[4]

The other attempt to influence industrial policy is represented by Arthur Henderson's co-operation with Lloyd George. This made him hated by the anti-war movement. Sylvia Pankhurst, for instance, poured scorn on how, as President of the Board of Education, he was unable to prevent the release from school of children of eleven and upward to work for a pittance.[5] His main business was to advise on labour questions. While Arthur Henderson probably saw this as defending labour's interests and was able to intervene on behalf of individuals, the net gain was undoubtedly the government's. It was incorporation rather than co-operation at which Lloyd George excelled – exhausting his Labour allies in numerous committees. Henderson gave a certain Labour legitimacy to the war. His advice could be read not at its face value as an effort to safeguard workers, but as an indicator of what the state could get away with. Sylvia Pankhurst maintained it was Arthur Henderson's 'inside knowledge' which was useful to the government and their reason for tolerating the Labour man. She believed his position was insidious and made him a 'dangerous enemy of the rank-and-file movement'.[6]

Eventually the conflict of loyalties became too extreme. Arthur Henderson resigned from the Cabinet in August 1917, after the Cabinet turned down a proposal to send Labour delegates to the proposed International Socialist Congress at Stockholm.[7]

The integration of labour movement figures like Henderson in the war effort meant they contributed to the extraordinary growth of the state. This was a process Lloyd George presided over from the moment he became head of the Ministry of Munitions in mid 1915.

Arthur Lee, a conservative politician who was to become Parliamentary Military Secretary at the Ministry of Munitions until July 1916, described the situation in November 1915: 'The Ministry of Munitions was then in embryo, indeed its headquarters consisting almost literally of two bare rooms furnished with trestle tables and a few kitchen chairs.'[8] Within a few months it had grown into the biggest state department, taking over two hotels and several other buildings. By 1916 there were five thousand people working in the Ministry of Munitions.[9]

Moreover, this administrative emporium extended the areas of state responsibility to include the health, feeding and housing of munitions workers, problems of entertainment, alcohol consumption and morale as well as industrial arbitration and intelligence. The war thus consolidated a trend in social liberalism towards a state with increased powers of intervention. Lloyd George brought in initially a group of civil servants who had been involved before the war in the new liberal welfare legislation in the Board of Trade and Unemployment Insurance Department. William Beveridge and Hubert Llewellyn Smith were among them. It was these men who helped Lloyd George to break the Clydeside shop stewards' organization.[10] There was thus a repressive element in the new social liberalism along with an attempt to come to terms with some working-class demands. Broadly, the concept of welfare was accepted and assimilated – the concept of workers' control was not.

This connection between social reform and national efficiency was to have a lasting effect on twentieth-century politics. The state's responsibility for social welfare gave it a new legitimacy. The working-class voter was offered a stake in the system, modest gains – but on certain conditions. In one sense it represented a recognition of the power of labour interests which could not be ignored in England at least; in another it presented a hegemonic challenge to the inchoate vision of a new social order based on free association which was an element in the socialist movement of the day. It prevailed not in the creation of a new liberalism but by making an impression on leading elements in the new Labour Party. It provided a means of accommodating socialism within the restructuring of the capitalist state.

The administrative power of the Ministry of Munitions launched Lloyd George into a new phase of his career. The maverick radical was replaced by the respectable war minister, acceptable to leading members of the business and financial world. Lloyd George was quite as flattered by their acceptance as Lieutenant de Valda was by the hospitality of the Sheffield industrialists. Lloyd George boasted in his *War Memoirs*: 'The Ministry of Munitions was from first to last a businessman's organization. Its most distinctive feature was the appointment I made of successful businessmen to the chief executive posts.'[11] It was this aspect of the Ministry, of course, which enraged workers. The appointment of William Weir, a factory owner on the Clyde, contributed to the Glasgow shop stewards' bitterness.[12]

During this period, Lloyd George drew closer and closer to the Conservative rebels around Carson, particularly F.E. Smith. Smith had had experience working in the press bureau on censorship. As Solicitor-General, he dealt with a great deal of legal business in connection with the new legislation which gave the state greatly increased powers – the Defence of the Realm Act and the Military Service Act. From November 1915 he was Attorney-General.[13] The conscious politicization of the law which F.E. Smith brought into these offices indicates how the war not only effected a closer integration between politicians and capital but also between state and judiciary. Again the increasing powers of the state, which had been observable before the war, were consolidated in wartime and re-established as the norm after the First World War.[14] The militant right-wing iconoclasm of F.E. Smith served in the period of innovation during the war and was less suited to the post-war attempt to adapt some of the structural changes of war to the normality of peacetime politics.

Despite the unifying purpose of the war, the tugs and pulls of differing politics and social outlooks were apparent among the dominant class. There were many contradictory and conflicting strands in the Coalition which acted as a check on the absolute power of any particular group. One was the irritability between the military and the politicians close to Lloyd George which could erupt into overt hostility. Tussles over skilled workers have already been mentioned. A farcical example of friction was F.E. Smith's visit to France in February 1916, when, because he was without a pass, the army arrested him and kept him in custody, and he was summoned before Adjutant-General Macready.[15] Nor was the War Office enamoured of Lloyd George's patriot capitalists. From a different point of view, they regarded them with the same cynicism as did the rebel shop stewards. Lloyd George bemoaned the War Office's coldness to arms manufacturers. 'They were treated as if they were greedy supplicants for profitable war contracts.'[16]

1916 saw the Easter Rising in Dublin and the prosecution of Roger Casement. Casement had tried to deliver guns and recruits, decided the rising was ill-fated, was arrested by the British and accused of treason under an ancient Act of 1351. The principal prosecuting counsel for the Crown was F.E. Smith. His closeness to Carson and known Unionist politics made the trial a political contest. The uncertain interpretation of the Act, the interested aspect of the legal prosecution and the death penalty contributed to furious opposition. British intelligence circulated forged diaries of Casement which smeared him as a homosexual.[17] The British government dithered about whether to hang him. Curiously, at this point the paths of F.E. Smith and Basil Thomson, head of the Special Branch, crossed. Thomson and Captain Reginald Hall were prevented from publishing a book about Casement's interrogation because it showed the prisoner in too favourable a light![18]

Ruthless, arrogant, determined to succeed, F.E. Smith was a buccaneer politician who thrived amidst social upheavals. His politics were volatile. He supported Home Rule in 1910, then switched sides in 1912, backing Carson's Ulster Rebellion.[19] Defying Parliament, F.E. Smith said, 'We hold ourselves absolved of all allegiance to this government.'[20] The Ulster rebels were not prosecuted and were outraged at the thought of the government sending in troops against them.[21] Carson made no secret that friends in Court circles had assured him of immunity from any penalty.[22]

F.E. Smith also changed his line on women's suffrage. In 1910 he was adamantly opposed not only to the vote but indeed to 'the intrusion of women into the field of politics'.[23] But he supported the Sex Disqualification Removal Bill after the First World War.[24]

F.E. Smith made a dashing figure in the newspapers with his liking for art and music, his heavy consumption of brandy and cigars, and his extravagant wife, Margaret.[25] His photograph on a postcard did a brisk trade before the war as a right-wing political pin-up. This was much to the distaste of more established conservatives who recoiled from such vulgarity and so little pretence to political integrity. In turn, Smith was contemptuous of the 'middle-aged dullards'.[26]

F.E. Smith's friendships defied politics. It was through Churchill, then a Liberal, that he was drawn to Lloyd George – despite political opposition.[27] During the war, F.E. Smith found a role among the 'new men' whom Lloyd George brought into powerful positions in the state, settling into the role of hounding left-wing rebels through the judiciary with aplomb. Lloyd George detected behind the insolent, witty, invective a capacity for diligent paperwork – always useful – and F.E. Smith was kept busy.

As early as March 1916, there was a movement among some Conservatives to try and get Lloyd George to take a strong line against Asquith. In return they were prepared to recognize Lloyd George as Prime Minister.[28] A friend of F.E. Smith's, Arthur Lee, was busy on the task of bringing Sir Edward Carson and Lloyd George together. Lloyd George notes that through Lee's 'patriotic good offices he had seen quite a lot of Carson' in this period. The final obstacle to Lloyd George's leadership was Bonar Law who had to be detached from Asquith before Lloyd George could take over.[29]

In July 1916, Kitchener's new army was thrown into battle on the Somme. The offensive had tailed off in aimless disaster by November. There was a chronic shortage of munitions and problems with food supplies. In October 1916, it appeared that Asquith would try for peace. Lord Robert Cecil, a Conservative, furiously opposed any such move.[30]

In his *War Memoirs*, Lloyd George described this period in purple prose.

> It is hard for me to convey an adequate picture of the sense of frustration and tangled impotence which oppressed me during those closing months of 1916. There are nightmares in which one welters amid a web of fettering strands and obstacles, and watches, wide-eyed, some doom approaching against which the strangled throat cannot force a sound of protest or appeal.[31]

Lloyd George did not welter long in tangled impotence, becoming Prime Minister in the first week of December 1916 to the dismay not only of socialists like the Wheeldons, but also to that of the Liberal, old guard elite. Margot Asquith complained to her Conservative friend, Nancy Astor, on 17 December, of the 'moral shocks she had had in the last 10 days'.[32]

Lloyd George's loyal Conservative friend, Arthur Lee, was not particularly happy either, for despite his patriotic good offices Lloyd George, once in power, and apparently prompted by Bonar Law who disliked Lee, cold-shouldered his old ally. Ruth Lee noted in her diary on 8 December 1916, ' "A" has had a miserable day' because he was out of favour with Lloyd George.[33] Lee was ignored until 7 February 1917 when he was invited to breakfast with the Prime Minister, 'the first break in over two months' silence'. Shortly afterwards Lee met a 'radiant' Carson in the lobby of the House of Commons, happy about the rapprochement. Carson hinted that Lloyd George was very impressed with Lee's views on food – which had apparently been expressed during breakfast. Sure enough, on 14 February, Arthur Lee was put in charge of food production and Lloyd George was all charm. He confessed touchingly to Lee, who lacked a sense of irony, that he had felt so bad that Lee had not been given a post before he had been unable to see him. Ruth Lee recorded Lloyd George as saying, 'You see we weren't colleagues only we had been such pals.'[34]

Lee had learned, however, that his 'pal' could be ungrateful. He remained doggedly loyal to Lloyd George but he was hurt. Just before the ice broke, Lee wrote in his diary:

> On February 2nd, a plot was discovered to murder Lloyd George by shooting him with a poisoned dart, from behind some bushes, when he was playing golf at Walton Heath. The miscreants concerned were Sinn Feiners, but the man who frustrated their plans and secured their arrest before they could effect their purpose was my brother [Major Melville Lee], who was attached to the Secret Service Division of the Ministry of Munitions. Needless to say, he received no recognition or even thanks for this, but it was once more demonstrated that Lloyd George could not get on – however much he might try – without the help of the Brothers Lee.[35]

Arthur and William Melville Lee, like many of Lloyd George's supporters, came from relatively obscure families. Their father, a vicar, had died, leaving them impoverished; and Arthur was adopted. Arthur's marriage to a wealthy American heiress made a political career possible – it also gained him some influence with Theodore Roosevelt, which interested Lloyd George.[36]

Christopher Addison, son of a Lincolnshire farmer, was a different kind of outsider politically. He and his associate, Kellaway, could help Lloyd George round up Liberal support. But Addison had a personal loyalty to Lloyd George similar to Lee's.

Having gained office by allying with the far right, Lloyd George was seeking around for a new programme of social reconstruction with which he could again woo Liberal and Labour supporters. Addison was first given the Ministry of Munitions and later sacrificed. By the summer of 1917, Lloyd George had replaced Addison with Winston Churchill at the Ministry of Munitions. Addison was made Minister of Reconstruction, a rather premature role amidst war and industrial and social crisis.[37]

F.E. Smith too had been passed over when Lloyd George became Prime Minister – he simply remained Attorney-General. In his biography, William Camp observes: 'From the publicity point of view, he began well enough by prosecuting the Wheeldons, an eccentric family of conscientious objectors who had plotted to murder Lloyd George.'[38]

How convenient an opportunity for both Melville Lee and F.E. Smith to show zeal for Lloyd George's personal safety and strike a political blow against pacifism and socialism. But what if the Wheeldons were found not guilty and the charge of conspiracy rebounded?

F.E. Smith's son said that his father

> as Attorney advised a prosecution. The decision caused him some anxiety. It was connected with politics; if the prosecution had been begun, and had collapsed, there would have followed a great new disaster – loss of prestige. A law officer should never run the risk of the humiliating collapse of a prosecution, yet it is even more dangerous not to act when serious crime is being contemplated.[39]

The Attorney-General must have known the evidence against the Wheeldons was inconclusive and wagered on the prevailing climate of panic and abhorrence of anyone who opposed the war. As Tony Bunyan comments in his history of the political police: 'The use of the beliefs and life-styles of defendants in political trials – although theoretically inadmissable – is a consistent feature of state prosecutions.'[40]

F.E. Smith had already used this in Casement's trial. Again in the Wheeldon case he was able to pull it off. The embarrassing Alex Gordon was shipped out of the way, the day saved for law and order, and F.E. Smith had a public show of devotion to Lloyd George.

Rival Intelligence Agencies

The shifting nature of political alliances and the rapid turn around of assumption about the legitimate use of law and power throw some light on the uncertainties among the intelligence office. Though the government had long used agents, their number and the scope of their work expanded vastly in the First World War. The exposure of the Wheeldon 'poison plot' brought their activities out into the open. It revealed the pressures upon them and the contradictions among them.

The men involved in establishing the case against the Wheeldons found their way into the Ministry of Munitions Intelligence Unit from quite different social circumstances.

F. de Valda had gone to sea at sixteen. Having some education he had taught young ladies French in Australia, leaving the school in a mildly scandalous cloud. Then he had worked on plantations in Jamaica and Central America and been an explorer. He lived a lonely life, seeking adventure; his autobiography reveals him as quite self-consciously bragging of his prowess as the devil-may-care machismo individualist who might have been a mercenary in another era.[1]

Herbert John Walsh Booth left no autobiography. His life comes into view as a series of appearances and disappearances. Before the First World War he appeared at the Cock Inn, a pub kept by a widow, Mrs Firmin, married her after five years and then vanished. Her elder daughter, Miss Firmin, read about his role in the Wheeldon trial. Booth himself also had a daughter by an earlier marriage; she kept a pub.[2]

Booth said in his evidence at the trial:

> I am employed by the Ministry of Munitions. I entered their employ on September 15th 1916. I have been engaged making certain enquiries of various organizations, amongst others, one, the correct name of which is the Independent Workers of the World Movement and other similar organizations. In connection with those duties, I employed Mr Alex Gordon. He reported to me daily, I reported to Major Melville Lee.[3]

He said he was also under 'Major' Labouchere.[4] According to F.E. Smith, Booth had worked as a clerk to a barrister, G.D. Purcell, before joining the Ministry of Munitions unit.[5]

Though Booth took on Alex Gordon and had experience of the legal profession, contemporaries believed he was the 'brawn and guts' in the duo and Gordon the brains.[6] Booth certainly seemed to have a problem with details. Apart from his slip about the dogs already mentioned in the discussion of the trial, the 'Independent Workers of the World' at the beginning of his statement has turned back into 'Industrial Workers of the World' later. And 'Major' Labouchere was a Colonel.[7]

Booth brought into the witness box the diary 'in which he entered from time to time the incidents of his relations with the Wheeldons'[8] – perhaps he was reminding himself of his own statements?

But he appears to have presented himself well in court. The *Derby Mercury* described him as 'a clean-shaven man about forty years of age who gave evidence with quiet self-possession'.[9]

Booth was used again in 1917 to spy on David Kirkwood and other Clydesiders. Following this he vanishes from the record, to reappear in the Second World War in the unarmed combat commandos. He died around 1950 in Kings Cross.[10]

Alex Gordon (whose real name was Francis W. Vivian) was a more psychologically bizarre character. The prosecution kept him away from the court, apparently embarrassed. As Tom Bell put it, they 'point-blank refused to put Gordon, their chief witness, into the witness box for cross-examination'.[11] After the trial, he was paid £100 and given £5 expenses to go to South Africa.[12] He did not come back to Britain until 1919. But he appears to have been still seriously disturbed about his part in the conviction of Alice, Winnie and Alf. He entered the office of the *Derby Daily Express* saying he was willing to sell information to anyone about anything. He brandished a revolver and showed the bullet he intended to use to settle something. The police were sent for and removed him. He turned up at another Derby newspaper and received money for a meal. Then the *Express* reports the Police Court Missionary offered to pay his fare to Leicester.[13]

Three weeks later, he gave a statement to the *Daily Herald*. The interview provides illuminating details of the wandering schizophrenic life of the men who were taken on by the Ministry of Munitions to do the dirty work connected with wartime intelligence. Gordon stated that he had been a member of a socialist group before the war, apparently the British Socialist Party.[14] Colonel Labouchere confirms that he was 'an ardent socialist and member of the BSP before the war'.[15] Gordon told the *Daily Herald* that socialists assumed he knew more about their organization than he did. 'I have only had a superficial conception of their activities – extremist or otherwise. Although I have always been sympathetic with the ideal Socialist Movement, I have really only been on the fringe of it in actual practice.'[16]

After leaving the BSP in 1915, he joined the army. Then somewhat mysteriously he left: whether he was discharged or deserted is unclear. He was writing articles for the *Leicester Mail* about the testing of spiritualist mediums to see if they were fakes. Vivian, alias Gordon, was approached by 'X' (Booth most likely or possibly another agent) who claimed to be an 'ideal socialist' collecting copy for a book on the difference between non-violent and 'extremist action' of a kind which would help the Germans. 'X' reported on Vivian to his 'governor' and returned saying he would receive £2-10s a week and bonuses if the copy was 'coming in well'. He intimated that the governor wanted exciting copy but 'you must get facts'.

'X' suggested Vivian should go to investigate the IWW in Great Tongue Yard in East London. He assured Vivian, 'No names will be published.' The information would not harm the individuals observed. 'You will be able to state the case as to the militancy and the attitude of any people who may be there, towards the war.'[17] Vivian recalled that 'I thought it was a decent job and there was more money in it than I had been getting. I had had a lot of worry and misery, and I did not want to lose this chance.'[18]

After much wandering, the two rather amateur agents managed to find where the Wobblies met by going to a police station and looking at a map. Once inside the meeting, Vivian was given a friendly welcome. There were two Americans and some books in a foreign language which he thought was Hebrew. He asked for some literature which they gave him including a copy of the syndicalist newspaper, *Solidarity*. A man who spoke English noticed the police spy's boots were very worn out 'and he actually gave me a pair'. Vivian reported what had happened to 'X' and was asked to draw a plan of the place. The IWW centre in Great Tongue Yard was later raided by the police and people were arrested. Vivian claimed he saw no connection.

Next he was sent to a place in Fitzroy Square. The 'governor' had heard that enemy agents and pro-German people went there. Vivian arrived at the 'Communist Club' and again was received most civilly by 'foreigners' in 'evening dress'. He had to sponge off them as 'X' kept him loyal through penury and fear. 'I was hanging onto this blessed job and hoping it would come all right. I was thinking of my wife and what would happen if the police pulled me up.'[19]

Vivian was sent to Manchester and told Booth there was nothing to report. Almost immediately afterwards a tramway strike developed. Booth, almost certainly annoyed at Vivian's lack of insight, broke off all contact. Vivian panicked. He must have realized he had to send in a compensatory sensational report. He did not tell the *Herald* about his contact with MacManus, around 7 December, or his trip to Barrow – another area of rank-and-file organization – on 9 December.[20] On the 13th, Vivian told the Ministry of Munitions Intelligence Unit what he imagined they wanted to hear and reported the existence of a 'Directorate' 'composed of fanatical unbalanced and generally dubious agitators' with a large following, wanting to stop the war by rendering the production of munitions impossible.[21]

Either he convinced Melville Lee or simply fed the Major's desire to find an organized conspiracy. Ruminating on the strike movement early in 1917, Melville Lee reflected that the leading spirits in the 'Revolutionary Ring' who led the rank and file were deported from the Clyde. He had selected a master-mind, after noticing that the majority of these deportees had been students at a 'so-called' economics class run by William Paul.[22]

Under pressure, Vivian had evidently tried to ensnare other socialists into plots with no success.

> I was not consciously a Secret Service man [Vivian wheedled in the *Daily Herald*]. By the time I was told that, the Government had got me. I suggest that it had – and nobody knows better than me – it had a hold over me and a very strong one too, that made it absolutely impossible for me to come straight out into the limelight.

Asked what he meant by 'hold', Vivian replied:

> Economically, I mean. I never had my money properly. I did on one or two occasions get a £3 bonus, but they were isolated instances. I never got the 50 shillings in one heap. I always had to 'beg' to get money to go on with. I could not do anything else. I was always in a state of chronic hard-up-ness.[23]

The *Herald* statement is illuminating about the psychological state of mind of an ex-socialist who became an agent. But it leaves many unsolved problems. Vivian's interview still does not explain why he went to the Wheeldons at Derby and it creates a further mystery about the hold Booth had over him. Booth seemed sceptical of Vivian's investigative abilities. When Vivian told him, 'there are some people here who want to poison Lloyd George and Arthur Henderson,' Booth responded sarcastically, 'only two'.[24]

The retrospective view was to be that the Wheeldons were abnormalities. This was not Melville Lee's analysis immediately after the trial. Instead he promoted Vivian's conspiracy into the big time. For him, the significance of 'the Wheeldon Case' did not consist in the successful persecution of two women and a man, but in the revelations about the 'aims, motive designs and mental attitude of a revolutionary sect'.[25] These were minimized in the trial but were, as Lee put it, 'the sign posts which should guide us to an understanding of the serious side of the business'.[26]

Lee was convinced the 'points of contact'[27] indicated not a loose network responding to the state's measures, but a wide-spread conspiracy. Shared sentiments and political and personal links congeal in this spy's mentality into organized conspiracy. The 'conspiracy' then begins to get out of hand. Lee noted other people saying the same things against Lloyd George as Alice Wheeldon – some were aldermen! He concluded not that other people might have just cause to oppose the Prime Minister, but that the 'conspiracy' was even more widespread. Winnie Mason said other elementary schoolteachers in Southampton shared her views. Reports were coming in from Cardiff of disaffected schoolteachers.[28] Apparently even the infants were unsafe.

Melville Lee, unlike Gordon, was not capable of entering the world of assumptions of his opponents. He gives them a homogeneity of views and a cohesion which glossed over feuds and political disagreement. Every report, spiced up to feed his fears, confirmed threats to law and order and to the production of munitions on several fronts. This situation of crisis justified agents.

It is interesting that their spying had still to be strenuously defended as legitimate state business. The judge at the trial justified it, declaring that: 'Unless the government employed secret agents, it would be impossible to detect or prevent such crimes as these.'[29] And the Attorney-General, F.E. Smith, made a similar point: 'No Minister would be worth his place if he refused the responsibility of employing secret agents to watch people of the Wheeldon type.'[30] Secret agents could be assailed as a waste of money and an intrusion into personal liberties. But secret agents with a plot were unassailable. They had a product – conspirators.

On the other hand, they were skating on thin ice. Overtly inaccurate information could rebound.

De Valda was dubious when he heard of the 'plot'.

Scares of this type were not uncommon and all news like this was viewed from the outset with some suspicion. It was of course very attractive to become mixed up with something really 'hot' but the fear of making a fool of oneself dominated over impulses to leap at conclusions.[31]

The poison convinced him, he claims. Was this really the case or was a decision taken to accept Vivian's account because the Ministry of Munitions agents decided the creation of a crime would forestall the even greater crime in their eyes of bringing production to a halt? The end of saving the British state in wartime might justify the means. During 1916 there was considerable suspicion on the left that the government had planned provocative action. Perhaps it was rather that the atmosphere of government fear created a climate in which this was a viable course of action for their more abject minions. Then, in their concern for security, they were prepared to turn a blind eye to some of the unconvincing details.

There was a less high-falutin influence upon the agents – rivalries between the various government intelligence departments. Their very existence was part of the unprecedented new growth in state machinery. Lloyd George had extended the Ministry of Munitions to include food, health, social welfare, industrial relations and security. Munitions were already sparring with the War Office about the overenthusiastic recruitment of skilled workers and about the boundaries and definitions of surveillance. The Wheeldon case introduced a new complication: the Home Office. Labouchere had to go through Basil Thomson, Assistant Commissioner of the Metropolitan Police and head of the Special Branch, in order to get authorization to open mail. Although he got permission, there was a certain awkwardness. As a policeman, Thomson regarded the army officers as amateurs. He saw himself as rationalizing surveillance and professionalizing it when he was asked 'to take over the service with my own trained men'.[32]

The gathering of intelligence was becoming competitive. Small departments had sprung up to do particular kinds of security work. Before the war, the Special Branch numbered about fifty men: it guarded royalty and ministers, watched out for bomb plots, observed Irish rebels, anarchists, suffragettes, Indian students and aliens. The police watched political and industrial groups.[33] Labouchere's unit was established within the Ministry of Munitions to safeguard wartime munitions production. When Lloyd George was at the Ministry of Munitions they reported to him. But he asked Basil Thomson to report to him when he became Prime Minister,[34] presumably because he lost the direct link with Ministry of Munitions intelligence. MI5 had begun as one officer and a clerk in 1909, watching for German spies and reporting to the Director of Military Operations. It began to monitor political groups and industrial militants after the war, when it really grew.[35]

The proliferation of small units created muddle and expense. But a single large secret service also threatened politicians. It was a long-standing battle. Writing about MI5, Nigel West observes:

> There were those in high places who did not always like to see one department of the secret services growing unduly powerful and there were others who often thought that intelligence gatherers should all be together under one roof and one control. So from time to time attempts were made to merge the various branches.[36]

Survival strategies were used successfully by Kell at MI5.[37] But Labouchere was less successful and the unit was to pass into the hands of Basil Thomson. At the time of the Wheeldon case, its future was still uncertain. Ironically, the very success in finding a 'conspiracy' blew its cover.

Despite the interdepartmental rivalry, Thomson's political assessment of the situation was not dissimilar to Melville Lee's. 'Pacifism, anti-conscription and Revolution were now inseparably mixed. The same individuals took part in all three movements. The real object of most of these people, though it may have been subconscious, appeared to be the ruin of their country.'[38]

He was more inclined to see his opponents' views en masse, as psychological eruptions and contagions. Major Melville Lee thought more of conscious alliances between subversives. Thomson waxed lyrical with metaphors of disaffection. 'There is a rapid evolution in political unrest. Subversive societies are like the geysers in a volcanic field. After preliminary gurgling, they spout forth masses of boiling mud and subside, while another chasm forms at a distance and becomes suddenly active.'[39]

However, when dealing with individuals, he tried to make some distinctions. There were self-seekers who 'would sell their own grandmothers' and there were 'virtuous people who think it highly improper for a government to keep itself quietly informed'.[40] There was 'that blighter' Roger Casement, 'an idealist not a self-seeker, but extraordinarily vain', and James Connolly whom Thomson saw as 'very able' and 'most dangerous because he was not self-seeking and he represented a class [the transport workers] who had real grievances'.[41]

Thomson also had a professional pride in his trade as a policeman and liked expounding upon the art of investigation. He held that it required good organization, hard work and luck in about equal proportions.[42] He preferred to keep a low profile and accumulate information over the long term without attracting too much attention: 'The great art of acquiring information is to have friends in every grade of society in as many countries as possible.'[43]

He was convinced of the dangers of an anti-war alliance with revolutionary elements within it. But he was also highly suspicious of the flamboyant style of the army men and suspected them of provocation. In *The Story of Scotland Yard* he recounts how 'a military officer, who had been appointed intelligence officer to the Ministry of Munitions with the duty of keeping the Ministry informed of impending strikes and sabotage, walked into my room at Scotland Yard and proceeded to unfold a fantastic story.'[44] This was none other than Colonel Labouchere, telling him of a plot to assassinate Lloyd George while playing golf at Walton Heath Course on a Saturday by firing a poisoned dart from a blow-pipe which would cause first lassitude and then a seizure. Thomson asked for the name of the informant, which the Colonel was reluctant to reveal. He maintained that his source had become anxious on hearing Thomson's name and had 'made a condition that his name should not be disclosed'. Nor did he want to come and see Thomson.

> That set me thinking; either the agent was a person with a criminal history, or he had invented the whole story to get money and credit from his employer. But I did not confide my misgivings to the Colonel; on the contrary, I proceeded to take down the

names and addresses of the persons concerned as if I believed in this fantastic plot.[45]

Basil Thomson was in an awkward position. He had been asked to work out a scheme to take over all spying on political and industrial groups, but this entailed delicate bureaucratic negotiations with various departments including the War Office and Labouchere's own outfit.[46] The border between nominal and real authority was still unclear. When the Liberal Christopher Addison replaced Lloyd George at the Ministry of Munitions on 14 December 1915 and began changing policies, his predicament grew.

Thomson could not afford to dismiss Labouchere's information even though he was uneasy about the story. So he gave permission for the Wheeldon letters to be opened and purported to be shocked by Alice Wheeldon's language and opinions of Lloyd George when shown a photograph of a letter the next day. But he still suspected something: 'I had an uneasy feeling that he himself might have acted as what the French call an agent provocateur (an inciting agent) by putting the idea into the woman's head, or if the idea was already there, by offering to act as the dart thrower.'[47]

Consequently, Thomson insisted that 'Alex Gordon' come to London. He arranged for a CID officer to be downstairs to get a searching look at the agent as he came in. 'There walked into the room a thin, cunning-looking man of about thirty, with long black greasy hair.'[48] They had records of Gordon's fingerprints and two cards, each bearing Gordon's photograph but each with a different name, neither of them Gordon! Thomson adds, 'We had to use the man, there was no alternative. We could only observe whether he would come with credit through his cross-examination.'[49] In the event they decided it was not wise to risk letting Vivian into the witness box.

But the mood was changing as Addison settled in at the Ministry of Munitions. One of the few Liberals who had stayed loyal to the new Prime Minister through Lloyd George's turn to the right, Addison nonetheless had a radical reforming past, firmly opposing Lord Carson's Ulster Rebellion (in which F.E. Smith had been involved) and was concerned with welfare and health in particular. His wife, Isabel, was to his left, favouring Home Rule, and had been involved in the suffrage movement.[50] Throughout 1915 and

1916, Addison had shown himself concerned to minimize industrial unrest and prepared to back repressive measures only if he was convinced they met specific dangers.[51] His first priority was to increase munitions production, not hunt 'conspirators'.

Back in August 1916, under pressure from Arthur Henderson, Addison had been 'inclined to agree' that 'at least some' of the deported Clydeside organizers should be allowed to return. This met with fierce opposition from Jack Tennant at the Scottish Office.[52] Towards the end of January 1917 David Kirkwood returned to the Clyde, and on 31 January Addison met a deputation from the Amalgamated Society of Engineers and local shop stewards who pleaded that Kirkwood should not be arrested. Addison accepted this suggestion on condition that Kirkwood did not get involved in any movement to reduce the supply of munitions.[53]

Addison and his under-secretary and close associate, Kellaway, certainly disapproved of the use of agents like Vivian. On 30 January 1917 Labouchere used Vivian to visit a British Socialist Party meeting at Chandos Hall, claiming, incredibly, to be a delegate from Arthur MacManus. Kellaway sent a memo to Addison on 9 February objecting to the report from Vivian and calling the use of agents provocateurs 'monstrous'.[54] Addison concurred.[55]

The use of known and hated agents was not likely to calm down militancy in the munitions factories. A report from F.W. de Valda of the New Organization conference noted the support of the shop stewards for the Wheeldons and their hatred of Booth and Gordon. Neil Cassiday (Coventry), Ramsay (Leicester) and Murphy (Sheffield), spoke about the Wheeldon case and described the two spies – unaware that they were being watched by yet another.[56]

Umberto Woolf wrote to Kellaway on 12 February 1917 to say, 'some time ago we arranged to disassociate ourselves from Colonel Labouchere as far as possible and use Scotland Yard only. I think the time has come to make this break absolute except possibly Irl. [Ireland?] Wales and Scotland where he has I understand useful officers.'[57]

By March, Gordon had become a macabre celebrity. Questions were asked in the House of Commons about the use of Alex Gordon. Ramsay MacDonald pointed to the dangers in the use of 'agents provocateurs' who 'make their money out of the manufacture of crime'.[58] W.C. Anderson, a Labour MP for Sheffield, tried to get the Labour Party to investigate Alex Gordon.[59]

Although militant workers knew the munitions shops were 'riddled'[60] with spies, the publicity surrounding the Wheeldon case brought this to the attention of a wider public. Though this did not raise widespread protest in 1917, it spread unease.

Basil Thomson was exasperated and harassed by the 'revolutionary press' which 'tried to spread the belief among its readers that enormous sums were being lavished' on spying. Thomson was indignant at the accusation that he 'went around with bulging pockets corrupting honest working men'. On the contrary, he claimed 'the most useful and trustworthy information was furnished gratuitously and the corruption was all on one side'.[61]

In retrospect, the *Manchester Guardian* more or less accused the Ministry of Munitions intelligence department of creating labour unrest in the war.

> During the war, a system of industrial espionage was established in the Ministry of Munitions. That department learnt in course of time what a dangerous instrument it was. That system, introduced under cover of war, has now been transferred to the Home Office. Some day the whole truth of the proceedings of this kind that did so much to embitter the munitions workshops during the war will be made public, and the sooner the better. Many competent judges believe that these methods of spying were at the bottom of a great deal of the industrial unrest during the war.[62]

William Melville Lee must have grown increasingly frustrated as his reports of ever-extending conspiracies fell on deaf ears. He hinted mysteriously that Mrs Wheeldon and Winnie Mason were on 'terms of intimacy' with an unnamed individual identified prominently with the strike movement.[63]

On 10 March, a rather alarming report on Gordon was communicated by an anonymous informant. Walter Hill, the Sheffield shop steward,[64] was being pressed by W.C. Anderson MP to give evidence about Gordon. Hill stated that Gordon had told him lurid stories of kidnapping Lloyd George and 'C' and also that Gordon offered poison and bombs to the ASE men in Leicester and Coventry and to MacManus – who all turned him down. But Walter Hill refused to give evidence unless questions were confined to the case.

The government informant observed that there seemed to be something against his character that he was afraid might be exposed.[65]

J.M. Davison, the wealthy anarchist, offered a reward for the discovery of Gordon.[66] It was not surprising that some socialists believed the authorities sent him to South Africa not only to cover their traces but to save his skin. The extraordinary way in which Gordon continued to attend socialist meetings and conferences after the Wheeldon trial should have indicated that the 'conspiracy' Melville Lee was so convinced about was a chimera. It would have been easy to get information out through a centralized, top-down, underground organization warning people about Alex Gordon. But what existed was a series of interlocking networks and circles rather than a cohesive centralized project. As it was, news took time to travel through the semi-permeable membranes of the anti-war movement.

Eventually the publicity resulted in the supposedly secret agents turning into public figures and in a victory for Basil Thomson's intelligence empire. De Valda glumly records: 'on account of the publicity the case inevitably attracted to myself, further service with the secret XYZ organization was rendered valueless. I was transferred to a department controlling the rationing of motor spirit – an agonizingly dull occupation.'[67]

The zealous, romantic little intelligence units filled with gentlemen adventurers full of self-important dash and purpose, taking over hotel rooms, hobnobbing with top industrialists and dallying with glamorous lady spies passed into John Buchan novels and became a literary genre.[68] Vivian and Booth plodding through the back streets of East London, scrounging cash and staying with second-hand clothes dealers proved less memorable. MI5's development was to be low-key, long-term scrutiny, and well out of the limelight.[69]

The Wheeldon case presents a bizarre cameo of the state in action. Divergent strands and interests were jealously collecting information on the labour movement and opposition to the war. As de Valda says, 'there was little liaison and co-operation'.[70] The approach varied, oscillating between a panic-struck conviction of the existence of a widespread revolutionary conspiracy, which should be dealt with through decisive repression, and a desire to damp down smouldering resentment caused by the excessive demands on workers because of the war effort, the evident prosperity of employers and their integration within the state, and the desperate state of military operations against the Germans. Amidst such ruthless ambitions and political earthquakes among the mighty, it was hardly surprising that one small intelligence unit committed hara-kiri and was gobbled up by the Special Branch. Before its demise, it dragged down to destruction a family of lower-middle class socialists from Southampton and Derby.

Poison and its Aftermath

When Alice Wheeldon entered Aylesbury Jail she was fifty years old. She faced ten years' penal servitude. She had been in custody since the end of January, appearing in court in Derby early in February for five days and then having to repeat the ordeal in the Central Criminal Court in March for a further five days.[1]

Conditions inside the prison at Aylesbury in 1917 have been recorded because it contained a distinguished inmate, Constance Markiewicz, imprisoned for her part in the Easter Rising and grieving at the death of so many of her friends – especially Connolly: 'The day began at 6.30 a.m. Prisoners washed and dressed and ate their breakfast of six ounces of bread and one pint of tea (usually cold) in their cells.'[2] Women like Alice and Constance on hard labour were given an extra two ounces of cheese and a small piece of bread at ten o'clock.

> Lunch was at twelve and consisted of two ounces of meat, two ounces of cabbage, one potato, thick flour gravy and six ounces of bread; this was varied on Thursdays, when there was hard, cold suet pudding with black treacle, and on Fridays when these prisoners ate boiled fish. Supper at about 4.30 p.m. was a pint of cocoa or tea and six ounces of bread.[3]

In the centre of every cell door there was a carved and painted eye, with pupil, eyelashes and eyebrow. Outside, a sliding disc meant the warders, who were women and who were underpaid and inclined to be bad-tempered and vindictive, could spy on the prisoners without being observed. The eye was worse than the harsh regime, according to both Constance and a friend she made in prison, a tough Irish woman nicknamed Chicago May.[4] Its effect on Alice Wheeldon can be imagined.

Constance Markiewicz was kept away from the other prisoners. But on one occasion she and Alice encountered each other. Anne Marrecco writes in her biography of the countess:

Once Constance met a Mrs Wheeldon in the passage who had been convicted (unjustly some thought) of an attempt to assassinate Lloyd George. Constance greeted her warmly saying, 'Oh I know you. You're in for trying to kill Lloyd George.' 'But I didn't,' protested Mrs Wheeldon, as she was hustled away from dangerous contact with the Irish rebel.[5]

Alice Wheeldon served nearly two years, going on hunger strike several times in protest. Her health deteriorated. Winnie and Alf also went on hunger strike. Towards the close of 1918, in a changed political climate, they were released on licence by the Home Office 'as an act of clemency' at 'the express wish of the Prime Minister'.[6]

Reuben Farrow, her old political opponent, poignantly describes Alice Wheeldon's lonely return to the station in Derby. She was dazed and weakened and he had to help her. But the trial had branded her and neighbours ostracized her.[7] Sylvia Pankhurst says that the clothes business was ruined by the government persecution. Alice 'made the best of it' by growing tomatoes.[8] Hettie, who had been desperately campaigning for her family's release, had lost her job as a teacher because of the trial and could not get another. She worked on their allotment to grow food to keep them.[9]

Alice began to pick up the broken strands of her political involvement. Tom Bell came visiting with his friend Arthur MacManus. Sylvia Pankhurst went up to the Derby Labour Party Conference and met Hettie and Alice, whom she describes as ' "mothering" half-a-dozen comrades with warm hospitality in a delightful old-fashioned household'. The comfort was carefully maintained by hard work and thrifty management.[10] There appears to have been little sign of the mysterious Mr Wheeldon. The *Derby Daily Express* said Alice Wheeldon 'lived apart from her husband'.[11]

There was an influenza epidemic that winter. The local medical officer of health reported that it could have serious lung and bronchial complications which left even the young and healthy weak. For anyone who had gone through privation and ill-health it could be fatal.[12] A few months after Alice's release both she and Hettie caught the 'flu. Winnie and Alf were both seriously ill with pneumonia. The illness proved fatal for Alice. Her age and her sufferings in prison left her too weak to recover. She died in February 1919.

The *Derby Mercury* reported that the funeral was attended by 'a score or more of relatives and friends who were attired in everyday garb, not one of them being in black customary to such an event. Navy blue, green, fawn and mauve were the dominating colours.'[13] As the plain coffin was about to be lowered, William Wheeldon pulled a red flag, about three and a half foot square, from his pocket. It fluttered in the wind and he placed it over his mother's coffin 'amid an oppressive silence'.[14]

The coffin was lowered and it appeared to be all over, 'but one of the mourners, Mr John Clarke, struggled up the bank of the slippery soil and, standing bareheaded, looked into the grave of the departed and delivered a funeral oration which can only be described as sensational'.[15] It was a remarkable effort to reconcile the death of a loved comrade with a pantheistic view of nature – 'the great sustainer and destroyer of the universe'.

He said, 'Mrs Wheeldon was a Socialist. She was a prophet, not of the sweet and holy by and by, but of the here and now. She saw the penury of the poor and the prodigality of the rich, and she registered her protest against it.'[16] She had faced 'ostracism and calumny in life'. She was the 'victim of a judicial murder'.[17] John S. Clarke's accusation was made more dramatic because he was on the run when he appeared.[18]

Hettie, Winnie and Alf were all too ill to attend Alice's funeral. Besides William Wheeldon and John S. Clarke, Arthur Mac-Manus, Willie Paul and Tom Bell were there. There was Mrs Land, who was mentioned in the letter from the CO who wrote to Hettie from the detention camp, and Mr W.M. Land, along with Mr Parker, presumably Bert Parker, the healthy food masticator and CO from Derby ILP. Also from the Derby anti-war network were Mr and Mrs Marshall, relations of the Wheeldons; the Haywoods, who were sympathetic neighbours, and Mrs Robinson. Mrs Ramsay, mother of David Ramsay of Leicester, was also present; David Ramsay had just been arrested under the Defence of the Realm Act for saying he was proud to be a Bolshevik. Other mourners whose identities I have not been able to establish were 'Mr Thomas Davidson, Miss Emily Smith, Mr C. Botham and Mr Lees'.[19]

In her tribute to Alice Wheeldon, Sylvia Pankhurst remarked of the 'plot' trial, imprisonment and tragic death: 'A sordid story and one which the Lloyd George government will doubtless wish to forget.'[20] But in fact the Wheeldons' case was not forgotten. In their subsequent accounts, F.E. Smith and Basil Thomson perpetuated the characterization of them as abnormalities who were sufficiently dangerous to require firm repression. But Alice Wheeldon's friends raised their voices in protest against the conspiracy charge, and the role of the spies and of the authorities. John S. Clarke wrote a bitter 'Epitaph of Alex Gordon', in which, around the corpse of 'filthy Alex':

> Maggot-worms in swarms below
> Compete with one another
> In shedding tears of bitter woe
> To mourn – not eat a brother.[21]

W. Mellor in the *Daily Herald* reviewed the Hammonds' *History of the Village and Town Labourer* and reflected on the years after Waterloo: 'Then it was Oliver, today it is Booth and Gordon. Then it was Sidmouth, today it is Basil Thomson. Then the loyalty of Trade Unionists was sapped by bribes; today "the Special Branch of Scotland Yard" is everywhere to be found.'[22]

Dr Chandler, the Sheffield SLPer, carefully reconstructed the case of Alice Wheeldon in 1936. Tom Bell in 1941 and Willie Gallacher as late as 1966 remembered the case in their biographies and were concerned to record the injustice which they believed had been done to her and her family.

Bearing the Burden

John S. Clarke concluded his tribute to Alice Wheeldon by saying:

> If Mrs Wheeldon could speak, she would tell us to go back home not with love and sympathy, but with intense hatred against

what fills the world with warfare, poverty or crime and all such as that. She would tell us to go away to help bear the burden she has had to lay down, to fight more fearlessly than before, so as to obtain that glorious time when peace and joyousness shall fill all life.[1]

In their different ways, this is what they did, of course, though events moved rapidly and the bearings of politics shifted. The women's movement was no longer focused on a single issue but there were wider concerns with which Alice would have been in sympathy. The Women's Peace Crusade and the Women's International League for Peace and Freedom, in which Catherine Marshall was involved, continued to work for peace after the war.[2]

Jessie Stephen worked with Sylvia Pankhurst, campaigned for birth control and then worked in the Labour Party. She continued to struggle for a better life for women as a socialist and trade unionist.[3] There were many women like her in the labour movement. Immediately after the war there was a determined movement to improve the social circumstances of working-class women's lives which covered issues like maternity, health, education and leisure. Mrs Farrow's speech at the Derby Women's Co-operative Guild in October 1919 indicates a politics which was ostensibly moderate but which had far-reaching implications for social transformation.

She started with the predicament of women as mothers, but instead of confining women in the domestic sphere she sought the expansion of politics – and indeed socialism – to include the needs of everyday life. Every mother should receive a pension for each child born to her. Women should not rest contented while babies were deprived of milk through high prices but should demand municipal control of milk. There should be municipal baths, better housing, heating and lighting. There should be greater democratic control over the supply of energy. Teachers should be better paid as a step towards improving the education of working-class children. There should be municipal cinemas 'where children could be shown pictures which would bring the best out of them and give them a love of things beautiful'.[4]

The experience of ILP members on local councils made the locality an obvious arena of politics. There was a grass-roots municipal socialism which has been overridden in historical memory by the

Webbs' more elitist approach. The co-operative movement retained, amidst dusty ledgers and compromise, some consciousness of 'that glorious time when peace and joyousness shall fill all life'[5], and the Women's Co-operative Guild displayed an expansive creativity in the reforms it deemed necessary. It still carried the utopian vision amidst the domestic nitty-gritty.

Interestingly, this feminist-influenced current in labour politics of making demands around maternity affected the post-war Socialist Labour Party. Towards the end of 1919 *The Socialist* was arguing for the full maintenance of mothers, married or unmarried, for six weeks before and six weeks after birth, and for nine months if the baby was being fed by the mother, with restoration of jobs.[6] William T. Goode spoke at an SLP meeting in Manchester on 'Women's Position in Soviet Russia' and was met with 'bursts of applause' when he stressed the endowment of motherhood.[7] Manchester, as Jill Liddington remarks, was 'a city where socialism and women's suffrage had long gone hand in hand'.[8]

The SLP reading list expanded somewhat. Along with Marx, Engels, Nietzsche, Kautsky, Bax and de Leon, there were now Olive Schreiner's *Woman and Labour* and *The Story of an African Farm*, H.G. Wells's *Ann Veronica* and Marie Stopes's *Wise Parenthood*.[9]

Hettie reviewed *Factory Echoes and other Sketches* by R.M. Fox in *The Socialist* in August 1919. Fox was a socialist in the North London Herald League; a fierce opponent of the war, he edited the NLHL paper *The Rebel* immediately after the war. In a style which resembled John S. Clarke taking the long view, Hettie wrote of the love of pageantry, the desire to merge with the 'thoughts, feelings and aspirations' of a throng of people: 'Life itself presents one vast procession, ever moving along, now gaudy and gay, now sombre, silent and sad.'[10]

But to be part of this procession is only to know a part. It is impossible 'to view the whole structure of society as it has been and as it is'. Without this total picture it is impossible to judge how to act. Pursuing the strategic vision, Hettie wrote: 'This can be reached by scaling the wall of separation on the ladder of working-class history and Marxian Economics, then and only then, will they be in a position to see what is and what has been and to prophesy what *must* be – organizing their forces accordingly.'[11] The aim was not simply to be spectators but to acknowledge our 'responsibility' to 'show' others.[12] Her statement expresses acceptance of the separation of conscious Marxists, which differs from the stress in the wartime shop stewards' movement on merging any distinction between visible leaders and participants.

Around this time, late in July or early in August, Hettie and Arthur were married. The Derby Socialist Labour Party Secretary at 907 London Road, 'Miss H. Wheeldon', transmogrifies into 'Hettie McManus' in *The Socialist* of 21 August.[13] And from then on, it is 'Mr A. MacManus' who is the Derby secretary.[14] I have not been able to find further trace of Hettie Wheeldon – except uncertain rumour. Doris Alison knew Arthur MacManus in 1921 but does not remember seeing his wife. She thinks she heard people saying his wife went 'a bit mental' and died in childbirth.[15] Harry Young knew MacManus in the early 1920s and never heard about Hettie. He remembers Arthur with a woman called Billie.[16] In 1926 in his *Famous Trials*, F.E. Smith believed Hettie had died 'not long since'.[17] Hettie was thirty at the time of the trial in 1917 so she would only have been in her mid thirties when she died.

Winnie and Alf Mason are similarly elusive. I have found only a note in *The Socialist* in February 1919, thanking 'comrades and friends' for 'numerous kindnesses and expressions of sympathy during the past two years and for the strenuous endeavours made on their behalf'.[18]

A 'Marshall Wheeldon' is mentioned along with Willie Paul as connected with the Derby Clarion Club. (*The Clarion* was a socialist newspaper with recreational clubs organized around it.) In 1919 the Derby club was the base for the Workers' News Agency, which distributed *The Socialist*.[19] This could have been William as his initials were W.M. William we know to have got a job with the co-op in Burton-on-Trent. His post was in danger when it was discovered that his mother was Alice Wheeldon, but a petition from local labour movement people safeguarded it. He was interested in spiritualism, like his mother, and inclined towards anarchism. He married and raised a family in Burton-on-Trent.[20]

While the family's history disappears from view, the sensational nature of the trial and the continuing vilification of Alice must have caused lasting and unavoidable pain. We can only speculate on how Alice Wheeldon's imprisonment and death affected her family and friends, for there is little recorded about personal feelings, even of the most prominent political figure in the story, Arthur Mac-Manus. It is hardly surprising, however, that Harry Young remembers Arthur MacManus as 'solemn and serious',[21] in contrast to Tom Bell's earlier picture of the ardent romantic. He had known little but years of poverty, exhausting agitation, prison, pursuit by the authorities and personal tragedy. Nor was he alone. The commitment demanded of this group of revolutionary socialists was rigorous and severe. Tom Bell mentions in passing that he was forced to leave Liverpool in autumn 1916 when his younger boy, Lawrence, died of peritonitis, his older son Oliver developed pneumonia and an empyema, and his wife broke down under the strain. It was far from the idealistic days of their courtship. Capitalism demanded a heavy price from its enemies within.[22] The shop stewards' movement was a hidden history – the painful and difficult balancing of personal responsibility and public commitment.

The public activities of Willie Paul and Arthur MacManus are easier to trace because of their role in industry and politics. The Ministry of Munitions Intelligence Unit included a thumb-nail sketch of Paul in their 'Rough List of Names and Addresses of Individuals connected directly or indirectly with the recent strike at Sheffield': 'Prominent socialist, holds classes, was mixed up with Clyde trouble. Is in correspondence with MacManus and Murphy. Possibly the most dangerous man of the lot.'[23] And Melville Lee describes Paul as a conscientious objector, an advanced socialist and a writer of some power and distinction.[24]

After the imprisonment of Alice Wheeldon and the Masons, Willie Paul's organizing energies turned towards Coventry. In Coventry dilution and deskilling had occurred before the First World War. It was a centre of the newest and most technologically advanced sector of vehicle and aircraft production – in which Willie Paul developed quite an interest. Better, practical links existed between skilled, semi-skilled and unskilled than in the more traditional centres of industry. When a strike broke out in November 1917, funds were raised for young women in lodgings put out by the strike. Even the clerks came out in sympathy.

Paul and other SLP members – Tom Dingley, who was also in

the IWW, and Neil Cassidy, who worked at the Coventry
Ordnance Works – developed the Coventry Workers' Committee,
in close connection with the strongest local trade union, 'The
Workers' Union'.[25] 'The agitators,' wrote the local Ministry of
Munitions official in May 1917, 'were more of the ultra-socialist
and pacifist type than of the shop-steward type.'[26]

Circumstances varied from town to town, but the different positions and interests of skilled and unskilled, of men and women,
always presented serious problems. There were continuing contradictions in a move to extend democratic control from the
defence of craft privileges and a call to unity which came from political leaders who were men of relative privilege. Conscious to vary-
ing degrees of the need to overcome inequalities, they were also
part of the problem themselves.

J.T. Murphy was frank about the real antagonisms which made
it difficult to transcend divisions from above: 'We men and women
of today have now to pay the price of man's economic dominance
over women which has existed for centuries. Content to treat
women as subjects instead of as equals, men are now faced with
problems not of their liking.'[27]

There were not only the diverse experiences of different towns
and different sections of the workforce; there was a problem about
how to take action that affected living conditions outside work.
There are several attempts to overcome this limitation. In the summer and autumn of 1917, the issue of food prices was taken up by
the shop stewards in Barrow, Manchester, the Clyde, Birmingham, Coventry and Sheffield. In Coventry and Sheffield men were
leaving the munitions works to help their wives in the long shop-
ping queues. This grievance brought closer links between
organized workers and the domestic problems created by the war
economy.[28]

There was also an internal organizational awkwardness in the
shop stewards' movement. The workers, mainly men, came
together because of industrial battles. Their families and loved
ones suffered hardship and anxiety as a consequence. Yet there was
no role for them in the rank-and-file groups.

Early in February 1920, the National Conference of Shop Stewards' and Workers' Committees, with Arthur MacManus presid-
ing, unanimously decided 'to set up economic classes for women

interested in the movement and also for the children'. It was argued that while the men were kept in touch with the movement through workshop committees, there were many women who would welcome these classes which would also 'be helpful to the movement generally'. They also decided they needed to educate the children, 'the hope of the future'.[29] The sadness behind this rhetoric was that their course of absolute political involvement had left them with less to give their own children not simply in material terms but in emotional care and attention.

Shortly after Alice Wheeldon was sentenced, the network of shop stewards' committees attempted concerted strikes. They had been working to achieve better national links. The May strike movement of 1917 was the largest of the war, involving 200,000 engineering workers in Manchester, Sheffield, Derby, Liverpool, Birkenhead, Leeds and Newcastle, over the extension of dilution to commercial work and the exemption of skilled men from conscription. Nonetheless it collapsed – largely because of the differing and divided circumstances of skilled and unskilled workers.[30] On 15 May, a national delegate conference of strike committees was held in London. Its proclamations were suppressed by the censor.[31]

Three days later, leading members of the National Committee of Shop Stewards were arrested, including Walter Hill and Arthur MacManus. Tom Bell observes:

> F.E. Smith (Lord Birkenhead) was the Counsel for the Prosecution. It is doubtful if a more spiteful, hateful enemy of the workers ever existed. He blustered and threatened to send them to the front to be shot, etc. but a more subtle hand was at work. The majority of the prisoners signed. 'Mac' refused and didn't sign. He was eventually set free with the rest.[32]

Arthur MacManus was one of the SLP delegates at the Leeds Convention on 3 June 1917, a gathering of 1,500 British socialists of varied persuasions to express solidarity with the Russian Revolution. MacManus, Gallacher and Bell went to expose the ILP platform of Ramsay MacDonald and Philip Snowdon. There were many people there prepared by the war and the Russian Revolution to countenance changes which would have seemed inconceivable before 1916. For some it was only a superficial mood; for others it marked a watershed in how political struggle was conceived.[33] Soon after the Leeds Convention, the first fully representative national conference of shop stewards was convened in Manchester on 18 and 19 August 1917.[34]

Shortly after the Leeds Convention, Lloyd George allowed the deportees to return to Glasgow. Arthur MacManus spoke at the reception to welcome them. He talked of the need to develop the political character of their agitation.[35] This was an emphasis which the limits of rank-and-file industrial action were beginning to make more evident.

In January 1918 Lloyd George sent Sir Auckland Geddes to Glasgow to speak to the trade unions. The Women's Peace Crusade which had been started by Agnes Dollan, an ILPer, and Helen Crawfurd, a suffragette, organized among women with 'kitchen-meetings, street-meetings, parades, leaflets and poster boards'. At the meeting with Geddes, Arthur MacManus got up on a seat – because he was short, no doubt. Geddes was amazed at the reception MacManus received. Gallacher says,

> in a brilliant speech he riddled the case for the continuance of the war, ending up with 'not another man for the criminal war for trade and territory. An immediate end to it. This is our challenge to the Government. For this we are fighting and will go on fighting.'[36]

The following month Arthur took Tom Bell to meet the Soviet representative, Litvinoff, in London. They went to the International Club in Charlotte Street, an old haunt of nineteenth-century European revolutionary exiles. Tom Bell's account years later still conveys the awe and respect he felt towards these emissaries from the land where all his dreams and thwarted yearnings were becoming reality. Internationalism was no longer a statement of hope but an historical bond. He was dazed by the 'babel of tongues', fascinated by the unusual but imposing appearance of the young Russian they met at the club in his 'three-quarter length black coat'. The Bolshevik political sophistication held a depth of understanding which stretched his political thinking. He observed the Russian intellectual making a conscious effort to use simple direct language towards the British workers. He took 'great pains to show us . . . the political implications of all our industrial activities, and to lift us above the mentality of the pure and simple shop steward'.[37]

This is a curious remark from one who had paced the streets discussing philosophy, irritated women comrades with his adherences to Belfort Bax, taken baby Oliver to economics lectures, worked with Connolly and Maclean. The prestige and power of the Russian Revolution and the more coherent political culture of the Bolshevik Party seemed to wash away the fragile comprehensions of the previous decade. In retrospect, these appeared child-like, infantile. The concentrated energy of a revolution-in-the-making overwhelmed socialists in other countries – even as they learned from the Bolshevik tradition, they lost touch with some of the understandings they had so painfully gained themselves. Their own efforts appeared paltry in contrast to the epic developments in the Soviet Union.

Tom Bell was convinced that the SLP must be linked to 'this great revolutionary movement going on in Russia'.[38] He returned exalted to work in Glasgow on a Tuesday to discover his job was filled because he'd taken the Monday off. His workmates saw it as a matter of individual choice and would take no action.

In December 1918, Arthur MacManus and Willie Paul were candidates in the election at Halifax and Ince. They were a franker pair than is customary among politicians. Willie Paul told the electorate: 'I am not fighting this fight to get into Parliament, I am conducting this fight to stir up discontent against the ruling class and to strengthen the political and industrial organization of labour.'[39] He added that he did not know how many votes he would get and he did not care. Arthur MacManus campaigned similarly. He declared a 'Soviet Republic for Britain', a working day of six hours, a thirty-six-hour week, maintenance for all adults with extra for parents and mothers of families, pensions for the aged, infirm and sick. It was to be a co-operative commonwealth based on workers' and soldiers' councils.[40]

The form of the election campaign was an impressive mix of industrial agitation and political education. Bell, MacManus and other SLPers visited every factory and workshop in Halifax with their fourteen-point programme for a Bolshevik Britain. 'Little Mac' stood on 'the top of machines addressing the workers on the class issues of the moment'. With a trace of the old, earnest didacticism of the pre-war SLP, they distributed 40,000 copies of 'an excellently coloured map of Europe showing the imperialist division of territories',[41] illustrating the sources of wealth in these areas. Arthur MacManus told readers of *The Socialist*, 'Comrades we have a chance.' Echoing Connolly he added, 'if the time is ever ripe it is ripe now.'[42]

Arthur got 4,036 votes and Willie Paul 2,231 from the workers of Halifax and Ince.[43] It was not a bad effort but Bolshevik Britain failed to arrive in the House of Commons. Tom Bell again got the sack for being absent from work.[44] Still, it had been an ingenious way round the Defence of the Realm Act's gagging of political opposition. The election campaign was an admirable means. Undaunted, the SLPers declared, 'We are denounced as "British Bolsheviks". We do not seek to conceal our views. We are proud of the title. The SLP is the only political organization that stands wholeheartedly and uncompromisingly for the Soviet idea. Let it be known! We are the British Bolsheviks.'[45]

There was another enormous strike on the Clyde in January 1919. The Secretary of State for Scotland decided he faced not a strike but a Bolshevik uprising. The government sent six tanks and a hundred lorries up by train and placed central Scotland under army occupation. For MacManus and Gallacher it was prison again. The strike collapsed and similar industrial rebellions in Belfast, on Tyneside and elsewhere caved in.[46]

Rising unemployment was beginning to have an effect. The circumstances of wartime production which had made the shop stewards' movement possible were transformed. Assailed by the intensity and rapidity of industrial restructuring, battered by the arduous engagements of unceasing struggle and blighted with poverty and personal hardships, the small band of SLP comrades tried desperately to make sense of circumstance. Even without the impetus of the Bolsheviks, a desire for greater coherence, co-ordination and structure to all their efforts and suffering would hardly have been surprising.

The end of the war saw Arthur MacManus struggling for some means of sustaining and holding the movements from below which before the war had seemed sufficient in themselves. He now believed struggle itself was not enough. There had to be clear channels cut for rebellion to target the weaknesses of the ruling class.

Primarily the revolutionary potentialities of each succeeding ferment should be noted, and a conscious direction of our efforts towards securing unity of purpose, spontaneity of action, and a courageous grip of events. With the passing of each succeeding ferment is recorded a lost opportunity. To make the most of a crisis, the main point of action must be controlled by and in the hands of the revolutionary socialists.[47]

Arthur retained his theoretical non-sectarianism and the emphasis on the realization of consciousness in action. But the emphasis on the direction of a vanguard with an overview of the battlefield is more apparent than in his earlier stress on rank-and-file action: 'the mere blind, instinctive struggle of the workers against their masters cannot overthrow capitalism and establish communism. Into that struggle every revolutionary socialist must throw himself or herself and give the masses a battle-cry.'[48]

He polarizes struggle as 'instinctive' and the revolutionary socialists as conscious. The earlier syndicalist emphasis had stressed consciousness developing within action. But the shop stewards' movement, and the centralized power of the capitalist state it faced, had shown up the problems in this generous faith in action as the democratic educator. It lacked depth and did not probe beyond immediate uprising. It presented no strategy for taking power in society as a whole.

This was the strength of the Bolsheviks' revolutionary achievement. With hindsight it is not difficult to say there were a few snags there as well, for the 'higher consciousness' of the revolutionary socialist partly reflected existing privilege and was as subject to power struggles as the rest of human political affairs. But Arthur and his friends can hardly be expected to have had X-ray vision seventy years into the future. Struggling with the continuing problem of how rebellions for immediate needs in the here and now change qualitatively into movements for a new social order, and aware of the danger of the rank-and-file organizing being dissipated and becoming ineffective, Arthur MacManus saw the Russian Revolution as the needful synthesis.

He told the conference of Shop Stewards' and Workers' Committees in 1920 that the working class in Russia 'have gone to the roots, and have found a way out, and what is of even greater interest is that they have found the way out by means of just such committees as we are building up in this country. They call them Soviets, we call them workers' councils.'[49] He set his shoulders for a task they must accept collectively. The Russian experience meant 'an added obligation placed on our shoulders, that of not only shaping our organization to end the present system of capitalism but also of adapting our organization to maintain a better system in its place.'[50]

This is what J.T. Murphy later called more succinctly, 'Preparing for Power'.[51] In his pamphlet published by the Sheffield Workers' Committee in 1917, *The Workers' Committee: An Outline of its Principles and Structure*, Murphy had sketched out how workers' committees might develop into a wider form of social organization and take on issues of life in the community and distribution as well as democratizing production. A continuing theme is the conscious awareness of being part of an extensive process of economic restructuring and the accompanying transformation in organizational assumptions. The emphasis on rank-and-file action goes with a powerful sense of 'responsibility' as a revolutionary socialist.[52] With its overview, its strategy and its conscientious commitment, the politics of the skilled craft worker was hurtled during the war onto a national stage.

By 1920 this had become international. MacManus, Bell and Paul advocated the SLP's fusion with others into the new Communist Party. Old hostilities went deep. Arthur MacManus had clashed with Philip Snowdon of the ILP during the negotiations for unity.[53] The connection to the Labour Party, the role of parliament, were big obstacles and the SLP majority turned against the new party. Tom Bell gave up the editorship of *The Socialist*. MacManus, Bell and Paul called a breakaway meeting, the Communist Unity Conference in Nottingham, and were expelled. MacManus and Bell then concentrated on the preparation for the Unity Conference, working closely with the Comintern representative.

They were taking in a new set of assumptions about political organization.[54] Lenin's theories of how to organize were barely known. Their acceptance was by no means automatic. There were people like Mrs Bamber from Liverpool Council and L. Royle from Sheffield saying, why build up the Labour Party when you knew you would have to smash it in the future?[55] There was David Ramsay saying, 'Let the English comrades decide the question for themselves.' But how could there be an International if everyone decided for themselves, demanded the Bolsheviks. And how could such an amorphous body be held together without the directing ascendency of the Bolsheviks who had the confidence to assert their own leadership – in the interests of the international proletariat?[56]

The Comintern representatives were tireless in their explanations. Up got an angry Jack Tanner with a copy of *Solidarity* to demand of Zinoviev: '[is there] nothing more . . . to learn from the struggles, movements and revolutions of other countries. Have they come here not to learn, but only to teach?'[57] Willie Paul wriggled uncomfortably, acknowledging the weight of the Russian experience but unwilling to accept the denial of local circumstances and the elevation of Lenin's authority into a canon of obedience. They should not 'slavishly accept everything which he utters in Moscow. The very warp and woof of our propaganda is criticism and, as we believe in criticism, we are not above criticizing Lenin,' he declared. 'Lenin is no pope or god.'[58]

The pressures of ensuing events were to make this a difficult position to hold to over the years.

Arthur MacManus became the chair of the new Communist Party. Ironically he had to face his old opponent Arthur Henderson with the question of affiliation to the Labour Party. It is not known whether Arthur Henderson remembered that, a few years before, Arthur MacManus's late mother-in-law had been rumoured to be conspiring to murder him. This was one of the local circumstances Lenin missed out on from Moscow! Henderson had little trouble quoting MacManus's own articles in *The Socialist* on the iniquities of the Labour Party back at him.[59] And affiliation was, of course, rejected.[60]

MacManus visited Russia with Tom Bell and served as the British representative on the International's executive committee. In February 1922, he was one of four foreigners who sat in judgement on a critical document of the Workers' Opposition in Russia. This group, which included Alexandra Kollontai, argued the case of the workers against the production drives of the New Economic Policy. It was only two years since MacManus had chaired the British Shop Stewards' Conference. But socialism, it now seemed, could brook no militant rank-and-file opposition. The foreign socialists sat in embarrassed silence as Trotsky, Zinoviev, Stalin and Rudzutak refuted the arguments of Kollontai and the other oppositionists.[61] Harry Young shared a hotel with Arthur Mac-Manus and the Wobbly, Big Bill Haywood, in Russia. These revolutionary exiles were suspended from the events shaking Russia and were divorced from the politics of their own countries. Big Bill Haywood turned to amorous diversions. MacManus simply drank.[62] Claude McKay, the black socialist writer from Jamaica, describes MacManus at a party in Moscow, 'swaying like a tipsy little imp' and accusing a Russian who was a clerk in the Department of Investigations and Arrests of being a spy.

'Spy! Spy! I am not going to stay here, I am going home. Spy!' shouted Arthur in Glaswegian at the Russian who, roused to insulted fury, knocked his small opponent down and kicked him across the room. Arthur, McKay recalls, 'lay curled up like a half-dead snake'.

'You dirty little Englishman,' cried Venko. 'Go back and make your own revolution and don't stay in Russia to insult a real Communist.'

MacManus picked himself up and began shouting, 'I am not a Communist. I am an Anarchist. Anarchist. Anarchist.' A comrade clapped his hand over MacManus's mouth and, 'lifting him up like a kid, carried him out of the room'.

McKay remarks, 'I couldn't understand the meaning of Mac-Manus's outburst except perhaps that he, like some of the visiting comrades, was afflicted with spy mania.'[63]

In 1922 MacManus had lost some of his influence when the party organization was overhauled to bring it in line with the Russian model. But, along with Paul, Bell and Murphy, he was a leading advocate of the turn back to rank-and-file organization from 1926.[64]

In Britain, the authorities did not stop their surveillance and harassment. In April 1924, two Special Branch men were discovered taking shorthand notes underneath the speakers' platform at the CPGB conference. The local police were called and a young constable discovered he had arrested men from Scotland Yard.[65] In the General Election of 1924, the Labour government was defeated. A contributing factor was the publication of 'the Zinoviev letter' which was sent to Arthur MacManus and proposed armed warfare. The Tories presented Ramsay MacDonald as a Bolshevik dupe. The letter was in fact a forgery and the work of White Russians and British intelligence agents – though this was not known for certain until 1966.[66] In October 1925 MacManus was among a group of Communists raided and charged with seditious conspiracy and incitement to mutiny. The trial put the Communist Party executive out of operation but failed to find evidence of large sums of money from the Soviet Union. In his history of MI5, Nigel West comments, 'It was altogether a poor performance for an admitted six years of intermittent observation by the Special Branch.'[67]

Arthur MacManus died, only thirty-eight years old, on 27 February 1927.[68] His last activity was the 'Hands off China' campaign. As first President of the CPGB he was buried with honour in the Soviet Union. Tom Bell became National Organizer of the Communist Party. He died in 1944.[69] William Paul died in Derby in 1958. He, too, was a founder member of the CPGB and edited the *Communist Review* between 1921 and 1923. He became a Labour candidate for Rusholme in 1923-4. His book, *The State: Its Origins and Functions*, was influential on the left in the twenties. He was also active in the Plebs League, a Marxist education organization.[70] John S. Clarke could not accept Lenin's arguments of the need to work with the Labour Party. He never forgave Arthur Henderson. For Lenin personally he had the greatest respect and affection, but as a man, not a divinity. 'In spite of the heavy pressure of work which he, in common with everyone, had to face at that trying time, he always had a cheery word, a happy smile and a patient ear to lend to all.'[71] But he thought Lenin was misled about Britain. He never joined the Communist Party but continued to give Marxist lectures for the National Council of Labour Colleges and *Plebs* published his writing. He became a Labour MP and then a journalist, dying in Glasgow in 1947.[72]

They all strove to bear the burden Alice Wheeldon had had to lay down, even though the alignments of truth and justice were drawn without clarity and the post-war world yielded little enough of the 'peace and joyousness' John S. Clarke had prophesied by the grave in Derby in 1919.

Preparing for Power

If John S. Clarke were around he would undoubtedly draw many lessons from history in all this. Marxist historians, however, have become more self-conscious since his day, abashed by the recalcitrant present which trounces the past. The desire for those tidy lessons – a neat pre-school room with small desks in rows, ink-pots at the ready, dip-pens poised – is still a powerful dream of order. Even this is a psychological imposition – the clarity of the good old days.

Still we all turn to the past with some present concerns. Perhaps some confusions can be avoided by stating them.

My interest in the Wheeldons' story, beyond the personal drama, comes out of unanswered problems in the socialist movement now. For the case contains in microcosm a fascinating combination of interconnecting political strands, many long forgotten and some rediscovered in contemporary times as if they had never been tried before. Present, amidst the whirlwind of ideas and assumptions in the rapid events of the First World War, can also be seen the beginnings of a new phase of left politics which was to set the terms – for better or worse – of the traditions of socialism which are our immediate inheritance.

Error and circumstance have revealed sufficient flaws in those socialist assumptions, formed in the interwar period, to open enquiries which do not regard their direct predecessors as patronizingly as used to be customary.

Somewhere amidst the dour events of our century, socialism turned sour. It lost the capacity to fill people's hearts with hopes of pleasure, beauty, love and happiness. There were good reasons for this. Amidst the carnage and despair, a naive optimism based on falsehood is of little help to anyone. But in grappling with the loss of innocence which the exercise of power made manifest, precious understandings slipped away. Socialists – both reformist and revolutionary – made only desultory efforts to garner the visions of what could be. For they came to hold these of little account. If power was to be achieved, or taken, strategy was required – not dreams. Of course to try to make a new reality requires planning, but there was an imbalance. Behind the imbalance was a negligence which left the capacity to imagine stunted. The initiation of such an enterprise as socialism demands a human characteristic symbolized in the person who steps off the cliff into the unknown. In beginning to change what is, you have to wager with what cannot be known – because it is not yet.

There is then, necessarily, a risk attached to socialism. It is after all about beginning anew. The socialist movement's celebration of the ancient festival of spring, May Day, optimisticaily asserted the fertile awakening of the new, the step into the unknown. As the evidence mounted of the seriousness of the distortions which the risk could involve, the insouciant utopianism of the fool seemed frivolity. The desire to hang on to what appeared to be known, rather than uncovering what was not known, prevailed.

My compulsive curiosity about Alice Wheeldon and her friends is partly the consuming yearning to know what happened, shared by all who love to explore the past. It is driven too, though, by the conviction that socialists at this time need to take courage in both hands and set off to visit some earlier uncertainties. Not to be devil-may-care about it, but because the beginning of wisdom these days is to accept that the certainties we have inherited are inadequate.

This is frightening in the turmoil of engagement. It is ironically the case that radicalism often fosters a counterbalancing conservatism in the manner in which opinions are held. The most 'left' of us can clutch and huddle around received truths as if our lives depended upon their unchallenged veracity.

We would do better to take a leaf from Jack Murphy's *The Workers' Committee*, written in 1917: 'Thought is revolutionary; it breaks down barriers, transforms institutions, and leads onward to a larger life. To be afraid of thought is to be afraid of life and to become an instrument of darkness and oppression.'[1]

Even so it has been peculiarly difficult to divest ourselves of the consensus reference points passed on to us through the Labour Party, the Communist Party or its Trotskyist stepchildren. It is still less effort to take them as we find them, with a 'handsome-is-as-handsome-does'. It is an effort to recognize that before their emergence there were valuable understandings which have been consumed and squandered, that socialism involved a wider vision of a transformed society, on the part of both revolutionaries and reformists. It meant new kinds of relationships without alienation and hierarchy, and a more harmonious connection with nature. This was not in the realm of grand theory, but common knowledge, taken for granted and quite frequently discussed. The making of socialism involved changes in the here and now – for example, the attempt to develop the capacity for leadership in everyone and the conscious nurturing of transformed desire. Socialism was about the extension of freedom in society and against coercion from the state.

The socialist tradition never abandoned such concerns, but they ceased to be central and passionate and vehement. So we have to labour to reconstruct socialism as a vision of freedom. The aim was to bring freedom from exploitation, from the soul-destroying alienation of creativity in labour, freedom from want, from needs denied, and freedom from cultural humiliation, the subordination of potential humanity which class, race and sex oppression entails. Early this century socialists were still not too embarrassed to shout all this from the roof-tops or the street-corners or the market-place.

There is abundant evidence that what is called socialism today has not achieved this, and this is much less encouraging news to be shouting about. Nonetheless, if we are resolved that socialism is about extending the scope of freedom, it entails honesty about what has *not* been achieved in the name of socialism. It is not in the spirit of overweening correctness but rather the case of the beginning of wisdom being the confession of what is not known.

> One of our present dilemmas on the Left is the habit of thinking that we *already know* what the content and future of socialism is. We talk of socialism as if it were an already completed agenda: the script of a play which is already written and only waiting for someone to put it on stage.[2]

I think the habit to which Stuart Hall refers in the above quote goes deep. So much so that many of us can bumble along for years knowing we may not know ourselves but trusting that someone or some others do because they speak with greater confidence. So we defer the responsibility of working it out ourselves and come down with a bump to realize it is our business as much as anyone else's.

It may feel raw and vulnerable to open wounds and be explicit about what is not clear, even after the pain and tragedy of the events of this century, but it is also the means to renewal.

There have been several resolute voices castigating complacency. Significant among these in recent years has been E.P. Thompson's in reminding socialists that they have lost the capacity to imagine an alternative and have no commonly accepted understanding of the manner and process of transition from modern capitalism to a democratic socialism.[3] This has not been simply because of internal theoretical shortcomings but because external events devastated the terrain of assumption. The structure of capitalism changed and changed and changed again, dragging the rest of the world in its wake and leaving socialists' heads spinning.

One of the changes underway early this century was the consolidation of the powers of the state to intervene in people's lives. This involved the increase of surveillance and police powers, the acceptance of trade unions within a restricted economic bargain for wages, and the establishing of the welfare state. All have a direct contemporary relevance, for the central state has been and is being greatly enlarged in its powers. Liberties, including the limited rights of trades unions, are being curtailed, while the welfare measures, initiated early this century, are being whittled away.

This welfare has always been double-edged. Partly representing the gains and encroachments of both the feminist and labour movements over the control of resources, it has also served the long-term interests of a stable capitalist bargain with the oppressed. It gives even the powerless a stake in the status quo. Yet over time it also raised expectations. This is the radical truth in the mean-minded Tory slogan about a generation gone soft on welfare. The welfare, initiated by Lloyd George's new social liberalism and built upon by Labour, reconstructed the common sense of basic needs.

The present onslaught by the right is thus a resurgence of the seedy side of conservatism, the Scrooge in the Tory spirit. It is also, in a more sinister way, a howl for revenge against the restraints of democracy on class power. The right is prepared to use the consolidation of state power to coerce quite openly. Theirs is a rebellion against the enlightened conservatism which countenances reforms in order to preserve privilege and against the utopian conservatism of organic harmony.

In the state of shock which these innovatory right-wing strategies have produced on the left, two simple realizations loom starkly. The two strategic routes which opposed each other clearly from the early 1920s, labourism and communism, either regarded the state as a neutral force or assumed it would be taken over and mysteriously wither at some unspecified time in the future. Consequently, neither strategy led socialists to put detailed thought into how the actually existing state was to be dismantled and changed.

It is one of the bitter-sweet features of capitalism that the capacity to imagine an alternative becomes the more fantastic in the very process of reforms becoming achievable. For the Labour Party, the transformation of society was far, far in the future. The aim became the specific reforms in themselves, a more human capitalism with increased productivity, falling back 'upon the Utilitarians' earthly paradise – the maximization of economic growth'.[4]

Modern socialism has suffered from a polarization – a strategic absorption within and a politics of permanent opposition without. Socialism having in various ways hit hard times, there are considerable pressures to retire into one or other of these polarities. Both, however, are dead ends. Instead, extending the endeavour to balance anew the achievement of attainable goals with the gamble of what might be – that is a pressing requirement.

An apparent rout could yet be turned into an opportunity to advance on a new tack. It is time to get a bit crafty and turn a few tables. The bargain with the working class, which kept capitalism on an even keel, has been dissolved. This need not leave socialism an archaic memory. On the contrary it could be an opening for a renewed offensive. From the resistance against the attack on what has been assumed to be instead the opportunity to assert a new scope for trade union action and a more democratic and accountable form of welfare could arise. Making an explicit strategy of such an endeavour would make sense of many of the fragmented responses people have made in resisting the encroachments of the Conservative government in the last few years.

The politics discussed in Pear Tree Ward in Derby are not sufficient to provide contemporary redefinitions – times, after all, have changed and changed again. Still, they could remind us that there was a time when the two routes to socialism, of opposition and absorption, had not become such well-worn tracks that the reason for setting out on either had been almost forgotten in the arguments about which route was best.

The limits of syndicalism, its preoccupation with economic change at the workplace among mainly men workers, its emphasis on the act of industrial rebellion, its tendency to extol the politics of a pure rank-and-file opposition which ignores the difficulties, weaknesses and prejudices that make this rebellion problematic have been reiterated many times.

But those criticisms are too cut and dried. The dismissal of the historical moment of syndicalism's force as a movement is too absolute. It forecloses the potential of the extraordinary tumult which was syndicalism in its wider sense. For what was also there, counter-balancing the permanent opposition, was the recognition of the need to create a new culture, values and relationships.

Odon Por and P.M. Atkinson, for instance, write in the *Daily Herald* in 1912:

> Syndicalists perceive the tremendous difficulty of social progress. They know it could make no substantial difference to have a new social order with the human material of the present order unchanged. Accordingly, they endeavour to combine the new society with the creation of the new man.[5]

They quoted a French syndicalist, a clerk in the Post Office: 'A revolution does not improvise itself and it is necessary that in the industrial groups new ideas, new collective sentiments, should be born and should develop and prepare the social change.'[6]

The narrowing is there not only in the new 'man' but in the industrial group as the locus of rebellion. But in fairness to the syndicalists it should be said that their comments were not all male-bound, and that the precedence of the workplace was an aspect of Marx's thought as well. And it is not the case that syndicalism had no concept of transition.

Also, as we have seen, the emphasis on the workplace was in practice offset by the to-ing and fro-ing which Ken Weller has termed the 'the confused matrix of the grassroots movements'.[7] For instance, the article by Por and Atkinson was plonked down amidst schemes for co-operative housekeeping and articles on how motherhood could expand its social meaning in specific reforms. People everywhere in the 'rebel' milieu shifted between causes and movements just as the Wheeldons did in Derby. There are many such stories to be told.

People also carried opinions from several sources at the same time. As the years passed and circumstances changed, they shed a few and hung on to others. Socialists like Edward Carpenter and Leonard Hall were influenced by syndicalism but retained the vision of the co-operative commonwealth. The rebellious, anti-hierarchical, anti-state stance permeated the views of many people who would not be categorized as syndicalists. For instance, Bertrand Russell wrote in *The Ploughshare* in 1916:

In economic home policy the old State Socialism of the Fabian Society is somewhat discredited. There were socialists who rejoiced, in the early days of the war, that now Socialism had come. The Government controlled banks, railways, prices, everything. Now they have carried Socialism to the point of punishing all who will not take part in the war. If this is Socialism, the less we have of it the better. What is desirable is not increased power of the State, as an end in itself, but greater justice in distribution and, still more, better opportunities for initiative and self-direction on the part of those who do not happen to be capitalist. We need economic democracy as well as political democracy; we need the complete abolition of the system of working for wages. Something of the youthful revolutionary ardour of syndicalism is needed if labour is to have a free life. The men who do the work ought to control the policy of their industry.[8]

So political attitudes were not so neatly distributed and syndicalism was not sealed off from other strands of rebellious thinking. Thus for a time feminism bundled in with workers' control, anti-militarism co-existed with spiritualism and concern for the freedom of the Irish hobnobbed with municipalizing the milk supplies, without it occurring to contemporaries that this radical mix was especially odd. Perhaps the socialism they wanted was idealistic and inattentive to necessary administrative details – the Fabians' forte. But at least they had some notion of another kind of society. It is not possible to conceive strategies for transforming society as it is into society as it might be unless you let a few cats out of the bag about what you want. This may cause considerable argument – there are many wants and many visions. No harm in that. They could do with some airing.

Because the moment captured in *Friends of Alice Wheeldon* is one in which the two subsequent main courses of socialism, communism and labourism, were still unclear, consideration of the political assumptions of the period opens a source for imaginative reconception. Alice Wheeldon and her contemporaries acted without our retrospective knowledge of the versions of socialism which prevailed. The recreation of the moment of her notoriety is to enter the socialist past with a very different perspective.

The inchoate libertarian vision of the rebels against both the war and the state regulation of industry was to be overtaken and eventually dissipated, persisting in disgruntled and subordinate strands in the Independent Labour Party and the Communist Party. Its development halted, it was to be infantilized, labelled as a primitive form.

This was not only because of the efficiency of the Webbs or of the political machine Arthur Henderson developed, or even because of the evolution of modern capitalism and Keynesian economics. Rather, the anti-statist, syndicalist- influenced strand failed to provide an answer to areas of necessary action and to people's needs outside the workplace. Its supporters kept coming up against its limitations. This failure was particularly obvious after 1919 when unemployment eroded the shop stewards' strength. The political leaders certainly partially recognized this, seeking to form links with other issues and groups in the community. Some of the leadership – MacManus, Paul and Murphy – saw in Leninism a synthesis that transcended the dilemmas of rank-and-file workplace organizing, and they went into the new Communist Party – which was statist in a revolutionary way.

But the problems were evident to socialists who did not accept Bolshevism. The end of the war meant that the state was no longer overtly oppressive, except in particular moments of industrial rebellion or towards the unemployed demonstrations in England at least, Ireland and the Colonies always being another matter. So a blanket opposition to the state simply did not fit. It began to seem a rather cranky ideological hangover. There was considerable grass-roots pressure to make demands on the state which appeared to be more in accord with statist tendencies in the labour movement. For example, there was agitation from women in the feminist and labour movement for child benefits and improved maternity provision. The syndicalist-influenced left had tended to tag areas of social and personal life rather awkwardly onto industrial militancy. So when socialist feminists in the 1920s tried to follow through the ideas of workers' control in relation to sexual liberation, they found themselves with an awkward dualism. Men were to control work and women their bodies as if women did not work and men were without bodies.[9]

The absolutism of the anti-state strand left it without any

recourse for a whole range of needs. When it was evident that a fairer distribution of resources controlled by the state was required as well as changes at work, there were no clear arguments that this must be secured by direct democratic struggle, accountable and controlled from below.

There is a glimmer though, after the First World War, of the extension of a concept of control into aspects of life beyond the workplace. The glimmer was not revolutionary in the Leninist sense. It appeared in the politics of the Women's Co-operative Guild's vision of a co-operative commonwealth of municipal milk supplies and municipal laundries. It was there in the agitation for the right to birth control in maternity welfare centres.[10] Its most celebrated eruption was in the 1921 rebellion of the Poplar councillors led by George Lansbury against the failure of the government to give more help with the payment of poor relief. The councillors included several socialist feminists who had worked with Sylvia Pankhurst.[11]

There were more spasmodic moves for control over welfare measures from below. And there was a continuing consciousness among the rank and file of the ILP and the Women's Co-op Guild that socialism was not just about external changes, about voting the Labour Party into power or seizing state power through revolution. Socialism was also about extending the experience of democracy, of living differently. The Women's Co-op Guild called this caring and sharing. *The Miners' Next Step*, written by South Wales miners influenced by syndicalism before the war, called it 'solidarity' by which they meant the conscious acceptance of individual responsibility and the collective bond. None of these elements in the socialist tradition was entirely forgotten. The 'retrospective construction of tradition' is not all-powerful. People continued to remember but they became somewhat defensive about the relevance of their memories.

As for the means – these have received greater attention in modern times. No one can know if there is to be a once-and-for-all combat for socialism in an advanced capitalist country. Whether or not the conflict is specific or sustained – and the latter seems more likely – its outcome will be affected decisively by the extent to which Connolly's 'outworks' have been undermined and reconstructed. Not by a division of movements into those responsible for outworks and those taking the 'citadel' but by all subordinated groups in society developing from below forms of resistance to the control exercised by employers and by the state. The struggle to gain democratic control over the fruits of toil will thus take up new kinds of resistance as capitalism changes. It will always require expanding the scope for freedom, not simply guarding civil liberties but sustaining the rebellious clamour of the human spirit against the confinements and indignity of oppression.

The return to Pear Tree Ward, Derby, then, is not for answers. They are not there in the past. If they appear to be there they can misguide as much as they assist. The realizations of movements are not sufficient but they are a vital corrective to the dogmatic arrogance which is the bane of sectarian theorizing. In rethinking past history, the point is not to idealize 'the answer', but to reappropriate abandoned understandings. So while the politics discussed in Pear Tree Ward in Derby all those years ago is not going to solve contemporary dilemmas, it still holds elements too precious to be dismissed. These aspects of socialism give Murphy's phrase 'preparing for power' a wider meaning. If the coercive and controlling force of the state is to be transformed and our alienated liberties claimed, such an enlargement is vital.

And the reassertion of the forgotten interconnections and assumptions of these socialist rebels involves an astute recognition, which the maligned Reuben Farrow saw in the pre-war ILP. There are losses as well as gains from past ascendancies. At a time when many of the supposed gains have become somewhat threadbare, such a realization is an essential element in 'clearing the way' – for the creation of a socialism which, to echo Jack Tanner, knows how to learn as well as to teach.

Friends of Alice Wheeldon

Foreword

It was the outline of the Wheeldon case in Ray Challinor's *The Origins of British Bolshevism* (1977) which made me suddenly see a play. The bare account there contains its own immediate drama, and *Friends* is above all a dramatic tale. It is the story of a woman isolated and wrenched away from a familiar world by a remarkable concentration of political forces and accused of a conspiracy she denied to the last. It is a mystery as to why the British state should go to so much trouble to imprison three individuals who were not central figures in either the anti-war movement or the industrial unrest in the middle of the First World War. And all this takes place in a period where there is an extraordinary shaking up and recombination of political traditions and ideas as the war threw together socialists, pacifists, feminists and others in opposition.

I have presented the bare outline of the story in my Preface (pp. vii–ix above). Here, I will briefly try to reconstruct the social and political background to the events the play describes.

As suffragettes in the Women's Social and Political Union, Alice and Hettie Wheeldon must have known about the political fights between Christabel, Emmeline and Sylvia Pankhurst over syndicalism, socialism and alliances with men.[1] As left Independent Labour Party supporters before the First World War, they would also have been aware of the growing dissatisfaction with the Labour members in parliament, who gave no lead on how to oppose unemployment and who went along with the state welfare reforms introduced by the Liberals.[2] Many socialists feared the growing powers of the state, distrusted any reliance on it, and opposed the equation of state intervention with socialism which Leonard Hall, a socialist sympathetic to syndicalism and feminism, described as 'social bureaucracy'.[3]

Syndicalism represented an approach to political action rather than a tidy programme. In *Don't Be a Soldier*, Ken Weller observes:

> The term 'syndicalism' and 'industrial unionism' covered a wide range of different nuances and meanings – from the amalgamation of existing unions to the belief that industrial unions organising all the workers in an industry were a more effective weapon of struggle; to seeing the industrial organisation of workers as not only being the vehicle of revolutionary transformation, but also as a prefiguration of the socialist future.[4]

Hettie and Alice could well have come across such syndicalist influences directly, since syndicalists around Tom Mann had propagandized in Sheffield, Birmingham and Coventry.[5] Syndicalism and the anti-statist concepts of the Guild Socialists were also debated in George Lansbury's eclectic *Daily Herald*.[6] When Herald Leagues were set up as a means of distributing the paper, they became centres for diverse rebel strands on the left, and in some cases fostered a radical avant-garde culture. There was a Herald League in Derby which was linked to the Clarion Club before the war.[7] Hettie and Alice had copies of the *Daily Herald* and the (weekly) *Herald* in 1916[8] and undoubtedly had had some contact with the League.

At the same time there was the Socialist Labour Party (SLP), active in Leicester, Nottingham, Sheffield and Derby,[9] introducing a strand of revolutionary socialism which was influenced by the debates on the role of trade unionism in the American Socialist Labour Party, by James Connolly's encounter in the United States with the Wobblies and (though they would have been irritated with me for making the connection) by the syndicalist ideas around the engineering unions which Tom Mann had helped to bring over after his experiences in Australia and New Zealand. Though the British Socialist Labour Party members were careful to distinguish themselves from the syndicalists with their dismissal of politics, they were still influenced by their emphasis on rank-and-file workplace action and their distrust of leaders.

So when Willie Paul and Arthur MacManus came visiting in the war, bringing the debates of the Socialist Labour Party and the exhilaration of industrial struggles against wartime production methods, their outlook and ideas would not have been unknown to the two socialist feminists in Derby, even though the men came from a quite different left milieu in Glasgow.

In the years 1915-19, the theorizing about strategy and the implications of the struggle for workers' control and self-management were inseparable from involvement in the shop stewards' movement, nowhere more so than in Glasgow. As James Hinton, writing in 1972, said in his introduction to J.T. Murphy's 1917 pamphlet 'The Workers' Committee':

> The shop stewards' movement recognized that any struggle to restore undiluted craft privilege would be both undesirable politically and hopeless, and the movement attempted, with some success, to break down divisions between craftsmen and less skilled workers, to develop an industrial policy which united the interests of the two groups, and construct all-grades organization in the workshop. The leaders of the movement were revolutionaries who saw in the craftsmen's militant revolt against bureaucratic trade unionism the germs of a revolutionary spirit on which they could build. But the movement contained, as well, the germs of a merely sectional struggle for the restoration of lost status. Its development hung between possibilities.[10]

The wider implications were evident to the more politically conscious stewards. They were resisting not simply the encroachment of the employers' control but the reduction of human beings to the status of automatic workers. William Gallacher and J.R. Campbell were to sum up this process in 1919 as a tendency which would 'deny the worker responsibility, rob him of initiative, and reduce him to the level of some ghastly, inhuman, mechanical puppet'.[11]

Freedom and responsibility were constantly recurring themes in the writing of the socialists in the shop stewards' movement. Direct action was both a means of achieving specific objectives and a process of learning through the realization of qualities of freedom and responsibility.

The interplay of thought and practice in conditions of wartime repression produced both energy and contradiction. The period in which the play is set is thus a moment of great ferment. Even as the assumptions of revolutionary syndicalism find expression, there are contradictory pulls towards a new synthesis because the characters are facing the limits of workplace rebellion in practice. Mac-Manus, Paul and some of the other prominent figures in the rank-and-file movement were to find this new direction crystallized in Leninism after the war. But at this point, their ideas were in flux.

The tension involved in ideas that develop from such a movement must have been immediately recognizable to Alice and Hettie, with their experience of activism. While the suffrage movement was campaigning for reform of the existing constitutional process, the ferocity of the opposition to the vote pushed some of the suffragettes to defy the law. So as members of the Women's Social and Political Union (WSPU), the two women knew about the less benevolent side of the state. Direct action and distrust of parliament were part of suffragette political experience. Aspirations towards responsibility were part of feminism as well as syndicalism.

The connection between syndicalism and feminism appears surprising to us now because the history of this period has been transmitted along very specific channels. The syndicalist influence on the left and the shop stewards' movement have featured in autobiographies of men who went on to play a leading role in the Communist or Labour Parties. They have tended to regard it as an underdeveloped form of politics.[12] More recent histories written between the late 1950s and mid 1970s have focused on syndicalism and the shop stewards' movement because of disenchantment with both the Communist and Labour Party traditions. While giving syndicalism its due, they did not look at links or connections with other social movements, feminism or pacifism. And the shop stewards' movement was presented mainly in terms of action at the workplace, thus abstracting industrial militancy from the political and cultural networks which sustained it.[13]

The classic histories of feminism, too, with the exception of Sylvia Pankhurst's accounts which are London-based, missed out the links with socialism. The prevailing versions presented the patriotic right-wing perspective on the suffrage movement. The local

involvement of working-class and lower-middle-class women outside London and the overlapping of socialist and suffrage agitation
has only recently begun to be investigated.[14] Links between suf-
fragism and syndicalism appear particularly unlikely at first sight.
Feminists were campaigning for the vote, which seemed an insig-
nificant reform to the pure syndicalist, and the feminists directed
their political energies towards parliament, an institution which
syndicalists dismissed. Moreover, syndicalism, which concerned
the sphere of industrial production, completely excluded many
areas of women's lives.[15]

There were, however, shades of syndicalist influence amongst
both feminists and socialists. Socialists were prepared to argue that
the struggle in parliament needed to be backed by direct action outside – a tactic which would have been familiar to socialists who had
taken part in the suffrage agitation.[16] Socialists active in the suffrage movement, in industrial unrest and in Irish politics all had
reason to be discontented with Labour in parliament.[17] Moreover,
the suffrage movement in this period was about much more than
the vote. Like syndicalism, it carried an implicit assumption that
both people and social relationships were to be changed in the process of resistance. Feminists of every persuasion saw the process of
struggle as a means whereby women could come to exercise powers
they had not known they possessed. And there was a conviction
that when women had political power, the world would be differently organized.

Working-class socialist feminists emphasized the vote as a means
to other reforms – allowances for mothers, improved conditions,
divorce law reform, and better schools for working-class children.
These were integral to their vision of transformed relationships
between people; they were glimpses of a more harmonious connection to nature, and of a democratic conception of beauty in everyday life. While these notions were never completely lost in the
socialist tradition, they tended to be pushed to the sidelines and,
certainly from the late 1920s onwards, were widely presented as
'cranky', 'sentimental', peripheral elements.[19]

Feminism and the Anti-war Movement

During the war many people must have been surprised at the company they found themselves keeping. Sylvia Pankhurst, from the militant strand of the suffrage movement, found herself aligned with the constitutional suffragist Catherine Marshall. Members of the Socialist Labour Party met the arch-reformist and ethical socialist, Ramsay MacDonald. Quakers and anarchists, vegetarians and syndicalists together opposed the war. While old sectarian conflicts certainly died hard, the isolation and coercion that these groups encountered exerted a pressure towards unity in the face of tribunals, detention centre imprisonment and humiliating, sadistic cruelty from the military authorities. They needed each others' support. In these circumstances people relied on networks which were partly based on pre-war association, partly on the new circumstances. Behind the formal organizational opposition of the No Conscription Fellowship, it is possible to trace a shadowy informal network of resistance. There was support work for the conscientious objectors and their families. Also many socialist young men who opposed the war decided that rather than giving themselves up, they would go on the run. They joined what became known as the 'flying corps'.[20] Robert Barltrop in his history of the small socialist group, the Socialist Party of Great Britain, describes this as a

> brotherhood of men on the move, relying on their own resourcefulness and others' loyalty to keep away from the authorities . . . Often a group would stay in a member's house until some circumstances made it no longer safe. And often a member's wife or sister kept the police at the front door long enough for him to climb the back fence and run.[21]

The Wheeldons' house was part of a network like this in the Midlands. They were thus involved in the public side of the anti- war movement. Hettie was secretary of the Derby No Conscription Fellowship for a time in 1916.[22] But the Wheeldons were also part of a more covert side of the movement, sheltering and protecting men on the run, members of the Socialist Labour Party, the British Socialist Party and the Industrial Workers of the World, and individuals who were not in any organization.[23] They thus afford us a glimpse of aspects of feminist activity about which very little is known.

The feminist wing of the anti-war movement has been neglected until recently. It is in the process of being historically rediscovered under the impact of women's renewed activism in the peace movement. This political connection places Alice and Hettie in a context which linked opposition to the war with feminism and socialism. In 1915, prominent feminists formed a committee to prepare for an International Congress of Women, despite the war. They included Catherine Marshall, Sylvia Pankhurst, Charlotte Despard of the Women's Freedom League, Eva Gore Booth, the Irish poet, and Lady Ottoline Morrell, friend of Bertrand Russell. This developed into the Women's International League for Peace and Freedom. Catherine Marshall recruited Bertrand Russell to the No Conscription Fellowship in 1916. In the summer of 1917, Helen Crawfurd, a member of the Women's International League, and Agnes Dollan, an ILP member, launched the Women's Peace Crusade in Glasgow. Other towns followed their example.[24]

Gwen Coleman had been an organizer of the constitutionalist National Union of Women's Suffrage Societies in the west of England. She remembered the anti-war movement as the hardest struggle of all:

> Working for peace during the war wasn't easy, it was harder, much harder than working for the suffrage movement, that was child's play compared with what one put up with during the war. I mean you were a traitor to your country, you should have been shot at dawn.

When the war ended, Gwen Coleman experienced a tremendous sense of physical and psychological exhaustion, an indication of the pressures that women like the Wheeldons came under during the war:

> We were living in Leeds, mother and I, and things were pretty bad, we couldn't get any firewood or anything. I went for a walk on the moor, gathering firewood. I came to a wall, I stood by this wall and just the other side a lark went up singing. I put my head down on that wall and sobbed and sobbed. It was just something that this lark had, you know, that we'd done without for so long.[25]

State Intervention and Socialism

Not only were they in isolated networks and organizations that faced unpopularity, ridicule and attack. Not only was there considerable deprivation and hardship, but opponents of the war faced an unprecedented degree of state regulation of ideas, work and everyday life. The Defence of the Realm Regulation (DORA) promulgated in 1915 made it an offence to make 'statements likely to cause disaffection'. The newspapers were brought under government influence. There were panics against German spies, and moral outrage against shirkers was whipped up. When exhortation proved insufficient, two Military Service Acts in 1916 introduced conscription, to call up 'single men first', and then all able-bodied men except those who were exempt because they were working on munitions, railway work or other jobs essential to the war effort. Employment conditions were increasingly subject to government control but with an aim of increasing production, not protecting the workers. Women were particularly vulnerable to exploitation, working long hours, their health suffering through work on explosives and poisonous war materials, and in danger of accidents.

Even leisure was not outside the state's concerns. To get drunk or take time off could harm the war effort. Working-class women were stopped on the street and, under suspicion of intimacy with men in the armed forces, examined for VD.[26] Conscientious objectors had to go before tribunals – often consisting of local worthies who knew the radical young objectors from pre-war political battles.[27] If they refused to do non-combatant service, they were the responsibility of the army, who imprisoned them in military prisons and detention centres where their treatment could be harsh and humiliating, in some cases leading to death.[28]

Surveillance intensified. The government was concerned to trace networks of people against the war and to prevent them linking together. A special cause for concern was the discontent in industry. Workers resented the close ties between employers and the state and the intensification of exploitation in the effort to increase production for the war. The leaders of the shop stewards' movement knew that there were spies and agents provocateurs in their midst.

However, Lloyd George's extension of state powers was not purely repressive. Along with intensification of productivity and the regulation of labour, there was also considerable expansion in health and other kinds of welfare provision.

To the syndicalist-influenced left, these interventions were equated with repression. But the Independent Labour Party, although it had a strong libertarian element, was also campaigning for reforms *through* the state. Its strength in local government could be seen as the link democratizing state socialism and ensuring control over resources and provision for the working class. For new liberals, like William Beveridge, who believed in social reform, and for those Labour Party members, like Arthur Henderson, who believed that the war against Germany was just, these state reforms appeared to be progressive.[29] Some women trade unionists were more suspicious of Lloyd George but nonetheless saw there were gains to be made from negotiation with the government.[30] There were thus various shades of emphasis and interpretation among socialists as to the value of state intervention.

The experience of working within the state left a lasting mark on Labour's politics. When the Labour Party came to power in 1924, it drew on the experience of office gained in this period and on the tradition of social liberalism's welfare reforms.[31] On issues of surveillance and security there was considerable ambivalence. There was a pattern of protest in opposition and compromise in office.[32]

Stuart Hall recently observed that it was the 'statist-oriented brand of socialism' which prevailed in the ideological tussle. Survivors tended to get their version of events accepted, and as the years went by, people were liable to forget that the now dominant tendency had formerly been one among several. At the time, the pro-state position had

> had to contend with many other currents, including, of course, the strong syndicalist currents before and after World War I, and the ILP's ethical Marxism later with their deep antipathy to Labour's top-downwards, statist orientation . . . One of the many tricks which the retrospective construction of tradition on the left has performed is to make the triumph of Labourism over these other socialist currents – the result of a massive political struggle in which the ruling classes played a key role – appear as an act of natural and inevitable succession.[33]

The case of Alice Wheeldon presents a cameo of this observation.

While the play can be read and enjoyed as a story, there is a great deal more surrounding Alice Wheeldon's arrest and imprisonment than a purely personal tragedy.

It is the implications of the story which have continued to preoccupy me in the five years since I wrote the play. Feminism has been historically misrepresented – particularly the experiences of working-class women active in the Labour movement and of socialist feminists in the early years of this century. This distortion is part of a 'retrospective construction of tradition'.[34] But this is only one particular thread. The perceptions, priorities and alliances of the socialists also need reassessing. In the First World War, many assumptions which were to crystallize in the 1920s were still in flux. It was not only the development of the shop stewards' movement which 'hung between possibilities' – but the socialist enterprise and vision itself. And the contrary pull of ideas is very much part of the drama. For it was neither clear nor inevitable that the statist tendency would win out.

In the mid 1970s I sat opposite a Glaswegian socialist, Annie Davison, and listened as she explained rather shyly that the socialism she had known as a girl in the 1920s had been an 'idealistic' kind of socialism.

> They didn't want to have to – they didn't want to just vote Labour. They wanted their children to learn that socialism was a good way of life and what was good for one was good for all, and so this was a moral attitude they had. What I call myself is an 'idealist Socialist' and it's laughed at nowadays because the world has become so complicated. Idealism is not very popular nowadays because there are so many practical things that have to be decided where your ideals have to be pushed aside to some extent in order to get a result now. But I feel that a long-term result must be the real goal of socialism, and in the end the best, rather than trying to do something as a short-term measure. If the short-term measure becomes permanent, then it's no use, because the short-term measure is the wrong measure to me. That's not very well expressed, but that's what I have a feeling about.[35]

In returning to the interconnections of socialism and feminism in the early years of this century, I sometimes have to shake myself back into the present. I have a recurring dream of discovering a new set of rooms in a familiar house. Each time I return to the dream, I am puzzled. How could I live so long without realizing that just through a door and round a corner and down a passage there were unvisited rooms, waiting, neglected, commodious – new, sketchily defined possibilities.

When *Friends of Alice Wheeldon* was performed, I realized that my obsessive return to these connections – which were becoming so familiar I could hardly describe them all – was completely strange to many people. They were amazed by the political interconnections which I and a few others had come to take for granted. It is precisely the obvious, that which is assumed, which eludes history. It is too evident to remark upon.

The historical and political accounts are for those who are curious to know more of the ideas and activities of a small group of socialists and feminists at a time when their future 'hung between possibilities', and for those who are concerned to understand the manner in which the repressive power of Lloyd George's new state machinery crashed into the life of Alice Wheeldon, ending forever her existence as a private citizen. They will make sense to people who have begun to suspect that political ideas do not march around in tidy ideological blocks and check in at conferences for the convenience of historians. The play certainly does not end the story, for there are several doors left unopened. If others are encouraged to further investigation, some good will have been done, partly because an obscure and ordinary family was made to suffer for the fears, prejudices and ambitions of the mighty, but also because this confrontation carried implications which have a continuing resonance.

Alice Wheeldon's reluctant exposure to history brought her and her family much suffering. Perhaps it would have cheered her a little to know that her memory would continue to provoke, inspire and reveal possibilities much needed by later generations.

Friends of Alice Wheeldon *was first performed at the Rotherham Arts Centre on 30 March 1980 by DAC Theatre Company.*

F.E. Smith	Ian Jentle
Jessie Campbell	Val Oughton
Alice Wheeldon	Christine Cox
Hettie Wheeldon	Barbara Marten
Arthur MacManus	Fine-Time Fontayne
Willie Paul	Rod Arthur
William Wheeldon	Russ Ellias
Florrie Bates ⎱ Sarah Clarke ⎰	Joanne Lewis
John S. Clarke	Ian Jentle
Alex Gordon ⎱ First Policeman ⎰	Bryan Heeley
Second Policeman ⎱ Herbert Booth ⎰	Russ Ellias

Directed by Penny Cherns

Music arranged by Tim Myers
Designed by Maggie Quarry
Sound and lighting by Dave Cope
Scenery, Properties and Costume by Maggie Quarry, Kim
    Newby and Karen Wood
Stage Manager Annie Laws

Characters

F.E. Smith Attorney-General, a well-dressed, dashing, arrogant man

Alice Wheeldon an Independent Labour Party suffragette in her forties

Hettie Wheeldon her daughter, also an ILP suffragette, in her twenties, a teacher

William Wheeldon Alice's son, aged twenty

Jessie Campbell an ILP suffragette from Glasgow, in her early forties

Arthur MacManus a small, wry, wiry, likeable man in his mid twenties, a Glasgow member of the Socialist Labour Party and a shop steward

Willie Paul his friend, rather more aloof, theoretical and studious

Florrie Bates a Derby woman

John S. Clarke an ex-lion tamer and zoo owner

Sarah Clarke his wife

Alex Gordon (alias Vivian and Rickard) a government informer

Comrade Bert (alias Herbert Booth) a worker for the Ministry of Munitions

Two Policemen

A Wounded Soldier

A Note on the Songs

1. *Woman This and Woman That* was traced with help from the Fawcett Library for reprinting in the book by Kathy Henderson, Frankie Armstrong and Sandra Kerr *My Song is My Own*, London: Pluto Press, 1979. It appears to have been written in 1916 by Laurence Housman. We used it in the play as its music (a traditional folk melody) is far less turgid than many of the suffragette anthems expressing similar themes, and therefore more accessible to modern audiences.

2. *Yes, Let Me Like a Soldier Fall*, music by Vincent Wallace and words by E. Fitzball, appears to have been written originally for the Boer war and revamped, as were many Boer war songs (e.g. *Soldiers of the Queen*), for singing in music hall and other more formal venues before and early in the First World War.

3. *Bread and Roses* surely needs no introduction. It was written by James Oppenheim (1882-1932) in 1912 after he saw a banner carried by striking women textile workers saying: 'We want bread and roses too', during the well-documented Lawrence (Massachusetts) strike of that year. It first appears in print (I think) in *Industrial Solidarity*, an IWW publication. As were many other IWW songs, it was adopted, for some almost as an anthem, by women of the SLP, which had close links with America.

4. *The Police* lyrics translated from the German by J.L. Joynes and set to the tune of *Lass of Richmond Hill*. J.L. (Jimmy) Joynes appears to have managed somehow to reconcile his socialist ideals with his career as a teacher at Eton in the latter part of the nineteenth century. He was responsible for translating a variety of German socialist writings in the course of which he came across the original words of this song. He translated it loosely, set it to its well-known tune, and sent it to his friend Edward Carpenter for inclusion in *Chants of Labour* (1888) which Carpenter edited.

5. *Ballad of Law and Order* also appears in *Chants of Labour* and was one of many texts written and set to popular tunes (in this case *The Vicar of Bray*) by John Bruce Glasier (1859-1920). He wrote this song whilst still a member of William Morris's Socialist League; in the play, he is mentioned as one of the leaders of the ILP.

6. *England Arise!* was written and composed by Edward Carpenter himself. It, too, appeared in *Chants of Labour*.

All songs used have been cut to a greater or lesser extent as they would have been far too long in their full versions.

Tim Myers

A Note on the Play

The play was originally written for a touring company with a minimal set. The set was non-naturalistic, with a small number of props suggesting the different scenes. A number of the songs are sung between scenes – in front of the curtain, if there is one.

The overall feeling is one of claustrophobia and danger.

ACT I

Scene 1

A study. F.E. SMITH, *a dashing, arrogant figure, is working on a speech.*

F.E. Smith 'I confess that even if I were satisfied that every woman in the world wanted the vote, it would not influence me one bit. As for the statement that women are against war and that the female vote would make for a pacific spirit, even if it were so it would be an additional reason that would' . . . er . . . hmm . . . sway – no, disincline – 'that would disincline me to support this Bill, because as long as other countries are not taking a bias in the direction of peace I have no desire that we be prepared to take such a step.' Yes, that will do.

He takes out the speech

Now, on woman's right to the vote: 'A vote is not a right. A vote is not a right. A vote is not a right. It is a capacity which is given on approved public ground to such section of citizens as, in the opinion of the whole state, are likely to exercise that quality with benefit to the country taken as a whole.' Ha! That should deal with the damn fool issue of rights.

'I venture to say that the sum total of human happiness, knowledge and achievement would have been unaffected' – no, better say almost unaffected – 'if Sappho had never sung, if Joan of Arc had never fought, if Siddons had never played and if George Eliot had never written.'

He goes back to his desk

Then the tribute – ha! 'At the same time, without the true functions of womanhood being discharged throughout the ages, the very existence of the race and the tenderest and most sacred influences which animate mankind would have disappeared. Profoundly believing as I do that these influences are grossly marred by the intrusion of women into the field of politics,' etcetera, etcetera. Stress women not interested. Even if they were – pacific spirit. I imply the country unmarred by women voting. Vote is not a right. Sum total of human happiness not affected by women in the public sphere. End with women's true function. Hmm . . . yes.

Exit

HETTIE *stands in front of the curtains, dressed in suffragette colours of green and purple, carrying a banner with the words* VOTES FOR WOMEN, *sings.*

Woman This and Woman That

We went up to St Stephen's with petitions year by year;
'Get out!' the politicians cried, 'We want no women here!'
MPs behind the railings stood and laughed to see the fun,
And bold policemen knocked us down, because we would not run.

For it's 'woman this' and 'woman that', and 'woman, go away!'
But it's 'Share and share alike, ma'am!' when the taxes are to pay;
When the taxes are to pay, my friends, the taxes are to pay,
O it's 'Please to pay up promptly!' when the taxes are to pay.

When women go to work for them the government engage
To give them lots of contract jobs at a low starvation wage,
But when it's men that they employ they always add a note –
'Fair wages must be paid' – BECAUSE THE MEN HAVE GOT THE
VOTE.

You dress yourselves in uniforms to guard your native shores,
But those who make the uniforms do work as good as yours;
For the soldier bears the rifle, but the woman bears the race –
And THAT you'd find no trifle if you had to take her place!

O it's 'woman this' and 'woman that', and 'woman cannot fight!'
But it's 'Ministering Angel!' when the wounded come in sight;
When the wounded come in sight, my friends, the wounded come
in sight,
It's a 'ministering angel' then, who nurses day and night!

For it's 'woman here' and 'woman there', and 'woman on the
streets!'
And it's how they look at women with most men that one meets,
With most men that one meets, my friends, with most men that
one meets –
It's the way they look at women that keeps women on the streets!

You talk of sanitation, and temperance, and schools,
And you send your male inspectors to impose your man-made
rules;
'The woman's sphere's the home,' you say, then prove it to our
face:
Give us the vote that we may make the home a happier place!

For it's 'woman this' and 'woman that', and 'woman, say your
say!'
But it's 'What's the woman up to?' when she tries to show the way;
When she tries to show the way, my friends, when she tries to show
the way –
And the woman means to show it – that is why she's out today!

Blackout. Police whistles until lights come up.

Scene 2

A second-hand clothes shop and inner parlour, lower middle class, comfortable but plain. ALICE WHEELDON, *the proprietor of the shop and her daughter* HETTIE *are busy tidying up.* WILLIAM WHEELDON, *Alice's 20-year-old son is also present.*

There is a knock at the door. Four comrades from Scotland enter into the parlour: JESSIE CAMPBELL, *a robust woman in her 40s;* ARTHUR MACMANUS, *a small, humorous man in his mid-20s, with the voice and manner of an accomplished agitator;* WILLIE PAUL, *the same age, but classically handsome; and* JOHN S. CLARKE, *a tall, imposing ex-lion tamer, from the North East but now working in Edinburgh.* CLARKE *is bald and looks very different with and without his hat.*

Jessie You should have waited for us. I told you we were coming.

Alice We thought we'd better get started.

Jessie Och, the Wheeldon family are nae going to win the women's suffrage all on their own. Ye and Hettie'll be getting as bad as the Pankhursts soon. All drama and limelight heroics.

Arthur We needed a lift. Jessie gave us a lift down in the Clarion van.

John We're thinking of printing our paper down here.

They all sit down – ARTHUR *opposite* HETTIE *and next to* WILLIE PAUL, JESSIE *next to* HETTIE

Hettie Oh well, that should stir things up a bit.

Jessie And what'll ye be doing next, hen? Away up Chesterfield's leaning tower wi' a suffrage banner and a red flag?

Alice Jessie.

Hettie I heard you speak in Nottingham, Mr Paul, a couple of years ago.

Willie Against the man who wanted conscription.

Jessie You're unlikely to agree on other matters. He and John Clarke over there disagree about the importance of the vote, they dunna believe it has done the men any good, so he is of the opinion that it's not worth the women bothering with it. Arthur MacManus is one of our supporters though.

Willie Perhaps you'd like to get a sound impression of our views from some of our literature (*handing it out*).

Arthur You must sell our paper *The Socialist* in your shop, Mrs Wheeldon.

Alice I don't know. I can't remember the names of half your groups. What's yours called?

John It's the Socialist Labour Party.

Alice As long as I don't have to argue with one of those pale-pink, milk-and-water, flaming-Jesus-Christ kind of socialists like Reuben Farrow.

They enter the shop.

William Oh, she's off now.

Alice William!

William We have our splits down here. Reuben's a Christian in our
Socialist Society in Derby.

John Aye, this element is to be found in large numbers in the
Independent Labour Party.

Alice You've lost me there, lad.

Hettie I think what John's saying, Mam, is that it's important to
be clear where you stand.

Jessie *(Sarcastically)* Och, at all costs.

Alice Come and look what I've got in the shop, Jessie. Some lovely
blouses.

She takes her out but can be seen in the background.

William There's a fellow round here walks barefoot up Abraham
Heights at Matlock. He says he's taking restorative
draughts of the Earth's magnetism.

Arthur And are you sympathetic to this position?

William A bit too chilly for my liking. There's Bert Parker an' all.

Hettie His emphasis is on thorough mastication of simple foods.
He does exercises an' all that. He's very well on it. He's a
big strong lad.

Arthur I think the movement should confine its approach to
industrial and political questions. We're hampered by
faddists and cranks who want to air their views on religion
or vaccination and vegetarianism.

John Or even sex.

Arthur If we could form a really principled revolutionary
organization, we could form a consistent position on these
questions. It's awful difficult.

Hettie The virgin birth is the difficult one. At school I daren't even
give them a rational explanation for that in case the head
found out. Still when we do it at Christmas they're usually
too busy deciding who's going to be the shepherds and
angels in the Nativity play to bother.

Arthur But it's difficult to know what you can reconcile wi'
historical materialism. I canna abide those comrades who
have na' human feeling. But can you really accept, what
was it. . . .

William Magnetism and thorough mastication.

Arthur Aye, but what part have these to play in the emancipation of the working class?

William Oh, live and let live if you ask me.

Jessie (*Re-entering*) The Socialist Labour Party is never going to live and let live. You want all 300 of your members to be doing exactly the same thing at the same time. It warps the imagination. Now in the Clarion movement and Independent Labour Party we are for keeping the byways open.

Willie With no basic grasp or understanding of the basic Marxist works. You live and let live in your Independent Labour Party and who do you get for your leadership? Ramsay MacDonald. . .

Jessie Wi' the best pair of legs in the Labour movement. It's the truth.

Willie Bruce Glasier. Philip Snowden.

Arthur Aye, an' ethereal Ethel. It's all flowery language and no consulting the rank and file.

Willie It'll be respectable socialism they'll be promising you and always far in the future. It'll become more and more respectable and less and less of the socialism the closer they get to power. Och, your live and let live in the ILP.

Arthur You'll build your own little byway branches, tend them like rose gardens, and let Arthur Henderson and his Labour machine mow them behind your back. Even old Queer Hardie.

Alice (*Entering*) I'll have no sneering at Keir Hardie in my house. Whatever your views, fair's fair, he's done as much as anyone for votes for women.

Willie The ILP're full of sentimental talk about loving your fellow men and socialism being the kingdom of god on earth.

John But who wants it? I mean, anyone studying that kingdom must conclude that it's the inspiration of a criminal lunatic.

Willie But when it comes down to the concrete arguments they're pliant. They'll always stretch a point. And the ruling class makes sure it's stretched in their direction and not the working class's.

Alice I don't think it matters what you call yourself providing your heart's in the right place. I'm for direct action myself. That's what we've used in the suffrage movement.

Arthur At Singers in Clydebank last year we began to develop a completely new form of working class movement. So that when one of the women there was sacked we formed a strike committee wi' five representatives from each department.

The shop bell rings. ALICE *goes to answer the door.*

They were called shop stewards. Now I believe this has great possibilities.

Jessie Aye, and the management were canny too, Arthur.

Alice Hello, Florrie.

Jessie You know fine that you were nearly all out of work after that strike.

Alice I've some lovely little baby things in. They're as good as new. Look at this jacket.

Hettie Listen to the saleswoman.

Arthur But every man from Singers took that idea into his next job.

John You wait, we'll have a shop stewards' movement in factory after factory.

Arthur Singers is only the beginning.

Alice I'll put it by for you.

Hettie No sale again.

Alice What about these trousers for young Charlie Bates. Oh they grow out of them that quickly. They'd just fit him now.

Willie This form of organization is appearing in several other countries now. It is na' limited to Clydebank. It's among the contradictions the system has developed.

Arthur Och, it's the organization of the future. There canna be any doubt.

FLORRIE *and* ALICE *in the shop. The scenes are in parallel.*

Florrie How much are they?

Hettie Wait for it.

Alice Lets say tuppence. They'll wear ever so well. You have a good look round, duck.

Hettie If you take on the bosses at work, what about the police and the army – they'll use them against you if you get too successful.

Arthur Willie Paul is working on the problem, Hettie.

Lights on ALICE *and* FLORRIE *down in the parlour.*

Alice Well, you have to try and do summat early. There are some herbs that'll bring you on, natural-like. But it has to be within a few days really.

Florrie I just couldn't have another one. It were murder, Mrs Wheeldon. I'm bad for doing it. I'm a real bad woman for having done it.

Alice Florrie, women have had to do this from the beginning of time. It's not that you're bad. You're daft, that's all. Can't you get him to be more careful?

Florrie How can I? Not when he's been flaming drinking. I can't.

Alice Oh, bloody men. If they could have the babies for one year even, just one year. Mind you, my first, Mr Gossage, he was ever so careful he used to break off. Have you ever tried having a coughing fit? At the last moment, duck? That can shake it out sometimes.

Florrie He might get a bit mardy.

Alice Well it's better him getting mardy than. . . You have to stick up for your principles, gel. Old Wheeldon, I put him out of the house in the end. He comes and stays occasionally when he has a job that brings him round here. I'm better off without him, Florrie. I'll give you herbs to heal you, duck. You boil them and come here and have a nice bath. Here, have another cup of tea. I got so browned off with him. I used to lie there pretending I was fast asleep. He used to try and tiptoe round the bed. A drunk on tiptoe. *(Imitates him)* Burp, he'd go. Taking his trousers off. 'Are you awake, Alish?' 'Alice duck.' All luvvy duvvy. I felt like clouting him.

FLORRIE *is laughing despite herself.*

Florrie But you've got your business, Mrs Wheeldon. You can afford to have principles.

Alice Only just!

Florrie And you have all your meetings for company.

Alice Well they're not quite the same. But then again I get a lot of
them in here complaining that their old man just rolls over
and goes to sleep. Have I got special potions to give them
energy, like. I don't know why they bother myself. Still,
everybody's different, it'd be a dull world if we weren't.

Florrie Ah that's right enough.

Alice What we need is mothers' pensions, Florrie. Then we
wouldn't be tied to bloody men. The more children you
had the more money you'd get.

Florrie Well I'd be doing all right. Lady Muck I'd be. I'll be off
now, you've got company.

Light off in shop and up in parlour. WILLIE PAUL *is
reading some socialist literature e.g. Bebel.*

Alice (*Re-entering*) Oh that Florrie Bates. She can't even afford the
clothes I keep in my rag-bag. How she's going to manage
with another one I don't know.

William There's something I find it hard to put into words. It's
deeper than the power of the army or the police. It's how
we can um. . . How we can make socialism – you know,
the common weal.

Willie It is na' something hatched in the brain of a poet or in the
imagination of some idealist philosopher. (*Waves his arms
oratorically in a grand sweep*)

William (*Rather taken aback by* WILLIE PAUL's *speach but
standing his ground*) The point I'm trying to make is that if
you are pushed around and shuffled about all your life you
somehow come to expect it like. You wait for somebody
else to fill the space when there is a space – you let them
take away your chances even when you glimpse an
opening for a moment. That's how we get the Ramsay
MacDonalds and the rest.

Hettie Yes, I can understand that. I feel it myself, even in the
suffrage movement it were the same. We always end up
with the middle-class women in London speaking for us.
As if we were just nobodies. But they'd have been
nowhere without us.

William It's a physical feeling we're trying to describe. How do
you take something you've never taken in your whole life.

How do you make something when your eyes can't see what it is you're making. A few of them see something at one time or another. Like Keir Hardie. They have good intentions. They take a step forward and they look behind to see if we're with them. And suddenly we can't touch them. The old ways close round on them till they can't move in this direction or that. They feel powerless with all those people expecting things of them. So they begin to pretend they can do more than they can. I think that's the lie at the source which has turned on the working class.

Hettie And on women too.

John Exactly, this is why we in the SLP argue for a principled organization.

William It's not just a matter of stating principles. You say we are making our ILP branches like tending protected rose gardens and ignoring the real power in the Party.

Jessie We'd all acknowledge there was some truth in that.

William But there's more to it than meets the eye. We are doing something. We're learning to be gardeners.

Arthur Och, man!

William We must become people who will help others to grow.

Arthur It sounds like a mystical horticultural form of Fabianism to me.

Alice Well if it doesn't happen for all your militancy, when the dust settles you'll be left like Keir Hardie's been left, mouthpieces on a platform crying against the wind.

William You're not understanding my meaning, Arthur.

Bell rings.

Alice Oh that bell!

ALICE *exits.*

William It's not the Fabians' change from the top I'm talking about. It's change from below sort of thing. More than that it's not just a change in the workshop but in a man's whole being . . . *(adds hastily)* And in a woman's too. See how there's no real feeling on the woman question still in the socialist movement.

Hettie He's right. Oh, the men speakers give women lip-service now. It's the stock-in-trade of agitation because of the feminist movement.

William It's not just an outer change I want, it's an inner change – it . . . I wish . . .

Willie (*Quietly looking up from his book*) Wishes are not class power, William.

ALICE *enters very agitated.*

Alice Quick I need help. Florrie Bates. She's really ill. Tried to get rid of her baby. Summat went wrong. She collapsed at her front door. We'll have to take her to the hospital.

Jessie I'll come wi' ye, hen.

Alice She must've come to me for help. I was a bit short with her because of the meeting. Then I had company and we were all talking. We'll have to carry her.

William Don't fret, Mam. Me and Willie can do that.

Hettie (*Reappearing as they exit*) What's up, Mam?

William (*Shouting back as he exits*) You stay here with Arthur and look after the shop.

ARTHUR *is staring as if far away.*

Hettie That's the worst kind of inequality to my mind. You're robbed of your looks and your life by that endless work, work that begins again as soon as it's done. It marks your face, your hands, your belly. I'll never have bleddy kids.

Arthur My mother brought us all up in a but and ben. Just two rooms, Hettie. When it was near her time – they could na' afford a doctor – Mrs Hamilton came to her, my sister told me about it. She was evidently a wee old perfect old lady, she was. She was awful nice, my sister said, and she looked after her. Mrs Hamilton used to say 'Come on, hen, I'm going to give you some medicine.' She always had headaches when she was expecting a baby. Then Annie MacGregor would come and walk the children round Glasgow Green and they'd be given sweets. And when they got back there'd be another bairn. My sister used tae' think Mrs Hamilton brought them.

Hettie What kind of life is that for a woman? Jessie's right. She says birth control will free women more than the vote.

Arthur You're awful young to be discussing such topics wi' Jessie Campbell.

Hettie Huh! And Florrie Bates is awful young to be having four bleddy kids and one abortion which puts her life in danger and will probably poison her system.

Arthur But this is a particular case.

Hettie How many particular cases do you think there are, Arthur? They pass the same enema syringe all round these streets, they come to Mam for herbs to bring them on.

Arthur *(Shocked)* You canna make socialism just by helping folk, there are too many of them. Och, it's the capitalist system that's to blame, Hettie.

Hettie Well it's not only the bleddy capitalist men that make babies.

Arthur With socialism women will be able to have as many children as they want. There'll be good housing.

Hettie Well that's all very well. But how many do they want?

Arthur I expect they'll vary, but it's better housing – not birth control – that's at the root of the problem.

Hettie Even if we were all living in Buckingham Palace, we should still be able to decide.

Arthur Och, you can decide, Hettie. But that's just common sense. It's not a political question. You have to be careful. That's all there is to it.

Hettie It is a political question: it's to do with your own . . . *(uncertain)* You only have one life . . . *(gains confidence)* Jessie says every woman has a right to be mistress of herself.

A very long pause.

Arthur When I worked at Singers, you know, I used to point the needles. As fast as I reduced that mountain of needles a fresh load was dumped on the table. *(Sighs)* Day in day out it never grew less . . . One morning I came in. The table was empty. I could na' understand it. I began to tell everyone. There were no needles on the table, no needles, the mountain had gone . . . It suddenly flashed on me how absurdly stupid it was . . . spending my life like that.

Hettie What did you do?

Arthur I just turned on my heel. And I walked over the hills. I never even took my jacket off. But next day the needles were back and the next. So what do you do, hen?

Lights down

Prologue to Act II

Male solo – sung in front of the curtain.

Yes, Let Me Like a Soldier Fall

Yes let me like a soldier fall
Upon some open plain,
This breast expanding for the ball
To blot out every strain.
Brave manly hearts confer my doom
That gentler ones may tell
Howe'er forgat, unknown my tomb,
I like a soldier fell,
Howe'er forgat, unknown my tomb,
I like a soldier fell,
I like a soldier fell.

I only ask of that proud race
Which ends its blaze in me
To die the last and not disgrace
Its ancient chivalry.
Though o'er my grave
No banner wave
Nor trumpet requiem swell,
Enough they murmur o'er my grave,
He like a soldier fell,
Enough they murmur o'er my grave,
He like a soldier fell,
He like a soldier fell.

ACT II

Scene 1

*Boxing Day Dance of Socialists in Glasgow in a Glasgow
Labour Hall, December 1915. Cheaply festive.*

Willie It's getting harder to sell *The Socialist*. Arthur and Tom Bell

should be along soon. I don't know why they bothered to
stay up here. At first they were singing,
'Never mind about the gun,
Stay at Home'
But it's 'A Long Way to Tipperary' now.

Hettie In Derby there was a crush at the recruiting offices at first.
Now they say men are just deserting. William got a
dreadful letter threatening him if he didn't join up.

Willie Aye, it's going to be hard.

William Ah I think it's time for the entertainments.

Music ends. Applause.

Jessie Your King and country need you
Ye hardy sons of toil
But will your King and country need you
When they're sharing out the spoil.

Applause.

A lad went down to hell.
'What's your religion?' asked auld Clootie.
'Church of Scotland.'
'In that cage to the right.'
Another arrived.
'Your religion?'
'Church of England.'
A third and the same question.
'Roman Catholic.'
'Get in that double-barred cage at the bottom.'
A fourth.
'I'm a true-blue Orangeman.'
'That double-barred cage at the top.'
A fifth.
'I've no religion.'
'Are you sure?'
'Sure I'm sure.'
'All right,' says Auld Clootie, 'You can get a barrow and
bugger about the yaird. You'll no quarrel wi' anybody.'

Cheers and applause.

Comrades, here's John S. Clarke with one of his ballads.

John (*Recites dramatically*)

> *For King and Country*
> Simple Simon met the sly man
> Of and army corps,
> Who talked to him of 'scraps of paper',
> Guns and Huns and War.
> Simple Simon took for 'gospel'
> All the sly man said.
> Now there ain't a Simple Simon;
> Simple Simon's dead.

> *Laughter and applause.*

Sarah What do you feel now seeing suffragettes flag-waving and giving men white feathers? They can't do enough to get men into the army.

Jessie We're still suffragettes, Sarah. We've not got the vote yet. There's been splits before.

Willie Said the Socialist to the Suffragist,
> 'My cause is greater than yours!
> You only work for a Special Class,
> We for the gain of the General Mass
> Which every good ensures!'

> JOHN *and* SARAH *lead cheers. Some boos.*

Alice Gerrup there, Hettie lass. You tell 'em.

Hettie Said the Suffragist to the Socialist,
> 'You underrate my Cause!
> While women remain a Subject Class
> You never can move the General Mass
> With your Economic laws!'

> ALICE, JESSIE *and* WILLIAM *lead cheers.*

John 'A lifted world lifts women up,'
> The Socialist explained.

Hettie 'You cannot lift the world at all
> While half of it is kept so small,'
> The Suffragist maintained.

ARTHUR *runs in.*

Arthur We're in trouble with the paper-selling at Bath Street.
There's a gang threatening Tom Bell out there.

Jessie I'll go with you.

John We can deal with it, Jessie. It could get a bit nasty.

He tries to stop her physically.

Jessie You are speaking to an ex-member of the Women's Social
and Political Union, John Clarke. And you're telling me
to keep away from a few wee roughs in Bath Street.

Willie You're not as young as you were, Jessie.

Jessie We blew up Glasgow's telegraph wires a few years back.

Hettie Come on, Jessie. We're just wasting time arguing.

Jessie Only just a few wee years back.

Exit everyone except JESSIE, ALICE *and* SARAH
CLARKE. *They start to clear up.*

Sarah I don't see what you expect to get from the vote. It's got the
men nowhere having it.

Alice It's just a beginning.

Jessie It was the unifying slogan.

Sarah The women's movement has raised all kinds of questions.

Alice The unrest goes deeper than the vote. A nerve has been
touched. Such hatred of women came out. The spirits of
women will never be the same again.

Sarah You've just stirred up sex hatred. Now in the rent strike,
chucking whiting at the sheriff's officers, marching to the
shipyard to get the men out, we felt strong as women, but
we had a clear objective.

Alice But Sarah, there's some things that affect women as women,
if you know what I mean. You can't rely on men to
support you; we have to rely on ourselves.

Sarah It's a change in the economic system that's needed. Perhaps
it's because I'm younger than you are, but there are no
feminist battles left for us.

Jessie Och – I used to put acid in post-boxes in my maid's uniform.

Alice Most men will just use women if they can get away with it
and sometimes that just means having to . . .

Sarah But the leaders of women's suffrage are middle class. And
they're using you. Look how they've let you down now.

Jessie Opposition to the war is the main thing now and there's
middle-class women against the war too, and what about
Labour men?

Alice Look at that blooming Arthur Henderson.

Sarah Oh, when he spoke yesterday at St Andrew's Hall. Well he
could hardly get a word out. We drowned him and Lloyd
George.

Alice They couldn't get a word of their propaganda in. There was
about 3,000 in the hall singing '*The Reg Flag*'. It's the
best Christmas I've ever had. But I felt a fear in me too.
What if they bring in conscription. John'll be called up.

Jessie Sarah, you know Mac quite well don't you, hen?

Sarah Quite well. He's really friendly, but inside he's a private sort
of man, isn't he.

Jessie He and Hettie have been writing, oh, for about a year and a
half now.

Sarah You shouldn't worry, Mrs Wheeldon, Mac's really kind.
Everybody likes him.

Alice But what kind of life is that for a woman with a man rushing
about smuggling socialist papers from one country to
another. It'd be politics first all the time.

Jessie But Alice you always insisted on going to suffrage meetings.
You just took the children with you.

Alice Well that was different.

Jessie Why was it so different?

Alice It's different with men. You have to watch them like hawks
– the buggers. You know that Jessie. Look how they're all
round you at the ILP conferences – a single woman.
Wasps round jam. And the wives waiting at home.
Anyway if he's so flaming perfect, why did he send her
that book? He'd only known her a month then.

Sarah What book?

Alice That book about . . . well, Sarah, you're a married woman.

Jessie Dr Foote.

Sarah Oh, *Plain Home Talk*. It's only about popular health. It
never tells you what to do or anything like that. The
Americans wouldn't allow it.

Jessie Och, they don't regard it as a mucky book. They believe the working class has a right to knowledge. As Mac says, they're putting everything to the test. There's nae convention that won't be challenged under socialism. They're very advanced in Glasgow. I don't know what you think about it, Sarah, but I tend to think it's still expressing the young men's point of view.

Sarah (*Rather fiercely*) They've seen that having ten wanes in a but and ben crushed their fathers and mothers.

Jessie But the men can always escape to the pub or the meeting. It's the women who have to clean the same square feet over and over again. The women who give birth in these conditions. So it's the women who have the real need to match words wi' effective action. No, my argument is that the socialist talk is still up in the air. Our women need practical help. Like you give, Alice, but on a scientific basis. So they have the knowledge to decide for themselves whether or not to become mothers. This is where we need the direct action now, imagine every woman her own . . . mistress of herself.

Alice Can we get back to Hettie and Mac?

Jessie I don't understand your problem, Alice. You've always said you've brought your daughters up to look after themselves. You never worried like this when Alfred was courting Winnie.

Alice Well, Alfred is a quieter sort of boy altogether. He's involved in his chemistry and his studies. And Winnie's not Hettie either. Hettie is far more headstrong.

Jessie Och. Well, you bring up your daughters on direct action and then you're worried about the consequences. What's happened to your principles, Alice?

Alice Oh, don't talk to me about principles, Jessie Campbell. You don't know what it's like. All that passion and love you have for them. They grow up so quickly. You know them that well and then suddenly you feel you're losing them. It's as if you'd never reared them all those years.

Sarah You have to let go, Mrs Wheeldon. Hettie has to find her own feet. You can't live her life for her . . .

Lights.

Sarah Where've they got to? It shouldn't take this long. I'm going
to look for them. (*Marches towards the door*)
Jessie We'll all go.
Sarah (*Calling*). Wait. They're here. They're coming.

Enter WILLIE, HETTIE, MAC, JOHN. *They all look
rather scuffled and* JOHN *is not wearing his hat.*

Sarah Where's your hat gone?
John What kind of welcome is that? My hat, Mrs Clarke, is sitting
in an hospitable dustbin.
Sarah What's it doing in there?
John It was either my hat or me, Sarah. The bobbies followed me
down Bath Street. I led them quite a chase. I hid in a shop
door. Got rid of my hat and walked quietly off in the other
direction. It always works. They never recognize me
without it.
Willie I told you he'd be up to his circus tricks.
Arthur It's true, you look like a douce Glasgow businessman in
your hat.
Jessie Well, one on hard times.
Arthur Without it you look like Grock the clown.
John Huh, thanks very much!
Jessie Well it goes to show. When you take on patriots and law and
order – always do it in a hat. You might have to leave in a
hurry.
Sarah Well it's a good job I remembered to give it you.

Mock cheers.

John As usual Sarah's saved the day. Perhaps the heroine of the
hour will honour me with a dance.

Mock ceremonious bow. SARAH *laughs. Music begins.*
ARTHUR *and* HETTIE *dance together dreamily and
happily.* WILLIE PAUL *and* ALICE *dance rather
awkwardly.* WILLIAM *and* JESSIE *dance jokingly, not
very elegantly.*

Arthur I'm awful glad you could come to Glasgow, Hettie.
Hettie I'm glad too. I wish we could stay longer. Mam's worried
about the shop and all her lame ducks.

Arthur You could stay on till school begins.

Hettie Er, I suppose . . .

Arthur Jessie's got room. We've so much to talk about, hen.

Hettie Mmm. I'd like to see more of you, Arthur, to get to know you better. It's not the same, writing.

Arthur (*Tightens his hold of her involuntarily. Intensely*) Stay.

Hettie I'll stay with Jessie till school begins.

> *Pause,* ARTHUR *smiles.*

Oh the terms seem so long and all.

Arthur I'll be down in January or February. The Committee is working on a plan to resist conscription. Lloyd George is going to bring it in soon. We're getting ready. He'll try and break us on the Clyde. Especially after the reception he got at St Andrew's Hall yesterday. Our only chance is to widen the movement – form links all over. There's the miners and railway men on Tyneside. We've already contacts on Merseyside and down in Woolwich. (*Laughing*) And there's always the Wheeldons in Derby. I'll make sure they send me to Pear Tree Road. (*Pause*) This is the last dance.

> HETTIE *moves a bit closer.* ARTHUR *is still holding her on his arm. They are intensely aware of one another –* ARTHUR *is visibly affected by* HETTIE's *closeness. But he does not pull her to him.*

Sarah How are we going to get your hat back?

John We're not. I'll get a new one.

Sarah But it was nearly new.

John I'm not wearing a hat that's been sitting in a dustbin, Sarah.

Sarah You're so extravagant.

John Extravagant! I'll go without a hat if necessary. Where's the girl I married – who walked free as the air with me. Now your head's always full of trivialities like lost hats.

Sarah Your hat's not trivial. You'll catch cold without one. Then it'll be . . .

John Shh. (*Kisses her*)

William Jessie! You're not meant to be leading.

Jessie Och. You've no sense of rhythm.

Willie Our opposition to the Independent Labour Party is on a
scientific, not a personal or sectarian basis, Mrs
Wheeldon. We're not anti-political as such. We believe
parliament is a place where socialists must continue to
propagandize.

Alice *(Relieved)* Oh I think it's ending now.

> SARAH *and* JOHN *are still kissing.* ARTHUR *and*
> HETTIE *hold one another after the music stops. They gaze at
> one another.* HETTIE *makes a slight movement towards*
> ARTHUR. *He flinches slightly.*

Alice Hettie, join hands for the singing. *(Grabs* HETTIE's *band.
They form a circle and sing* England Arise. HETTIE *glares
at her mother and mutters about the words of the song.)* Shh.

England arise! the long long night is o'er,
Faint the east behold the dawn appear;
Out of your evil dream of toil and sorrow –
Arise, O England, for the day is here;
> From your fields and hills,
> Hark the answer swells –
Arise, O England, for the day is here!

By your young children's eyes so red with weeping,
By their white faces aged with want and fear,
By the dark cities where your babes are creeping
Naked of joy and all that makes life dear;
> From each wretched slum
> Let the loud cry come;
Arise, O England, for the day is here!

People of England! all your valleys call you,
High in the rising sun the lark sings clear,
Will you dream on, let shameful slumber thrall you?
Will you disown your native land so dear?
> Shall it die unheard –
> That sweet pleading word?
Arise, O England, for the day is here!

Over your face a web of lies is woven,

Laws that are falsehoods pin you to the ground,
Labour is mocked, its just reward is stolen,
On its bent back sits Idleness encrowned.
>How long, while you sleep,
>Your harvest shall It reap?
Arise, O England, for the day is here!

Forth, then, ye heroes, patriots, and lovers!
Comrades of danger, poverty, and scorn!
Mighty in faith of Freedom your great Mother!
Giants refreshed in Joy's new-rising morn!
>Come and swell the song,
>Silent now so long:
England is risen! – and the day is here.

They all walk out still singing. Sounds of 'Goodbye' off-stage.

Curtain

Scene 2

ARTHUR MACMANUS *asleep in bed, 25 March, 12
o'clock midnight, Glasgow.*

Banging on door. ARTHUR MACMANUS *half wakes up.
Two armed detectives burst in; the first particularly brutal, the
second softer, but sneaky.*

First policeman Get dressed.
Arthur What the . . .
Second policeman You're leaving Glasgow.
Arthur You've nae right to do this.
First policeman Get dressed.
Second policeman (*Ironically*) Since when have you been so awful
>fond of rights, laddie.
Arthur You've got nothing on me. What's the charge?
Second policeman (*Seizing* ARTHUR *by the neck of his pyjamas*)
>Blackmailing the government. Reducing munitions. You
>should be shot.
Arthur (*Talking desperately and obviously scared*) They're on strike

at Parkhead because the soldiers are being brought in.
Beardmore's clamping down on Davie Kirkwood.

First policeman (*Shaking* ARTHUR) Shirkers.

Arthur I work at Weir's. We're not even on strike. You've nothing on me I tell you.

Second policeman We're nae here to argue. This is from on top. We're under orders. You're in a spot of bother, laddie.

First policeman We've got you this time. We're going to smash you.

Arthur (*Retreating further into the bed*) I'll nae go.

First policeman (*Menacing him*) Get dressed, you fucking conchie. (ARTHUR *thinks better of it and begins to take his pyjama-jacket off*) Get dressed.

Second policeman Better come quietly, laddie. (ARTHUR *pulls his trousers on*)

Lights

Scene 3

Railway station, 26 March. ARTHUR *is waiting nervously, looking at the time.* WILLIE PAUL *arrives carrying a bag and pushing a bike.*

Arthur I was getting a wee bit anxious.

Willie I'm sorry, Mac. I've been trying to establish what's happened. Here's your bag and your bike. It can go in the guard's van.

Arthur Thanks.

Willie Things are awful confused. Davie Kirkwood and two others from Parkhead, Jim Messer and you from Weir's are all being deported.

Arthur Why us? It doesn't make sense.

Willie We don't know why they picked you. So far Willie Gallacher and Tom Clarke and the rest are all right. They're saying it was the strike meeting on Glasgow Green. They've clamped down on all reporting. They're using emergency powers to keep it hush-hush. It's what we've expected since Christmas.

Arthur Aye, but they caught us wi' our pants down. They must be getting quite detailed information. This strike is a bloody shambles. The real issues of conscription and dilution have got lost. Kirkwood's been like that *(crosses fingers)* wi' Beardmore at Parkhead and now he's turning on his golden boy. So Davie says all out and expects backing.

Willie The Committee's met. Willie Gallacher's against a strike over Parkhead. He said Davie's been going it alone, accepting dilution, flirting with the management, listening to Beardmore's flattery, breaking up the unity of the Committee. He can stew in his own juice.

Arthur Well they've got us then, damn it!

Willie Willie Gallacher's talking of going to London to try and get the deportation lifted.

Arthur Bloody waste of time.

Willie Well, you never know.

Arthur Of course you know. That's playing it on their terms.

Willie We're not in a strong situation. Here's your train coming.

Arthur We should defy the ban. We should present an organized challenge. March into Glasgow. Let them put us in jail wi' John Maclean. He's the only one wi' the guts to defy them.

Willie *(Bundles* ARTHUR *towards the train)* You haven't even left yet. It's a good thing I bought your ticket. I've this for you too. The Defence Committee took a wee collection.

Arthur Will you thank them for me.

Willie Aye. Can you see Davie Kirkwood marching wi' ye? Or Wheatley supporting you on the Defence Committee? Davie'll make windy threats, then you won't see him for dust.

Arthur *(Acknowledges that* WILLIE *is right)* Well he's a good lad in his own way.

Willie He's a good lad, but he's nae basic principles. So he's not at all consistent and he's vulnerable when they praise him for his intelligence. There's no relying on Davie. Stay a wee while with John and Sarah in Edinburgh and then find yourself work in England.

Arthur I'm so browned off wi' working, Willie. I'm awful weary. I want some time to think . . . to live. I need a breather.

Willie Remember Singers.

Arthur Och no, not more needles.

Willie When they sacked you from Singers you took the shop stewards' system of organization all over Clydebank. It'll be all over England this time, Mac.

Arthur Aye, we took more than that. We showed the workers could do for themselves what their officials were too cowardly to attempt. Once people just *see* that happening. It's so simple . . .

Willie It'll be all over England this time. Och, they can smash a committee but they canna' touch an idea when its time has come, man. It's an ill wind . . .

Arthur Ideas wear awful heavy sometimes. Perhaps your ill wind will blow me to Derby.

Willie Get on the train.

Arthur Bye Willie. And thanks. (*He makes to go.*)

Lights fade. Curtain

Scene 4

The next day. Tea at JOHN *and* SARAH CLARKE's *in Edinburgh. They live in a small house crowded with stuffed birds and animals as a result of* JOHN's *circus life, and fossils and ancient flints because of his interest in archaeology and ancient history.* ARTHUR, SARAH *and* JOHN *are having tea.*

Sarah More tea, Arthur? My cake should be ready soon.

Arthur Thanks, Sarah.

John How do you feel?

Arthur I still feel shaken, John.

John Aye.

Arthur We've been expecting something like this. We talked about it on the Committee and Willie's been on about the function of the state over and over again at meetings. Between equal rights, force decides, an' all that. But it doesna' matter. Your sense of strategy and theory. It all falls away. I felt like a wee boy in my bed at home. And the bobbies – they looked enormous. When they come for you, you're just a wee boy in your bed. Sticky wi' fear. It all falls away. It seems unreal like. Och, committee meetings. There's the backbiting, but you know your strength lies in the action the men will take. You can count on men out there in the light of day. But alone in the night, I just wanted to say, why me? It's nae right. It's not fair. I havna' done something bad. I'm just Mac. It's all a mistake.

Sarah They're all shaken by it.

Arthur *(Hopeless defiance)* We should all march back into Glasgow.

John Well, no chance of that.

Arthur *(Despairs)* Everything's stacked against us.

John They caught you off-guard. You lost a skirmish. So you retreat in an orderly manner and plan the next attack from a better position.

Arthur Aye, under the bed.

John It's not like you, Mac.

Arthur Och, I feel like a rest.

Sarah You could go and see Hettie.

> ARTHUR *looks up and smiles but doesn't say anything.*
> Well I'll go and get it.

John What are you on about now, Sarah.

Sarah You've a mind like a sieve. Smell. Where's your nose?

John *(Sniffs)* Something good? I remember, the cake, the cake. Sarah baked a seed cake in your honour.

> ARTHUR *looks very pleased.*
> Wheel it in, love. We're all waiting.

Sarah *(Cross)* Oh slave, live for ever! *(Marches off)*

Arthur You better look out. She'll be away joining the suffragettes.

John No chance, Arthur. I know my Sarah. She knows which side her bread's buttered on – rather, marged, I'm afraid, at the moment. I'll leave the suffragettes to you. Are you going to Derby?

Arthur I've no plans at present. *(Pauses)* I need to take a breather.

John Shh, a minute. *(Smiles)* Listen. *(Dives into cupboard)* Got one.

(Brings out a mouse) That's the third. I have to get rid of them when Sarah's not here. *(Disposes of mouse)* Nice family the Wheeldons. The mother's a bit fierce. Watches over her brood a bit.

Arthur *(Refusing to be drawn)* Mmm. Young William was trying to say something to me a while back. When I met them. I mean he hasna' any grasp of Marxian principles . . . But he's got a point.

John What was it?

Arthur It was awful confused. These splits with Kirkwood. And the bobbies coming that night. Look what the women have been through. There's something missing.

John You're getting very soulful, Mac.

Arthur But you know what I mean.

John I do. But I don't know what it is.

Arthur Mmm.

John There's an awful lot of cranks about in the socialist movement. You become astral-planey.

Arthur Oh aye, right enough.

John And once you get into these questions you can develop a martyrish attitude like the Quakers and some of the suffragettes. Take me, persecute me. Ye'll never break me. I'll die witnessing first. If you're not a spider, then you better be the fly. I'd rather be neither myself.

Arthur But you kind of write about it.

John Well, my verses can be taken as jokes. It doesn't commit you.

Arthur All the phrases – scientific socialist an' all that. They're clanking in my head. The bearings are missing.

John But what are the bearings? I . . .

Arthur Those phrases. They couldna' touch my fear. I couldna' say to Willie even. How do you really face them, John? So they will na' come back. How do we learn what we've never known?

John *(Shakes his head)* I heard Willie say once that socialism wouldn't mean we jumped from society into chaos. The revolutionary movement will have the structure of the new system sort of built up and developed within the old one, ready to replace the old system when it's finally destroyed.

Arthur But they'd never let us. If it's a threat at all . . . Look at what they've done to the Committee . . .

Enter SARAH with a seed cake and oat cakes and tea.

Sarah They're hot. Better eat them now.

They all munch oat cakes and drink tea.

Arthur This is the life. I'll be away biking tomorrow if it stays fine.

Sarah I'll pack you a picnic then.

Arthur Don't trouble yourself, hen.

Sarah It's no trouble. *(Excited)* Shall I cut the cake? I've never made one like this before.

John *(Slightly humouring her, a bit patronizing)* You cut the cake. Ever been on a horse, Mac?

Arthur In Glasgow? No!

John You could have a ride at the stables. I'll be teaching there tomorrow. Arise Sir MacManus. A-rise, get it? *(Groans from ARTHUR and SARAH)*

Sarah Tch. There you are, Arthur.

Arthur Thanks, hen. I think I'll keep to my bike. I can think things through on my bike. Have you a map, John?

Bites cake. A peculiar expression appears on his face, but he doesn't say anything. Chews slowly. Takes another bite cautiously. SARAH senses something and looks nervous.

John Ughh. Sarah. You trying to poison us? Ughh.

Sarah *(Very upset)* Oh, what's wrong with it? Let me try. Ah. It's terrible. It's bitter.

Arthur I thought it tasted funny.

John What have you put in it?

Sarah *(Nearly in tears)* I followed the recipe. I followed the recipe Jenny gave me. I'll go and get it.

John *(Very concerned)* Oh dear, she'll be all upset now. Here, eat some more oatcakes, Mac. Go on, take another one.

Sarah Flour, sugar *(sniff)* I queued for an hour for the sugar. Two eggs, I've been saving them, lard *(sob)* . . .

JOHN puts his arm round SARAH.

John Oh Sal.

Sarah . . . lard, half a teaspoon of suet, marge, seeds, a little milk, a teaspoon of baking powder. I put them all in. I don't understand it. Cream the lard and margarine, add salt and sugar, add the eggs and flour alternately. Then add milk – yes, I did do that right, beat the mixture well. Perhaps I didn't beat it well enough. How long is well? Oh Mac, I'm so sorry.

Arthur It's the thought that matters hen.

Sarah But the cake matters too. I added the seeds. Stirred in the baking powder. Bake in a prepared tin for two hours. I was so worried I'd burn it. It wasn't burnt. *(Sniff)* It looked beautiful. *(Sniff, sniff)*

John Let me try and reconstruct the making of the cake. Give me Jenny's recipe, Sal. *(Screws his eyes up)* Sarah, pass me those seeds. *(Holds recipe and seeds together)* Sally Clarke.

Sarah What is it?

John Jenny wrote caraway seeds.

Sarah Well.

John You put in canary seeds. You put canary seeds in the seed cake.

ARTHUR *and* JOHN *laugh. Slowly* SARAH *begins to laugh.*

What do we need the capitalist class for? We've saboteurs in our own homes.

A knock at the door.

I'll go.

JOHN *goes to answer it, still laughing.* ARTHUR *puts his arm round* SARAH.

Arthur Aye, you're right, the cake was important too. It's terrible when you put your soul into something and it doesna' work out. But really, you know, the laugh was a better tonic than any cake. Your canary seed has blown away my fear, Sarah.

SARAH *smiles, very happy.*

Sarah I was so upset to hear about the police coming in like that. I'd set my heart on that cake.

Arthur The oatcakes were awful good.

Sarah Were they?

Enter JOHN *with* WILLIE PAUL.

Willie I came as soon as I could.

Arthur Any news?

Willie They're still keeping it all hush-hush. We're waiting for Gallacher to get back. I've got a wee surprise.

HETTIE *enters.* ARTHUR *is amazed and overwhelmed to see her.*

Arthur Hettie!

Hettie Oh Arthur, I'm really glad to see you.

He takes her arm. They walk a few paces, wrapped up in one another.

I went straight up to Glasgow. Jessie sent us a telegram. She took me round to Willie's. He was just leaving. I had to come, Arthur. It must have been terrible.

Arthur *(Dramatically)* Well, you've both had a very close escape.

Willie How do you mean?

Hettie Have they been here? Arthur, what's wrong?

John Just a little poisoning incident.

Hettie What? What do you . . .

Arthur It's all right, Hettie. We're teasing you.

Hettie Oh don't.

John Sarah put canary seed in the cake by mistake.

Arthur You know, my head feels awful strange. It seems a wee bit light on my body.

Sarah That's right, blame my cake.

Arthur I think I could fly . . . flap-flap. I'm away.

All laugh.

Willie Canary seed. The war's driving us all mad. Hettie and I have been making a few plans.

Arthur Plans?

Willie Well, someone's got to keep their head on their shoulders.

Groans from the rest except HETTIE *who looks very serious and businesslike.*

It's perfectly clear they'll be following up this particular offensive against the shop stewards' movement. Lloyd George will na' lose the chance to push home the advantage he's got now. He's bound to tighten up the terms of conscription. He's out to smash the shop stewards in munitions.

Sarah John won't be exempt.

Willie No, we'll be needing a place to stay.

John Aye, why hand yourself over to them? What have you to gain.

Willie Hettie has made a few enquiries.

Hettie There's a farm at Arleston outside Derby. It's owned by Mrs and Mrs Turner. They are close to the ILP. They are willing to put men up. It was an old abbey. There are outhouses and a bit of the old walls left, covered with ivy. There's a bell tower. They keep themselves to themselves. No one knows them very well round there. John could go.

Willie I've found a place in Littleover where we could put the paper together. It'd be quieter than Glasgow. I could bike there from Arleston.

Willie You'll have no choice, John. It'll be that or jail.

Arthur If you canna' be the spider, dinna' be the fly.

Lights

Scene 5

JOHN S. CLARK *sitting on a chair in front of the curtains, reads two poems he has written. They may be abridged if necessary.*

The Worm's Banquet

20 million Christians by charlatans enticed
Picked up their guns to follow Jesus Christ.
From Britain, from Belgium, from Russia, from France,
They swore to make the Germans cut a sorry dance.

Every little lawyer monkeyed with the laws,
Every little parson greased his ugly jaws,
Gave a benediction, blessed 'em with a prayer,
And told them how the Son of Man
Was bustin' to be there.

Orators aroused them with perorating rhyme
Labour leaders grunted like a herd of fattened swine,
Climbed with the boss class upon the workers' back
And 'stead o' better ways gave 'em all a gas attack.

Soon they were at it – weltering in slime,
Tearing out Teutonic guts with piety sublime,
Ships with regularity their carcasses disgorge
A loving gift to Davy Jones from brother Davy George.

Trenches full of reeking blood burst from slitten veins,
Trodden down with human pulp, battered bones and brains,
Corpses and sunshine – putridity and smell
Satan with a chuckle – says a paradise is hell.

Two heathen Chinamen stared at all the bother –
One with a curious grin whispered to the other,
'Each little Christian man butchering his brother.
Ain't they got a funny way of loving one another.'

The Voluntary System

The modern British Tommy is a credit to his nation,
He is absolutely full of dour and damned determination.
His four-and-twenty vertebrae are never known to sag
Unless he's *bent* on wiping out an insult to the flag.
And the reason for it is
He is *free* to do his biz
For the British never use coercive measures to enlist 'em
But stake their all on what they call the Voluntary System.

Pooh! The British have no use at all for what is called conscription
They wouldn't use compulsion – or things of that description.
Then each heart gives a single beat, each brain a single think.
And the reason for it is
They control the bally biz
That will go to hell – and – Tommy if the Germans come and twist
'em
So the free are all released to save the Voluntary System.

But the war was not a picnic as was at first anticipated
And the Tipperary trippers they were mostly spiflicated
So the ministry decided not to ask for further aid
But to pass an Act of Parliament to call a spade a spade
And the reason for it was
Absolutely just because
It wasn't naked niggers that had risen to resist 'em
But a folk who never swanked about a Voluntary System.

Scene 6

*Picnic at Arleston near Derby. A bright sunny day. All sitting
on a rug finishing the food.*

Hettie Vesta Tilley!
Willie Let's have an easier one for me, Hettie.
Sarah And me.
Hettie All right – a really easy one.
Jessie If you were a suffragette, who would you be?
Hettie I couldn't be a suffragette. It's too horrible.
Jessie I'll change it then. If you were a member of the working
      class, who would you be?
John I don't see –
Hettie The hangman . . . I'd be the hangman.
Others Ughh.
John A member of the working class!
Sarah Well, I'll ask you a nasty one then. If you were a poison,
      what would you be?

Alice Ugh, it's getting too morbid, this game.

Hettie Curare.

Sarah What's that?

Hettie *(Melodramatically)* It's poison American Indians use on the tips of their arrows.

Florrie Ugh. *(Shudders)*

Hettie It's a crystal. You drop water on it and it goes a chocolate colour. It takes a bit of time to work. Then you fall into a deep sleep – a kind of coma. Then you're dead. Dead as doornails.

Sarah Oh, she's really revelling in it.

Alice How on earth do you know about awful things like that?

Hettie Our Alfred told me about it. He's got some in the lab in Southampton.

Arthur You've provided us with considerable detail, Hettie, but I'm none the wiser. I must have the same kind of brain as Willie. If you were an insect what would you be?

Hettie A louse – sucking other people's blood.

John Lloyd George. It's got to be Georgie – may he pass on speedily into the hereafter.

Alice I'll say amen to that.

Hettie Oh, you'll set her off John.

Alice Thousands and thousands of boys' lives on his hands.

> *Lights change to denote passing of hours.* ALICE, JOHN, SARAH, WILLIE *and* JESSIE *exit.*

> *Later:* HETTIE *and* ARTHUR *walking.*

Hettie What'll you do now?

Arthur How do you mean?

Hettie Will you accept work?

Arthur Not you as well hen. I've enough with Lloyd George, the Ministry of Munitions and the Socialist Labour Party. They're all asking the same question.

Hettie I just wondered like.

Arthur As it happens the Ministry of Munitions has been so kind as to fix me up with employment. They never bothered themselves in peacetime. It takes a war . . .

> *They start to kiss*

Hettie Where'll you be?

Arthur The Cunard Company in Liverpool.

Hettie It's not that far. Oh. (*Very pleased*)

> HETTIE *and* ARTHUR *stay entangled together for some time in mild spooning.* ARTHUR *pushes* HETTIE *gently away.*

Hettie What's wrong?

Arthur I didna' want this to happen.

> HETTIE *recoils.*

> No I don't mean . . . that I didna' want you . . . I've wanted you since I first saw you . . . You're an awful fine woman . . . (*speaking with difficulty and embarrassment*) I mean that I . . . I canna' touch you without . . . er . . . wanting you more than I should. There's nae time for us to be courting.

Hettie They won't know where we are. William might, but he won't say aught.

Arthur I didna' mean that. I'm no the man for you.

Hettie Well, there's summat wrong if there's no time to love. There's summat wrong, that's all.

Arthur (*Puts his arm round her*) Shop stewards are like sailors, hen. But they have meetings, not girls, in every port. We have to bring the shop stewards' movement together. We've failed to stop conscription.

Hettie There's not only you to do it, Arthur. The whole ILP's against the war.

Arthur It's just sentimental.

Hettie Mam and I have been giving out our peace pamphlets.

Arthur There's no power behind you. Nae power. The main resistance must come from the organized rank-and-file workers.

Hettie The organized *skilled* rank and file. What about the women or the unskilled men – the dilutees?

Arthur We're making efforts to get all the men.

Hettie And . . .

Arthur And the women behind us.

Hettie Behind you!

Arthur Och, with us!

Hettie What about the rest of us, like? What are we meant to do? Sit back and watch men die in thousands?

Arthur We have the bargaining power. There's no way your peace pamphlets from the ILP, with a leadership that's turning both ways, or fine speeches, move Lloyd George and the rest. We're fighting a war, Hettie. The enemy is within the gates. We canna' expect politicians like Lloyd George to respond to appeals to their conscience. His political reputation's bound up with this war, you know. Who'll want the warmongers in peacetime?

Hettie Will they want revolutionary shop stewards in peacetime either? You need to strike about prices or something popular. Tch. Oh I'm sick to death of arguing with you about politics. At least you can still get to Derby if you work at Cunards.

Arthur But what kind of courtship is that? Love between committee meetings. It's impossible.

Hettie (*Cross*) Don't you think I can decide who I want to love, Mac. I've thought about politics and all that, like. I'm against the war just as much as you. It's been a lot of work starting our No Conscription Fellowship branch. (*She is upset*)

Arthur But what kind of future have we got, Hettie?

Hettie I'm not bothered about bleddy future, I want my life now.

ARTHUR *softens but shakes his head.*

Arthur That's what I'm saying. There's no abstinence in you.

Hettie (*Appealing*) You know what the song says though.

Arthur What?

Hettie 'There's a good time coming.'

Arthur That's just capitalist propaganda.

Hettie Well, we're only young once.

(*Chants*) Annie made a pudding, she made it very sweet. She daren't stick a fork in it for her life's sake.

Arthur What's that?

Hettie Oh, just a rhyme we used for skipping. Is that capitalist propaganda too?

Arthur I'm not sure about that.

Hettie Ah! (*Mischievously*) I'll tell you what definitely is capitalist propaganda.

Arthur (*Not very interested*) Hmm?

Hettie I saw this picture in the White Hall cinema. There's the young officer. He really likes this girl, if you know what I mean. They start spooning. He's getting all worked up . . bites his lip. Then he asks her . . .

Arthur What?

Hettie If she'll . . . you know.

Arthur Hmm.

Hettie She goes all trembly.

ARTHUR *is getting interested despite himself*

But they don't. She says 'no' after all. 'You would never respect me.'

Arthur (*Interested*) What does the fellow do?

Hettie Well it gets boring then. There's this long middle patch. She's in despair and he struggles with his conscience like. You just want them to get on with it. Until at the end you see them all radiant and coming down the aisle. I were that relieved for them. I don't believe in monogamy and that. It's just private ownership. Bebel and all that. But I were still relieved. He's got his arm in a sling – the wounded hero. She's got him. I could just see him all blonde and pink. You're meant to think, isn't she lucky – wounded too. He won't be able to escape easily, will he? She'll be able to show him off to everybody. 'They were so glad they had waited' comes up on the screen, and the music, and 'The End'. Arthur, what are thinking of?

Arthur I was thinking of Mrs MacManus.

Hettie Who? (*Sits bolt upright in horror*)

Arthur My mother.

Hettie Oh you bugger, you had me worried there. Arthur – don't you know what you can do . . . to stop you getting . . . You could get some of those thingymebobs like . . . That they make for the soldiers. Florrie said Frank Bates had them with him on leave.

Embarrassed silence

Arthur Well they're not completely reliable. If anything went
wrong, Hettie, what would we do? I'm wandering up and
down the country. If the resistance to the war builds up,
we could be . . .

Hettie Don't start on that again.

Arthur You never know when the time will be ripe . . .

HETTIE *puts her hand over his mouth.*

Hettie Until you try.

Lights dim

HETTIE *and* ALICE *sing*

Bread and Roses

As we come marching in the beauty of the day,
A million darkened kitchens, a thousand mill lofts grey
Are touched with all the radiance that a sudden sun discloses,
For the people hear us singing, 'Bread and roses, bread and roses'.

As we come marching, marching, we battle too for men,
For they are women's children, and we mother them again.
Our lives shall not be sweated from birth until life closes;
Hearts starve as well as bodies; give us bread, but give us roses!

As we come marching, marching, we bring the greater days.
The rising of the women means the rising of the race.
No more the drudge and idler – ten that toil where one reposes –
But a sharing of life's glories: Bread and roses! Bread and roses!

Blackout

(These are optional inserts before Act III. If included they should be read like news bulletins by a voice offstage.)

July 1915 *Sheffield Daily Telegraph*

'Lathes and machine tools for shell turning are being installed at the large works as rapidly as they can be obtained. The appearance of numerous machine shops in the East End marks quite a new departure in local industry, and before the end of the war Sheffield promises to be an engineering centre of some consequence.'

George Hodgkinson
'I came to Coventry just after the war started. It was well known for motor cars and motor lorries and its organization, tooling and know-how were easily grafted onto aeroplane work. I was machining engine cases, solid rings of metal like cheeses, for a plane called BEZC, it was something of a challenge, working to fine limits, 100th of a millimetre . . . It was only as the war went on and their craft interests began to be affected that some of them began to realize that there was another war going on, here on the home front. The employers had no conscience at all about war aims and the workers were only pawns in their game . . .

'As the war went on and the manpower problem got more acute, they began what they called "a comb out", which was typical of their attitude, treating working-class people as though they were lice. And as time went on anti-war arguments began to have their effect.'

ACT III

Scene 1

The Engineers Institute, Sheffield, 15 November 1916, 5 minutes to 4 o'clock.

ARTHUR MACMANUS *is in the chair at a shop stewards' meeting – about Leonard Hargreaves, a Sheffield worker conscripted into the army.* HETTIE *is standing outside wearing a coat and selling* The Tribunal, *the paper of the No Conscription Fellowship.* WILLIE PAUL *could either be with her on stage or, if it is possible to arrange it, giving out leaflets to members of the audience. If fire regulations allow and a motor bike can be obtained, he could have a motor bike parked on stage – though it may be difficult to find one from this period! The leaflet could be headed,* 'Repeal the Acts'. *This was the title of a real NCF leaflet around this time. Or it could serve to inform members of the audience that later they will be required to become shop stewards and file on to the stage and off again when the meeting ends.*

Arthur Is it agreed, then, if we have received no satisfactory reply from the government about the reinstatement of Leonard Hargreaves by 4 p.m. that the strike will be called?

Shouts from the audience of 'Yes' and 'Aye'.

Voice Hargreaves must be back in Sheffield in person before we return to work.

Arthur Is that the feeling of this meeting?

Shouts of 'Yes'.

At 4 p.m. all stewards present will immediately proceed *(drops his official labour movement chairman tone and adds jokingly)* at the double *(laughter)* to your factories and inform the stewards on the day-shift of the decision to down tools.

There are two hundred of you at this meeting. We expect 12,000 men out in Sheffield alone. *(Cheers)* Jack Murphy is liaising with Mrs Wilkinson and the National Federation of Women Workers in Sheffield. *(Sexist noises)* We're not forgetting the dilutees. *(More cheers)*

We've already sent men to prepare for sympathetic strike action and to gain recruits for the No Conscription Fellowship, the organization which supports resistance against conscription. They're in the Clyde, in London, in Coventry, Manchester and Liverpool.

At 4 p.m. a fleet of motor cycles will leave for all the main industrial towns in Britain. *(Cheers)*

Willie *(Outside)* Right, lads, Group One is to go southwards.
You've got your routes to Lincoln, Gainsborough,
Nottingham, Leicester, Rugby, Bedford, London.
Group 2, Derby, Coventry, Birmingham, Rugby and
London. Group 3 goes to Manchester, Liverpool, Bolton,
St Helens, Barrow. Group 4, Leeds, Halifax, Bradford,
Keighley. Group 5, straight up to Newcastle, over to the
East Coast, north to Edinburgh and Glasgow.

Hettie Are you sure you'll be able to drive that thing, Willie?

Willie There's nothing to it. It's the same principle as a push bike.

Hettie Well it goes a bit faster.

Willie Nae problem.

Arthur *(Inside meeting)* Arrangements have been made to reinforce
the motor cyclists. Delegates are also going by train.
These delegates are to stay in the big centres until you're
recalled. There'll be a lot of contradictory reports put out
by the press. And keep a sharp look-out for government
informers. The Ministry of Munitions has created its own
spying department. Some of us have experience of that on
Clydebank. It's three minutes to four.

Willie *(To Hettie outside, pulling out his gold watch)* We've three
minutes to go. It's pretty certain the strike's ON NOW.
They'll be coming out soon. Shall I take some papers?

Hettie Don't you have to drive that thing down to Derby?

Willie It'll only take a few minutes to sell them. Let's have a look.
Och no mention of the strike.

Hettie What did you expect!

Arthur Right, two minutes to go. I'll just sum up so you know the
case we're putting. The local Amalgamated Society of
Engineers here in Sheffield has been harassed throughout
this summer with the constant conscription of its
members. The exemptions granted by the Trade cards
have been continually re-examined. All the men were
eventually released. However last month Leonard
Hargreaves, who was a fitter at Vickers, was conscripted
into the army. Management allowed this to happen by
withholding his exemption papers.

Voices in audience Shame. Bring him back.

Arthur The Hargreaves case is a deliberate violation of the pledges

given to the skilled engineers on military service. We
must take a stand on this case. This strike is for the
reinstatement of Leonard Hargreaves. *(Voices cheer – they
can come from the audience)*

Voice *(offstage)* It's nearly 4 o'clock.

Arthur And against the dangers of industrial conscription.

Voices cheer again.

Arthur The ASE district committee has merged with the shop
stewards' committee in Sheffield. Jack Murphy
forwarded the resolution of the ASE Executive to the
Prime Minister on November 9th. We have one minute to
go.

   We have links now with other skilled unions. The
broadest possible basis of resistance is necessary. I don't
have to remind you again of our experience on Clydebank.
The government may now be preparing another list of
wanted men to deport from Sheffield.

Voices Let the fuckers try.

Arthur We must make a determined and united stand now.
Right, you're off lads. Oh – and buy a paper on the way
out.

*Men from audience rush on to stage and out again, if this is
possible to arrange.* ALEX GORDON *and* HERBERT
BOOTH *could be among them.*

Hettie Here they're coming. Buy *The Tribunal*, paper of the No
Conscription Fellowship. One halfpenny. News of
Clifford Allen. A letter from the trenches. Fenner
Brockway on the Australian opposition to conscription.

Willie Russian socialists and conscription. Police raid Russian
socialist groups in London.

Hettie Buy *The Tribunal*, only a halfpenny. Midlands Peace
Convention. Read all about it. Barratt-Brown presides.
Norman Angell, 'Why Freedom Matters'. Join the No
Conscription Fellowship.

*Hettie rushes after the men to gain recruits and buyers for the
paper.* GORDON *could buy a paper.* WILLIE PAUL
remains on stage selling The Tribunal. *When the hubbub dies*

*down, a wounded soldier or an unskilled worker appears
either on stage or in the audience and recites bitterly:*

Soldier/Worker 'Don't send me in the Army, George,
    I'm in the ASE.
    Take all the bloody labourers
    But for God's sake don't take me.
    You want me for a soldier?
    Well that can never be –
    A man of my ability
    And in the ASE.'

Silence falls.

To give HETTIE *time to get ready for the next scene*
WILLIE *could pack his papers in the saddle of the bike. He
could then try to start the bike.*

Willie Damn. It's the same principle as a push bike. But it will na'
start. Damn it.

*He can either get it going eventually and ride off on it or, if the
fire regulations do not allow this, he can glance furtively
around to make sure no one can see his difficulties and simply
wheel it off. Noise off-stage could indicate his trying again
and finally starting.*

Sung – by either a woman or a man – in front of the curtain.

Our Good Friends the Police

Where three men meet together
There some detective dolt
Sees signs of evil weather
And noses out revolt.
To run them in
He is not slow
Less careless he be found,
For 'tis his duty still to show
He makes the world go round.

Chorus
Long live the good police
Long live the good police

Our gentle friends
Our good kind friends
Our dear friends the police.

If 'eer a mortal sneezes
Or looks too gay or grave,
Straight by the ear he seizes
So manifest a knave.
And if by chance
He sneezes twice
Arrests him on the spot,
Before the scamp can do it thrice –
Plain signal of a plot.

Chorus

Tune: *Lass of Richmond Hill.*

Scene 2

Pear Tree Road, in the shop parlour, 26 December 1916.
ALICE *and* HETTIE *are cleaning up after supper.*

Alice Why are you being so mardy, duck?
Hettie I hate bleddy Christmas.
Alice Well it's over now. You can have a nice rest before school
starts.
Hettie How can I have a rest. Socialism takes too many evenings,
if you ask me.
Alice Well you're not secretary of the NCF anymore. Mr Farrow's
doing that for you.
Hettie But you never can get away from it in this house.
Alice Well, what am I to do?
Hettie (*Upset*) I know, Mam. I'm sorry.

ALICE *shakes her head.*

Hettie (*Sighs*) I'm three days late coming on this month. I feel
really nervy.
Alice Hettie you're not . . .

Hettie No, I haven't, if that's what you're thinking. Have you got
  something to bring it on, Mam?

Alice He's no good for you.

Hettie *(Angry)* Don't you think I'm the one to decide that, Mam?

Alice I'm telling you Hettie. I know men.

Hettie Well it didn't do you much good with my dad.

Alice Less bleddy cheek from you, my girl.

Hettie Well you're insulting Mac.

Alice He's a good lad. I've nothing against him.

Hettie Well why isn't he good enough for me then? Lordy, he's a
  fitter, Mam. He'll always find work when he wants it,
  whatever his views.

Alice When he wants it. He's always coming and going. There's
  something . . . He's a waywardness in him.

Hettie That's one of the things I love in him.

Alice All that shop steward business and the Socialist Labour
  Party. I'm not against his politics like. I believe in workers
  standing up for their rights. Get on the make while the
  making's good, if you know what I mean. And he's
  helping the boys to escape. But those organizations.
  You'll have to play second fiddle, like. What'll happen
  when you have kids?

Hettie I won't.

Alice Huh. I've heard that before.

Hettie But Mam, my father's hardly ever been round. He's always
  off on jobs.

Alice So I know what it's like, Hettie.

Door knock.

Who can that be?

Hettie Don't forget, Mam.

Alice What?

Hettie Summat to bring me on.

Alice Shh. *(Opens door. Off-stage voices.)*

Man's voice Mrs Wheeldon?

Exit HETTIE

Alice Yes.

*A man steps inside and shakes hands. He has a long thin face
and sunken eyes. His hair is rather long. It is black and greasy
and thin on top. He is about 30 years old. He is dressed rough.*

Alex Gordon The name's Gordon. Alex Gordon. Ferdy Kearon
gave me your address.
Alice *(A little wary)* Oh come in. How do you know Ferdy?
Alex I got out with him.
Alice Oh.
Alex Yes. Did you hear about that spot of bother they had with
him. They got him into a boat. So far so good. But his
hump was spotted. Gave him away. That's done it now.
We'll have to start all over again. Even Ireland is too
dangerous since the rising. I've been helping men out of
the camps down south. Now we send them all the way to
America with the help of the IWW – the Wobblies. You
know them? *(Alice nods briefly)* Ferdy says your son's in a
camp. *(At the mention of her son all* ALICE's *wariness goes
and she pours out her fears)*
Alice I'm desperate with worry about William. They've done some
dreadful things to him. The officers are the worst. They
took all his clothes away and left him naked in the cell. It
was freezing cold. They put the army uniform in the
middle of the floor. They can watch them and they never
know. If they so much as touch that uniform they say
they're trying to join up. Our William didn't touch it. I'm
that worried. He's not a strong lad at all. I don't know
what they'll do to him next. I'm not getting my sleep at
night. When I lay down, these pictures – horrible pictures
just spring into my mind's eye, like. You heard they shot
those young miners from Durham. And they smuggled
objectors from up in Richmond in Yorkshire to France
and pretended they were deserters. It was only chance it
were found out. They sent them through Southampton
and nobody could stop them. My younger daughter
Winnie and her husband Alfred are in Southampton.
They didn't know anything about it. It was so hush-hush.
Alex Are they against the war as well?
Alice Winnie's a real socialist, she is. She's completely against it. . .

Well Alfred is too. They've got an NCF group down
there. Actually Alfred thinks we take it a bit too far, if you
see what I mean. He's a quiet lad, you know, the educated
type. He teaches chemistry at the college.

Alex Do you trust him?

Alice Who?

Alex This chemistry teacher, Alfred.

Alice Oh he's always willing to help.

Alex They're tightening up all round since Georgie took over.

Alice Damned buggering Welsh sod – he has to live up to his own
promises now. He should be shot himself. It's old men
make the war and young men who die in them.

Alex Mmm.

Alice They were just practising. Then they tried it in Ireland. You
know, forced feeding, prison, breaking up presses,
seizing papers and pamphlets. They killed them and all
after Easter. Lloyd George, he's as slippery as they come.

Alex They've got dogs guarding the camps down in London.

Alice Are they vicious?

Alex They've trained them to be vicious.

Alice Ohh.

Alex We need to get rid of them before we can get the boys out.

Alice They like aniseed, dogs, you know.

Alex We need something stronger. Do you think your son-in-law
would have any ideas?

Lights

Scene 3

29 December, in the second-hand clothes shop, 8.30 p.m.
FLORRIE *and* ALICE *are sitting in the shop.*

Florrie You shouldn't worry about Hettie, Mrs Wheeldon.

Alice I worry about Hettie. I worry about William and Alfred who
they might call up and I worry they'll find Alex
Macdonald before we can get him away. And there's all
the others. We get terrible letters from men in the camps,
Florrie. They're so brave.

Florrie It can't be as bad for them as it is for those that are on the front.

Alice But everybody's against them. They kept this boy knee deep in water in a trench, tied up . . . He nearly died. He was there for days.

Florrie Well they do that and worse to the soldiers. I don't see what else they can expect with thousands getting killed all the time.

Alice Two wrongs don't make a right, Florrie.

Florrie Between you and me I wasn't sorry to see the back of our Frank. Well you have enough of them and their moods, don't you. It was quite a relief at first. But now I feel quite luvvy-duvvy for him at times.

Alice Oh listen to her. You know what they say, 'Absence makes the heart grow fonder.'

Florrie I'm going to get myself a set of those new teeth for when he comes home on leave.

Alice What's wrong with your own teeth?

Florrie The false ones are much whiter. I'll flash him a dazzling smile with my 'pots'. 'Florrie,' he'll say, 'I never saw you in your true beauty before.' He'll take me in his arms then
. . .

Alice Your bleddy teeth'll drop out.

Florrie Tch. I'm going to get my hair henna-ed and all.

Alice You'll be giving my shop a bad name, Florrie Bates.

Enter GORDON *with a big, beery man, aged about 40.*
ALEX GORDON *is dressed 'rough', still.* BOOTH *is dressed smartly, but not quite swagger.* FLORRIE *is quite impressed.*

Alice Oh!

Alex This is my friend Bert. Mrs Wheeldon, Comrade Bert.

Florrie Well, I'll be going. (*Eyebrows slightly arched – a bit curious*)

Alice Bye-bye, Florrie. (*Relieved* FLORRIE *has left quickly*) We'll go next door.

ALICE *motions the men to follow her into the shop parlour.*

Lead straight into the following scene.

Scene 4

Pear Tree Road, in the parlour. ALEX *enters with* BERT, *a clean-shaven, burly man of around 40, full of confident bonhomie.*

Alice So you found one another all right.
Alex Herbert Norton – Alice Wheeldon, you can trust him.
Bert Call me Comrade Bert. Don't believe in ceremony. *(Seizes her hand and pumps it up and down)* From the Industrial Workers of the World – British Section of the Wobblies.
Alice Oh I've heard so much about the Wobblies. Sit down and tell me all about them. I didn't know there were any over here.

They sit down at the table.

Bert We brought a little something.

Pulls out bottles from pockets.

Alice Eh. How did you know I like stout?

ALICE *gets glasses.* BERT *pours out drinks.*

Bert The police raided us in Great Tongue Yard down in London. They came in – smashed the press up.
Alice Tch. They'll stop at nothing now, blooming sods. Lloyd George has given them the go-ahead. They're getting away with all sorts. *(To* GORDON*)* Hettie took it by the 7.15.
Alex Good.
Alice Right. We better tell Mac that William and Alfred and Alex Macdonald are coming. Will you write him a letter to Liverpool?
Bert Have another drink, Mrs Wheeldon. Mind if I call you Alice? Ah she's a woman after my own heart. *(Slaps* ALICE's *knee)*
Alice *(Stiffening suspiciously)* Oh yes!?
Alex Watch it, Bert, she was a suff. Burns churches down with petrol. You were nearly copped. But they never found you, did they, Alice?
Alice I . . .
Bert *(Nudge, nudge)* Let's face it though, Alice. A man's a man and a woman's a woman. Law of nature. Vive la difference.
Alice What do you mean?
Bert Even you suffragettes have to admit it, if you're honest.

(*Leering*) Get down to the nitty-gritty. Have you ever had
   your equality in bed?

Alice Really! (*Horrified*)

Alex (*Quickly in oily tones*) Excuse him, mam – he's a rough
   diamond. He means no harm. Mind your tongue, Bert, in
   the presence of a lady.

Bert (*Unabashed*) She's still a woman after my own heart, suff or
   not. Direct action, aye Alice?

Alice (*Flustered*) That's what I believe in.

Bert None of your vaporizing. Oh those SLPers, terrible I've
   heard. The inevitable contradictions of capitalism. Talk
   the hindlegs off a donkey – never mind the capitalist class.

Alice (*Smiles despite herself*) Well, they're not the only ones.

   BERT *fills her glass again. Puts his legs on the table.*

Alice (*Rather primly*) The Wobblies support the women's cause.
   Joe Hill wrote *The Rebel Girl* for Elizabeth Gurley Flynn.

Bert Oh Gurley. Like that we were. Beautiful girl.

Alice Er . . .

Bert And what about your Independent Labour Party here. Do
   they support the women's cause?

Alice Most of the leaders are mealy-mouthed hypocrites. They
   ponce off the movement.

Bert (*Slaps his knee*) That's my gel.

Alice Now Keir Hardie's gone, I wouldn't trust them as far as I
   could throw them.

Bert (*Laughing*) Alex says you're no friend of Lloyd George's
   neither. What's all this about hiding behind the bushes on
   Walton Heath with an airgun?

Alice (*Laughing*) You never know. No, seriously though, he's
   neither fit for heaven nor blooming hell. All those
   innocent lives. When you think about it.

   HETTIE *enters, stiffens at the sight of* BERT *and* ALEX.
   ALICE *is too carried away to notice her daughter.*

   If anyone should be done in, it should be him and George
   of Buckingham Palace. Royalty, they just ponce off the
   people.

   ALICE *sees* HETTIE *and looks embarrassed.* HETTIE
   glares at BERT *and* ALEX.

Hettie Had a few, Mam? (*Puts lipstick on*) I'm just going down to
   the pub. (*Takes her bag. Exit* HETTIE)

Alice That was my daughter. I should have introduced you.

Bert She seemed to be in a bit of a hurry.

Alice Treats the place like an hotel now. Paints her face. I don't know what she's thinking anymore. She's behind a mask all the time.

Alex All the young ladies do now. It's the war.

Bert Very nice too. We must be getting along. What's the best way to get a parcel through to London, Alice?

Alice Either go to the station or get the Midland Railway van to call and ask the carman to put it on the train. It's safer than the bloody Post Office. I know from my past experience as a postmistress.

Bert Right-o. (*Shakes hands with* ALICE)

Alice Now look here, when I hand the poisons over to you, I wash my hands of it.

Bert What size will they be?

Alice (*Holds up a finger*) There'll be four one-inch phials with different poisons in each. It'll fit in the little tin box I keep my old buttons in.

Bert We should work out a code.

Alice Oh! We did all that in the suffrage movement!

Bert Any ideas?

Alice (*Laughs*) What about, 'We'll hang Lloyd George on a sour apple tree.'

> *Exit* ALEX *and* BERT. ALICE *sits at the table, tries to read a pamphlet. She looks very tired and lonely. She sighs, puts the pamphlet away, goes off-stage to fill her hot-water bottle. Returns slowly carrying the hot-water bottle, shuffling as she walks. She seems to have grown older.*

Scene 5

Herbert Booth is unpacking a parcel.

Herbert Booth A pair of men's socks, must be for the men on the run.

One fruit pie.

A tin of treacle, must have been hoarding this.

A chicken, stuffed.

Ah ha. Four phials. Instructions from Alfred Mason.

'Powder in tube A sufficient for two or three doses.
Powder in tube C by injection only – an airgun dart will
do.
Powder in tube B by mouth or injection.
Powder in tube D injection only.
All are certain. All will probably leave a trace. But if the
bloke who owns it does suspect, it will be difficult to prove
it. Pity the dog if you can get close enough to them. Dead
in 20 seconds.' Dogs, dogs. He didn't say anything about
dogs. They can't be plotting just to kill dogs. Must be a
code within a code. Perhaps the whole family are
completely cuckoo.

Lights

Scene 6

ALICE's *home. Two* POLICEMEN *spotlit, knock on the
door.* ALICE *answers and starts when she sees them.*

Policeman You are charged, Alice Wheeldon, with unlawfully
conspiring with your daughters, Harriet Ann Wheeldon
and Mrs Winnie Mason, along with Alfred George Mason
(husband of the last named) to kill and murder the Right
Honourable David Lloyd George and the Right
Honourable Arthur Henderson, contrary to Section Four
of the Offences Against the Person Act 1861 and against
the peace of our Lord the King, his crown and dignity.

ALICE *makes no reply but seems to shrink hopelessly before
them. She is led off in silence.*

ACT IV

Scene 1

Trial scene, Old Bailey. A witness box. The jury is imagined at one side of the stage, witnesses are spotlit and the audience represents the main body of the court.

F.E. Smith Gentlemen of the Jury. You are faced with desperate and dangerous people, poisoned by revolutionary doctrines, obsessed with an insensate and vile hatred of their own country, sheltering fugitives from the Army. And doing their best to injure Great Britain in the present crisis. Their bitterness is great against the statesmen who have felt it necessary to resort to conscription by compulsion in order to win the war. You may find, Gentlemen of the Jury, some psychological clue to the actions of the accused in hatred which they feel for the two persons mentioned in the indictment, Mr Lloyd George and Mr Henderson. There is a movement amongst a very small portion of the population to avoid military service and to shelter those who had a plea of 'conscientious objection' rejected by the authorities. It is very difficult, Gentlemen of the Jury, to trace such persons. For reasons of security, the prosecution was unable to call Alex Gordon. But I would lay special stress on the evidence of Mr Booth who has brought into the box the diary in which he entered from time to time the incidents of his relation with the Wheeldons.

Herbert Booth *(in witness box)* I sent Alex Gordon to Derby because I thought there was special work for him there. I went to Derby on December 29th on the instructions of my superior officer, Major Lee. On my arrival he told me there were people in Derby who wanted to poison Mr Lloyd George and Mr Arthur Henderson. I arrived that night in Derby about 7 o'clock. I saw Gordon at the Midland Station. The next evening we went to No. 12 Pear Tree Road. Mrs Wheeldon was behind the counter.

She motioned us through to the shop parlour. I heard her say to Gordon, 'Hettie took it by the 7.15.' I told her I had been on the run since September as a moral objector. I think I told her one or two escapades of getting away from the police. And she said to me, 'You know about the Breadsall job, we were nearly copped but we bloody well beat them.' Mrs Wheeldon then showed me the stuffed skin of a snake shaped into a bracelet. She said, 'I wish I had a hundred of them. It's a poisonous one.' I asked her the best way to kill – er . . . poison Lloyd George. I knew from Gordon that she wanted to do this and from the fact that she was sending for the poison. She suggested the best place to 'do in' Lloyd George was on Walton Heath golf course. She said, 'We had a plan before, when we were suffragettes, spent £300 in trying to poison him.'

F.E. Smith I will read some portion of the correspondence of that engaging young woman Hettie, to her younger sister Winnie Mason. This is dated 14th January 1917. Let her speak in her own words.

HETTIE, *isolated in spot, speaks.*

Hettie Well, we shall see what the next move is. What about the big push in May and what about the dark nights round about January 23rd and the new Zepps. Missis, look out. The weather is bitter and if many spend the night in the cellar there'll be a plague of pneumonia.

F.E. Smith Our pacific young lady continues, Gentlemen of the Jury.

Hettie Still, it will serve them right what they get. Who can blame the Germans now for taking their revenge on rhinoceros-skinned, perfidious, canting Britain.

F.E. Smith It will serve them right, 'perfidious, canting Britain'. Is this the language of conscience? Is this the source of conscientious objection to the war – contempt for the people of one's own country? She writes . . .

Hettie Have you heard (but don't suppose you have) of the mutiny at Darlington. Five officers have been killed. Cannot get to know more naturally. Wish it would spread.

F.E. Smith Wish it would spread. Five officers murdered.

Hettie What about Lloyd George visiting the Holy See and God's Vicar? He might be seeing His Majesty himself soon. Pray without ceasing. Tell Alf as soon as the push becomes hot to make a bee-line for here and then things can be considered. I've several suggestions but haven't the time to put them into code now.

F.E. Smith You see, Gentlemen of the Jury, men may die in the trenches every day, but women like Hettie Wheeldon and Winnie Mason reserve their sympathy, their admiration and their succour for the shirkers who avoid the duty of protecting their country. They describe the men who are protecting them as slimy cowards. The whole outlook on life of these women is the same. They are of a completely diseased moral condition.

Turns back to address the full court.

Tell me Miss Wheeldon, what did you discuss with Gordon?

Hettie I discussed emigration. I said assassination was ridiculous.

F.E. Smith And the code you used?

Hettie I wrote to my brother in code for amusement.

F.E. Smith You used the phrase 'dirty cowardly English'.

Hettie It was copied out of a newspaper.

Isolated spotlight away from scene.

Arthur Our attitude is neither pro-German nor pro-British, but anti-capitalist and all that it stands for in every country of the world. The capitalist classes of all nations are our real enemies, and it is against them that we direct all our attack.

F.E. Smith You also hope the mutineers in Darlington would kill their officers.

Hettie No, I hope for the spread of a revolutionary spirit.

Arthur *(Spotlit)* You gave us war, we in return give you revolution.

F.E. Smith And how do you explain your blasphemous wish that Lloyd George might meet His Majesty?

Hettie I hoped he might be shot whilst he was in France. It's not blasphemous for me to speak of God as His Majesty because I'm not a Christian.

F.E. Smith You wish Lloyd George to be shot a few days before your mother obtains poison.

Hettie It was coincidence.

F.E. Smith You say you are not a Christian, yet you read the Scripture with your class and once a week you give a lesson upon them.

Hettie Yes.

F.E. Smith And if the boys use bad language in class?

Hettie I correct them.

F.E. Smith Could you tell the court what your attitude is to the war?

Hettie Certainly. I object to war on principle.

F.E. Smith Do you understand the cause of the war?

Arthur Neither a million dreadnoughts nor twenty lines of defence will save you from the curse of militarism nor the plague of international war.

Hettie No, I don't understand the cause of all this bloodshed. But I think the country's gone war-mad. So I help COs.

F.E. Smith I suggest, Miss Wheeldon, that you were in your mother's confidence.

Hettie No, I wasn't.

F.E. Smith I suggest furthermore that you acted throughout as your mother's agent and messenger in the poison business.

Hettie If I had heard of any poison plot, I would have stopped it. The only way of stopping the war would be if the soldiers dropped their rifles and refused to fight.

Lights change and become softer.

Alice *(in the witness box)* I remember Gordon calling on me in December. He said he was on the run from the police. He asked if he could stay the night. Gordon told me he had assisted two men to escape from an internment camp, one was called Kernan, the hunchback. I sympathized with Gordon's views on Conscientious Objection. We were talking about internment camps and he said these camps were guarded by dogs and there was one way in which Mason, my son-in-law, could help, with poison for the dogs. Gordon said he could help in the matter. I paid

Gordon's fare to Liverpool to see about the emigration
scheme. When the poison came I gave it to Bert . . . er . . .
Mr Booth. He copied the directions. Then we burnt the
document and a letter from Winnie in which she said
somebody would have to get very near the dogs to destroy
them.

F.E. Smith How long is your son's sentence?

Alice Eighteen months.

Isolated spotlight away from scene.

William We were placed with our faces to the barbed wire of the
inner fence. As the ropes with which we were tied
fastened round the barbed wire instead of the usual thick
wooden post, it was possible to tie them more tightly, and
I found myself drawn so closely to the fence that when I
wished to turn my head I had to do so very cautiously to
avoid my face being torn by the barbs.

F.E. Smith Were you active in attempting to assist men to escape
military service.

Alice Yes.

F.E. Smith How long for?

Alice Ever since conscription was introduced.

William *(Spotlit)* I had a black beetle in my mouth one day. This I
readily admit was an exception. Yet I mentioned it to a
worker and he told me not to say anything about it,
because the other prisoners may ask for one too.

F.E. Smith Did you trouble to find out whether the objections
were conscientious or not?

Alice I thought they would not go through these trials if they were
not conscientious objectors.

F.E. Smith Have you a strong feeling against Ministers
responsible for these acts and in particular against Mr
Lloyd George?

Alice Yes.

F.E. Smith And Mr Henderson?

Alice Yes.

F.E. Smith You regard him as a traitor to the labouring classes?

Alice Yes. I am afraid I have a strong antagonism towards them.

F.E. Smith There are certain epithets of a quite disgusting and

obscene kind which we have you using on the evidence of
Mr Booth. (*Changes tone to insolent contempt*) Do you
always talk like that?

Alice I have done recently.

F.E. Smith (*With cold sarcasm*) Ever since you became a pacifist?

Alice I probably said that I wished Lloyd George and Henderson
dead.

F.E. Smith And 'George of Buckingham Palace'?

Alice Probably, in my bitterness. But I never wished to take
anyone's life. I wouldn't have blood on my conscience.

F.E. Smith Do you deny that you were once party to a scheme
organized by the suffragettes to put a poisoned nail in Mr
Lloyd George's boot?

Alice I never did plan anything of the kind. We acted against
property not against life. He's not worth it.

F.E. Smith Is that the only reason? Be careful.

Alice I should not wish to have his death on my conscience.

F.E. Smith Why did you not mention the dogs on arrest or before
the magistrate?

Alice I didn't understand what they were charging me with.

F.E. Smith Thank you, Mrs Wheeldon.

Lights.

Later – summing up.

Now, was the poison bought, as the defence maintains,
for guard dogs? No dogs have ever been employed at any
of the internment camps. The accused were familiar with
the circumstances in these camps. Why would Alice
Wheeldon take the trouble to obtain poison for dogs
which she knows perfectly well did not exist? Gentlemen
of the Jury, I put it to you that in this case mere agreement
and participation constitutes conspiracy. There is not a
man on this Jury knowing what you now know of the
Wheeldons who would not say that the use of Gordon was
justifiable. If the case is not proved without Gordon's
presence to give evidence you are entitled to acquit the
accused. But nothing has been elicited to prove Mr Booth
unworthy of your belief in *his* evidence. As for the youth

of Mrs Wheeldon's daughters, their youth – with the
innocence of youth preserved – only shows more clearly
the degeneracy of their surroundings. You must decide.
Was the poison intended to kill guard dogs or is this story
a desperate invention to cover the conspiracy to murder
the Prime Minister and Arthur Henderson?

Lights out

(Suggested material between Scenes 1 and 2, ACT IV.)

From *Derby Mercury*, Friday, 9 March 1917.

A news boy

DERBY FAMILY ACCUSED OF ATTEMPTED MURDER.
THE SCENE IN COURT.
WAS THE POISON BOUGHT FOR DOGS?

A female solo, sung in front of the curtain.

Law and Order

Since all our institutions are in danger at this moment,
With notions which those socialists do their utmost to foment,
Against all their vile principles which truly most abhorred are,
Let every patriot invoke the power of Law and Order.
   (Repeat last 2 lines)

In every nursery and school and barrack room and prison
Let sheets be stuck upon walls conspicuous to the vision
On which in ornamental text with neat appropriate border
Set out the words, 'Sedition shun and reverence Law and Order.'
   (Repeat last 2 lines of 1st verse)

Scene 2

Arleston, March, early in the morning after the end of the trial. WILLIE PAUL *and* JOHN S. CLARKE *sit outside the farm.*

John Shall I go and see if I can buy a paper?
Willie Mac'll be here soon.

JOHN *paces around.*

Willie They're bound to get off, John. I don't know why F.E.
Smith risked prosecuting – there's no evidence.
John There's a London Jury with an influenza epidemic and
Zeppelin raids.
Willie There's only the word of a police informer to convict them.
John That was a damned silly letter of Hettie's.
Willie Silly, aye. But you don't get sentenced just for silly letters.
John (*Nervy*) I'm going to take the bike.
Willie Look, John – no way can they convict them.
John You don't want to know what's happened, do you?
Willie Calm down, John. I'm just being rational about it.
John Rational. You're so . . .

He is cut short by ARTHUR's *arrival.* ARTHUR *has
travelled through the night from Liverpool. He is white and
haggard.*

What's happened?

ARTHUR *speaks slowly and quietly, as if all the fight were
knocked out of him. They enter the house.*

Arthur Hettie's free.
Willie What did I tell you.
John (*Claps* ARTHUR's *shoulder, relieved*) And the others?

ARTHUR *silently hands him a copy of the paper.*

John (*Reads paper*) Oh no.
Willie Let me see. But this is outrageous. Alice Wheeldon – Ten
years. The judge says, 'The statute under which you have
been convicted limits the punishment for this crime to a

certain period of penal servitude. I can imagine no worse
case than yours and therefore I have no alternative as
regards you, and the sentence is that you be kept in penal
servitude for ten years.'

John She'll be sixty by then.

Arthur She'll never last. She's already weak after these weeks in
custody.

John What about Alf and Winnie?

Arthur Alf got seven years and Winnie five.

Willie The judge says here it was the 'bad wicked influence' of her
mother. You were right, John. We've failed them.

> WILLIE *sits down and systematically begins to read through
> the account of the trial.*

Arthur *(Weakly)* What are we going to do, John?

John *(Shakes his head)* You're asking me? We could track down the
agent provocateur. What's his name?

Willie Gordon. Alex Gordon.

John We could do that for a start.

Arthur Och, he was just their pawn.

John Well you can't be certain of that.

> *Pause.*

John Jessie's bringing Hettie straight back.

Arthur Aye.

John You could spend some time together.

Arthur I've got to get over to Manchester.

John For Christ's sake, Mac. You can't be everywhere. I thought
the shop stewards were against leaders – 'the ferment
creates its own organization' and all that. Let the ferment
ferment a bit by itself.

Arthur They need everyone they can get wi' any experience, you
know that John.

John Doesn't Hettie need you too?

Arthur Aye.

John Well.

Arthur I can come over sometimes. Look man, we're really
building on a broader base at last. We're linking up wi'
different unions through the shops. It's got the solid

> organization we had at Sheffield. But there's vision this
> time. It's going to be really big.

John Well, you'll go your own way Mac, whatever I say.

Arthur I've got no choice, John.

John I don't agree with that. We always have choices, whatever the
pressures.

Arthur What did Connolly say?

Arthur 'Nothing can be accomplished until the structure of the
industrial union is complete.' Hettie agrees wi' that, John.

John Oh aye.

Arthur 'Every fresh shop or factory organized is a fort wrenched
from the capitalist class.'

John What do we do with them once we've got them?

Arthur How do we know when the time is ripe? I asked him that.
He said, 'The time is never ripe until you try.' You have
to try, John.

John You try and F.E. Smith and his mates execute you if you
time it wrong.

Arthur Och, that's an awful cynical approach.

Willie He contradicts his own evidence here.

Arthur Who?

Willie That spy Booth. Listen to the instructions Alf sent. Booth
says he copied them out. There's a phrase, 'The bloke
who owns it. As long as you have a chance to get at the dog
I pity it.' When he's questioned by Smith he says the first
he heard about dogs was in court that day. The defence
doesn't even take it up.

ARTHUR *shakes his head helplessly.*

The man was a lawyer's clerk for twenty-four years. Riza
. . .

John Who?

Willie The defence lawyer – suggests to Booth that this would
mean he'd know how to get people convicted. But Riza
doesn't drive home the point.

Arthur (*Admiringly*) You should have been their defence lawyer.

Willie I'm not trained for the job. The defence was awful weak,
though the Derby solicitor – what's his name now?

Arthur Clifford.

Willie He just fades away after the trial in Derby. Any continuity
was lost. We should've . . .

Enter JESSIE *holding* HETTIE. ARTHUR *rushes to*
HETTIE *and holds her.*

Jessie *(To* JOHN *and* WILLIE) We need to get her to sleep
somehow. We've both been up all night.

Willie I'll go and ask Mrs Turner if she has something. *(Exits)*

Hettie *(Gabbling wildly)* They've got Mam. They've got her. It's
the clutching hand . . . They're . . .

Arthur Hettie love.

Hettie The judge said it was a lamentable case, lamentable to see
women – apparently of education – apparently – using
language – language which would be foul . . . foul, he said,
foul in the mouths of the lowest women. We're the lowest
women. Lower than the lowest. That's as low as you can
get you know. You can't get lower than that.

John It's all hypocritical rubbish, Hettie.

Hettie Nefarious. That's what he called us. Foul and nefarious.
Teachers of the young. We made him wonder whether
education was the blessing he hoped. *(She has a moment of
anger and clarity)* I'd like to see him before my class at
Ilkeston. *(Breaks down again)* I'll have lost my job.
What'll we do. Mam and Winnie and Alf . . .

Arthur Shh Hettie, you must rest, hen. *(Goes to hold her.* HETTIE
breaks loose. Holds up her arm)

Hettie See my snakeskin. It's poisonous you know. You've heard
of the Wheeldons, everybody knows about them. We've a
perverted moral sense. We've been plotting. Oh we've
been plotting. Plotting to stop the murder of millions.

Arthur Hettie. *(Moves towards her and holds her)*

Hettie We got given 300 quid to do in Lloyd George you know. It
was a suffragette plot. Plotting for years. Oh Mrs
Pankhurst came. Britannia, the great patriotic
suffragette. Britannia announces, 'No suffragette plot to
kill Lloyd George.' There was only Mam in the plot. Only
Mam. Alice Wheeldon the murderess. *(Collapses in*
ARTHUR's *arms)* It'll kill her, Arthur. They're out to kill
her. Just like they've killed them all. Jim Connolly, that

Casement, Joe Hill. Mam, she never went for the
limelight. She was just in Derby.

WILLIE *comes back with some tea.*

Jessie Here, drink this, hen.

HETTIE, *exhausted, drinks. Exit* ARTHUR *and* HETTIE

Jessie Well, this is a terrible thing we've allowed to happen.
Willie It seemed so certain she'd be let off.
John Never underestimate F.E. Smith – we should've learned that
by now – especially in court.
Jessie In the trial it was as if time had frozen. He stood there, it was
as if he held time. He could change the past and punish
the future. He had the moments, seconds, minutes,
hours, days like poison crystals running through his
fingers. And Alice's principles. They were just echoes,
bouncing round the room, mocking her own case. Her
world, our world, met his directly, face to face. They're
usually so apart. The judge, Sir Marcus Samuel, Lady
Aylesford, Lady Penrhyn – they let titled ladies in to the
public gallery. It was their peep-show. They trapped
Alice, fixed her with their horrors and fears. And their
world prevailed of course. They've as good as sent her to
her death. At least Alf and Winnie are young.
John But why Alice? There are hundreds of people sheltering men
on the run. There's nothing special about the network in
the Midlands.
Willie Riza asks Booth's superior Major Lee, 'Do you know
whether Gordon is an ex-criminal?' Lee says, 'I have
already explained to you that I do not know the man – I
cannot answer questions on matters beyond my own
knowledge.' The defence lets this drop. Then he says to
Lee, 'Why did you go to Derby?' The reply he gives is
interesting. 'I employed Booth to get into touch with
people who might be likely to commit sabotage.' That
must be sabotage in the munitions factories.
John A school teacher and a second-hand clothes dealer?
Willie Precisely. I think the evidence indicates they were pursuing
Mac.

John But Mac is against sabotage. We've had that argument again
and again.

Willie I don't think the intelligence department of the Ministry of
Munitions can always grasp the finer points of difference
between us. I think they were after Mac, but Alice fell into
their net on the way.

Jessie The same thought had occurred to me.

John It could've been this Alex Gordon trying to clean up his
copy-book with them. That might be why they wouldn't
let him appear in court.

Jessie Why would Booth go along with that?

John I don't know.

Willie Well they must get more credit for an assassination plot than
for finding a network that is just helping men on the run.
They've had quite a few convictions. It's only a £10 fine
after all. This is something sensational, and it can be used
to discredit the anti-war movement.

Jessie Aye, they must be very anxious not to allow the pacifists and
the shop stewards to get too friendly. Divide and rule.
Now Hettie and Arthur . . .

Enter ARTHUR.

Talk of the devil!

Willie Why do *you* think they prosecuted Alice, Mac?

Arthur Why? Capitalism will always devour anyone we do not
defend. They struck where we were weak. We'll have to
do the same to them.

Jessie Surviving's hard enough. I've been getting so much time off
work even Mr Pritchard's becoming edgy. I'll have to be
back by Monday. How long can you stay wi' Hettie, Mac?

Arthur I may have to go over to Manchester if the lads need me.
(Hastily) Hettie could come.

Jessie *(Indignant)* And wait outside shop stewards' meetings in the
state she's in now, Mac? You canna' do that to the lassie.

Arthur They may never send for me.

Jessie But . . .

John *(Quickly)* Shall we go for a walk. Clear our heads. Blow some
of the courtroom gloom away. We can make plans.

Jessie You and Willie go on ahead. We'll catch up.

Exit JOHN *and* WILLIE.

Jessie Now sit down, Mac.

Arthur What . . .

Jessie *(Grimly)* I don't usually interfere Mac, but there comes a point. Now you and Hettie are thinking of getting married.

Arthur How did you know?

Jessie Tch, I've got eyes in my head. How do you think anyone knows anything?

Silence.

Well?

Arthur We're thinking about it. What are you getting at?

Jessie You'll be staying here two weeks.

Arthur Look, Jessie, I canna' commit myself to that.

JESSIE, *furious, stands up and towers above* ARTHUR.

Jessie Arthur MacManus, you're not leaving this chair until I have your promise.

ARTHUR *looks sheepish, sullen and a bit frightened. They stay in silence for a moment.*

Well?

Arthur Look . . .

Jessie It could have been your own mother, Mac. What would you think of Hettie if she left you alone wi' that.

Arthur Och, that would be completely different.

Jessie And why is that?

Arthur Ach, Hettie's not a shop steward.

Jessie There are a few other wee things we lesser mortals do in this world. *(Pauses)* Has it occurred to you, Mac, that they could have got onto Hettie and her family because they've been following you?

ARTHUR *looks stunned.*

Why else should they single out the Wheeldons?

Arthur *(Hesitatingly)* As examples?

Jessie But why pick examples in Derby in the first place? I'm not saying it's certain. I'm saying it's possible.

Arthur Mmm.

Jessie Consider this. They check on Derby after the Sheffield strike. They must keep a watch on you and Willie Paul. They get the address of the NCF. And Alice walks into the trap.

Arthur Mmm.

Jessie I'm not blaming anyone, Mac. I think myself you have a personal responsibility to Hettie. She's the woman you love. But I have observed that it's women and wanes last in the revolutionary struggle, as far as the men are concerned. So I'll put it to you this way. It's your political duty to stay here with Hettie until she can get back on her feet. Will you be staying then?

Arthur Aye. Aye, I'm staying.

Blackout

(Suggested insert between ACT IV, Scene 2 and ACT V, Scene 1, based on F.E. Smith's later account of the Wheeldon case.)

F.E. Smith (*Standing in front of the curtain, reads aloud from a manuscript*) The mother and daughter had been suffragettes of a very extreme and unusual type. There was also that curious masking of Communism under the guise of pacifism which has become increasingly familiar to us since then. (*To himself*) Belligerent pacifists – a most unpleasant phenomenon. (*Reads*) The government was absolutely bound to keep a wary eye on people like the Wheeldons. You remember they were people of some education but little refinement. (*Talking to himself*) This universal education nowadays – a watering down is inevitable in my view. Knowledge without an overall sense of culture. Liable to act on impulse. (*Reads*) Such people can talk themselves into a belief that whatever they think fit to do is for some indefinable reason entirely justifiable and will indeed produce the advent of some vague millennium.

Now Mrs Wheeldon is of a different opinion to Mr Lloyd George. So it is obvious to her for reasons which she never did and probably never could give in intelligible form that he should be removed. And as for the Labour Minister Henderson who had the misfortune to assist his country in time of dire need, he appears merely as the traitor to the cause which for the moment has captured her sympathy. What the conspirators thought they would secure by murdering him – if indeed they thought at all – will probably never be clear to us. They hated Lloyd George and it may be that his death was all they wanted. They were not persons accustomed to reasoning and the most probable explanation is that they hoped that his successor would be terrified into abandoning conscription. How anyone outside of a lunatic asylum could have believed that such a result could be so achieved passes comprehension. Yet none of these persons were insane. At the express request of the Prime Minister, the Home

Office is now reviewing the Wheeldon case. The situation
at present is charged with the most pregnant anxieties.
But it is by no means hopeless. We are in a sense still at
war. *(Speaking as if in a court)* This inscrutable disease,
this bitter enemy of democracy – Bolshevism – has taken
a hold. Bereavement, the hysteria of hope deferred,
perhaps have contributed. The cure can only be time. The
immediate remedies are education and propaganda. We
have to remember that we are not the first to face great
danger. After the battle of Waterloo England passed
through similar anxious years. The unrest then as now
was not peculiar to this country.

ACT V

Scene 1

Outside Aylesbury Prison, 1918.

HETTIE, FLORRIE *and* JESSIE *wait outside Aylesbury
Prison on a visit to* ALICE. *They could have a bench to sit on.*

Hettie *(Upset)* How am I going to tell her?

Florrie You just tell her. You're going to marry him.

Hettie It feels as if we're doing it behind her back.

Florrie You're only saying you've got engaged. You can't wait ten
years, gel.

Jessie Aye it's just a convention really.

Hettie But customs and symbols go deep really. They've got all
kinds of thoughts and feelings and hopes in them. Not
only your own but of people you don't even know.
There's a power in them. You know that in your heart,
Jessie.

Jessie To tell you the truth, hen, I feel at a complete loss.

Hettie Well that's not like you.

Jessie People have different parts to themselves. You canna'
    expect them to be always consistent.

Hettie You've always seemed like a sort of bridge between us and
    Mam. You're her friend but you'd stick up for us as well,
    like.

Jessie Bridges can split in two, lassie. I'm Alice's friend as you say.
    She's in prison. She's weak with hunger striking. We
    share a memory of that kind of thing from the suffrage
    movement. I'm bound to Alice in more ways than one. I
    honestly believe that she will be hurt when you tell her
    you're engaged to Mac. But I've known you since you
    were little. I know when you're serious. I like Mac myself.
    And I can see your love for one another is true. I'm a
    woman who believes in freedom and in love for that
    matter. You canna' expect me to be clearer than that.

Hettie I feel so cut off from her and Winnie. I don't know what to
    say in visiting time – with the screws all round.

Jessie I think you are cut off. Not only by the prison – but
    something growing within you. Och, you'll have to go
    your own way, hen.

Florrie Of course she will.

Hettie But how can I with Mam and Winnie and Alf inside. It was
    my letter that did it.

Jessie Rubbish.

Hettie I should've watched what was going on more carefully.

Jessie So should we all.

Hettie But I was there.

Florrie So was I. I saw them.

Hettie But you couldn't . . . I mean you're not up in the politics of it.

Florrie (*Standing very firmly on her dignity*) You don't need to be a
    school marm to be able to judge character. There was
    something inside out about both those two men. Alice
    should have seen that.

Hettie Well I knew her best. I know what Mam's like. She's too
    friendly. It's always been her weakness. She'd be friends
    with any Tom, Dick or Harry that comes into the shop.

Jessie But there's nothing wrong in that.

Hettie You can't just be friendly. We have to be strong, organized.
    We're fighting a war, aren't we? Here in our own country.

The Enemy within – the clutching hand. That's what took
her in there.

Jessie There's more than one kind of strength.

Florrie Well, I still say Alice should've had more sense – she
should mind what she says to people.

Hettie But look at her now. It's clear to her what she should do.
She'll just hunger strike till she dies.

Jessie Hettie. Now look here, hen. If we learned anything from
the suffrage movement – anything at all from all those
years – it was that women will always feel guilty whatever
their circumstances. We've been struggling with that.
Our own weaknesses – and God knows they exist – but it
wasn't them that put Alice in there. The blame is not with
Alice. It's not with her friends either. You should never
forget that. The responsibility for Alice's fate is with
everything we are against – the whole system of inquiry
agents – och, they're mean and sordid men. It's with the
dictatorial powers that Lloyd George has assumed. Aye
and with conscription and the vicious politics of Tories
like F.E. Smith. And it's with that jury at the Old Bailey
– so consumed with patriotic hatred they would've
convicted anyone against the war on very slender evidence
at that time. Stop torturing yourself, hen. We've got to
use all our energy to try and get Alice freed.

Hettie But I still feel I've betrayed her. I feel I've let my own
mother down. I can make the political arguments as well
as you. It's not them so much. It's something to do with
women as women, if you know what I mean. Then I feel
angry as if I'm being blackmailed by her suffering. Then
I feel guilty again. And angry to feel that. And.

Florrie You're just going round in circles.

Hettie But I still feel I've betrayed her. I feel I've let my own
mother down. I can make the political arguments as well
as you. It's not them so much. It's something to do with
women as women, if you know what I mean. Then I feel
angry as if I'm being blackmailed by her suffering. Then
I feel guilty again. And angry to feel that. And . . .

Florrie You're just going round in circles. You have to make a
break . . .

Hettie I still feel I've let Mam down.

Florrie Don't be so daft, Hettie.

Hettie I feel it, Florrie. I'm just saying what I feel. We're all responsible for one another. Look what she's been going through in there. I mean not only the hunger strike – the conditions. She says it's absolutely filthy inside. They make this great parade about being clean. They get them polishing the brass and they have to scrub all the floors. But Mam said the huge tin ladle they serve porridge with was left in a dirty pail at night with the brush they use to sweep the toilets.

Florrie Ugh.

Jessie There is a certain sense in which Mac represents a – er . . . I don't know if I can put it well – a political difference. It's not simply that he's a man, Hettie. He is na' just any man after all. He's Arthur MacManus, shop steward and member of the SLP.

Hettie (*Laughs*) Why, because the SLP is opposed to the Independent Labour Party's legislative skin ointment and parliamentary pills?

Jessie Not really. Alice is opposed to them too if you think about it. She always wanted more than the vote. Well, I think it's a question of how you see being a socialist.

Hettie I think the Socialist Labour Party is trying to be clear. The Independent Labour Party and women like you and Mam in the suffrage movement, you were on about so much at once. You have to have a clear goal and then you can work out your strategy.

Jessie Och that's the kind of thing Christabel was always telling us.

Hettie Tch. Oh Jessie. You need to have the correct perspective. Just look at the prison buildings. From here we can't see them all. Alice can't from her cell window either. Now if we had a ladder we could climb up it. See the prison as a whole.

Florrie Well I'll give you a leg up.

Hettie Don't you see it's the same with the class war.

Florrie Where's the ladder?

Hettie It's the history of the working class – combined with Marxian economics.

Florrie Well you can count me out for a start. I'd never get my feet
on the first rung.

Hettie Of course you would, Florrie. You're a member of the
working class aren't you?

Florrie Well it depends what you mean.

Hettie We could start an economics class. If we went through
every word in Marx, Florrie, slowly. We'd understand it
all in the end.

Jessie It'll take an awful long time. There'll be two wee grannies
spouting about surplus value. The world would pass you
by.

Hettie *(Discouraged)* He did write a lot.

Florrie He could've left summat out too, Hettie. He never had to
live with aught like Frank Bates did he?

They all laugh.

Jessie *(Sighs)* It all seemed clear before the war. Now I don't know
where I am. Except we've got to do everything we can to
get Alice out. I think they're opening the gates.

Florrie They are.

Hettie I can't talk to her in there.

Florrie Come on, don't waste any of her time. It's too precious.

Exit

Scene 2

WILLIAM WHEELDON, JESSIE, FLORRIE,
SARAH CLARKE, JOHN S. CLARKE, ARTHUR
MACMANUS, WILLIE PAUL *stand singing* England
Arise. *People at the funeral were dressed in navy blue, fawn,
grey and mauve. It may be coincidence, but purple was one of
the suffragette colours.*

Jessie There was always hope in Alice. Even in the terrible
suffering at the end of her life – after her release. She was

terribly weakened by her time in prison. The fever left her
even weaker. The same fever that has affected Hettie and
Mac, which is why they can't be with us today. In the end
it was as if she just faded out of life. But we know Alice
was not simply a victim of the influenza epidemic. She has
suffered also from the persecution by powerful people in
the government and from the ignorant prejudice of many
of her neighbours who accepted the lies about her and
treated her as an outcast after she returned. I think this
isolation from her own people was the hardest part of it for
her to bear. Even when the suffrage struggle was at its
most bitter, she was always loved in her own street. Her
shop was the place to go when you needed help. Alice
loved company and she died a lonely woman. But those of
us who were her friends will not allow her memory to be
forgotten. We will always carry her, her life and her
politics in our hearts. They knew her best who loved her
most.

Alice's friends, WILLIAM WHEELDON *and* WILLIE
PAUL, *carry her coffin across the stage. They hold it ready to
lower it into the ground. As they stand round it,* WILLIAM
WHEELDON *takes a red flag about 3½ feet square from his
pocket. He holds it fluttering in the wind, silently (if wind is
possible to make on stage). Then he places it on the coffin. The
silence is oppressive for a moment. Then they lower the coffin
into the ground. Everyone looks as if the ceremony is over and
they are about to leave, when* JOHN S. CLARKE *struggles
up the bank – the soil is slippery. It may be difficult to have a
bank so he could perhaps come on alone or come to the front of
the stage.*

John We who stand here this afternoon, to take our last farewell of
our comrade Alice Wheeldon, cannot affect that feeling of
awe and reverence for a supernatural God that is supposed
to sustain the Christian in this particular hour of trial. It
would be hard to analyse our feelings on an occasion like
this. But an awe for Great Nature, the great sustainer and
destroyer of the universe. Nature is neither moral nor

merciless. She knows neither good nor evil; she knows only law inflexible, inexorable law. And when her laws are infringed or transgressed she punishes both guilty and innocent alike.

This afternoon we are faced with the climax of one of the world's most poignant tragedies. Don't mistake that – a tragedy. We are giving to the eternal keep of Mother Earth the mortal dust of a poor and innocent victim of a judicial murder – don't mistake it, it was a murder. Incarceration in a prison, the body starved by anxiety. Foul cold-blooded murder. We commit her to the grave where she is beyond further torture by society. She was a Socialist and was an enemy principally of the deepest incarnation of inhumanity at present in Great Britain – that spirit which is incarnated in the person whose name I shall not insult the dead by mentioning. He was one who, in the midst of high affairs of state, stepped out of his way to pursue a poor, obscure family into the dungeon and into the grave.

There are many ways of murdering our valiant women figures. There is a straightforward, brutal way of sheer murder, which killed Rosa Luxemburg. And there is the secret, sinister, cowardly and slower method, which killed Mrs Wheeldon.

Mrs Wheeldon was a Socialist. She was a prophet, not of the sweet and holy by and by, but of the here and now. She saw the penury of the poor and the prodigality of the rich, and she registered her protest against it. She gave her activities to mankind, absolutely unselfishly. But if Mrs Wheeldon could speak she would tell us to go back home not with love and sympathy, but with intense hatred against what fills the world with warfare, poverty or crime, and all such as that. She would tell us to go away to help bear the burden she has had to lay down, so as to obtain that glorious time when peace and joyousness shall fill all life.

JOHN, SARAH, ARTHUR, WILLIE *exit*. JESSIE *and* FLORRIE *stand uncertain over the grave.* JESSIE *shakes her head doubtfully. She looks confused.* FLORRIE *is weeping. The voices of the other mourners are heard singing* The Red Flag.

Jessie *(Softly, sighs)* What would you say, Alice, what would you be thinking. I don't know.

Lights fade. Curtain

Afterword, Fact and Fiction in *Friends of Alice Wheeldon*

In constructing the play I adhered closely to the outlines of the story. Thus the dialogue at the trial is from contemporary reports and the written statements of witnesses in the Public Record Office. I incorporated the language I found in the Wheeldons' letters which were stopped and copied by the police. I also kept to geographical details. For example, the scenes at Arleston are fictional but the Turners did in fact shelter conscientious objectors.[1] Hill Top Farm is still there.

Most of the characters are historical figures and the public incidents in which they are involved occurred, with the exception of the meeting which Arthur MacManus is due to go to in Manchester after the trial. Such a meeting was quite likely in the course of organizing national links in the shop stewards' movement, but I invented the particular incident.

I had, of course, no knowledge of what Willie Paul, Arthur Mac-Manus, the Clarkes and the Wheeldons discussed. Here I used information from memoirs, speeches and articles about the kind of topics that concerned them. Of the courtship between Arthur and Hettie, and the feelings between mother and daughter, I know nothing, and all this is invention. Though again it is probably not historically implausible. For instance, I made Arthur send Hettie Dr Foote's book on popular health and birth control, which might appear to be a somewhat forward thing to do. But he came from a most 'advanced' and earnest political culture in Glasgow. Free love and comradeship in marriage were on the agenda for the revolution as well as the reformist left. Arthur's friend Tom Bell explains in his memoirs, *Pioneering Days*, how Dr Foote's *Plain Home Talk* influenced his thoughts on marriage.[2] It is also likely that these young SLPers knew of the birth control debates among American socialists with whom they were in close contact.[3]

Florrie Bates is pure invention. She is there really to offset the highly charged political intensity, to show Alice among women neighbours. Jessie Campbell, too, I made up. But there was an initial inspiration in the character of the Glasgow working-class socialist feminist, Jessie Stephen.[4] I introduced her so that Alice could relate in the play to a woman around her age who had gone through similar experiences as a socialist in the suffrage movement. But I made her a tougher, less gullible, more head-screwed-on person than Alice. She is similar and yet dissimilar from her friend. Feminists after all come in many shapes and sizes. You can share the same politics in innumerable different ways.

Jessie also complements the younger Marxist men, representing a strand of contemporary Glaswegian politics which offsets and gives another context to their emphasis on workplace organization. This was a politics which grew up around the ILP, the Socialist Sunday Schools, the Herald League and the Clarion Clubs – where there was socialist singing, socialist acting, socialist rambling and socialist camps. There were also various women's labour movement groups with links to the suffragettes' organization, the Women's Social and Political Union. These diverse strands frequently interconnected within the local left community.

Activists might have had their differences, but they knew each other. They could be in the same family or street. Brothers, husbands, sweethearts, fathers, friends from the revolutionary and left groups or trade union movements were brought in on occasions to guard a suffrage meeting or speak at a Socialist Sunday School.[5] It was this family and community network in the Glasgow working class and particularly among the women in and around the ILP which linked into the suffrage movement and during the First World War sustained organization around rents and peace.[6]

I know nothing of Sarah Clarke's views. I made her suspicious of feminism and thus a contrasting voice. This wariness certainly existed among women in the socialist movement and perhaps was likely in a younger generation for whom the suffrage agitation was eclipsed by the war and who were able to observe that the heady dreams of freedom of an older generation were already turning sour as the years passed by.[7]

I was surprised to find that some of my guesswork was nearer to the mark than I realized. I discovered after writing the play that the real Jessie Stephen (rather younger than my Jessie) was in fact in Sheffield as an organizer for Sylvia Pankhurst's Workers' Suffrage Federation during 1916 when the Sheffield shop stewards' strike occurred.[8] So she was in reality not geographically so far away from my Jessie visiting Alice in Derby in the play. I knew that ideas of socialism as a new way of life and spiritual concerns interconnected with both the ILP and the suffrage movement but I really was guessing when I made William Wheeldon express these aspirations in the play. I subsequently learned William was an anarchist and both he and his mother were spiritualists.[9]

Even odder, I invented Alex Gordon's presence at the Sheffield shop stewards' meeting, because I imagined a link between the attempt to spread this strike and his arrival in Derby at the Wheeldons'. I subsequently discovered that he had in fact been in contact with the Sheffield shop stewards – with a letter of introduction from Arthur MacManus.[10]

Before the war the Special Branch numbered around fifty men. During the First World War it extended its activities not only to search for spies, but to collect information on the socialist movement as a whole and anti-war groupings. It was headed by Basil Thomson. Its activities overlapped with those of the newly formed MI5, and there was rivalry between the two departments. The picture was further complicated by the sprouting of several small intelligence units. One of these, attached to the Ministry of Munitions in 1916, was headed by an army officer, Colonel Labouchere. Under him was Major William Melville Lee who employed Herbert Booth and Alex Gordon.[11]

So Gordon and Booth are real enough in my play, but the ruling class who employed this shadowy army of spies and *provocateurs* are not portrayed. This is not because I dismiss their importance in the historical reality. Their action brought tragic results for Alice Wheeldon and her family. They are not represented because I was unable to make them convincing characters. Even when I gave Basil Thomson his own words, he turned into a P.G. Wodehouse slapstick comic and I abandoned the attempt. The problem was, of course, that while Glasgow shop stewards and Midlands feminists are within my ken, I have had little occasion to observe at close quarters gentlemen from the Special Branch, MI5 or members of the Cabinet. I had too little to go on and there was an atrophy of imagination.

John S. Clarke was a satirical poet and historian with roots in the self-taught pedagogic radicalism which was a nineteenth- century working-class heritage with its sweeping theories of ancient history and materialism, and secular alternatives to religion.[12] Willie Paul was a lecturer and theoretical writer best known for his study of the state. Arthur MacManus was destined to become the most famous of the three. At the time of the play, his friend Tom Bell portrayed him as excited by ideas and open to movements which were not necessarily socialist – women's suffrage and Irish nationalism.[13] But his real gift for workplace organizing developed in the wartime shop stewards' movement which arose in resistance to the intensified breakdown of skill demanded by the efforts to increase productivity and increase their hold over their workforce 'dilution'. Again and again, little Mac was able to gain his workmates' confidence. He was evidently able both to stick to the issues that concerned them and to arouse passion and hope for something greater. It was undoubtedly these qualities which made him a target for the fears and hatred of his opponents in the ruling class.[14]

The participation of MacManus and to a lesser extent Paul in the shop stewards' movement took them into a political situation which was more flexible and uncertain than the rigours of sectarianism. They found themselves doing battle at the interstices of transformation, where old forms of working were being replaced by new conditions of labour, as unskilled workers – women – were brought in droves into the war-time engineering industry to boost the production of munitions.

The story has its own momentum as a personal tragedy. I found when I was writing the latter part of the play, where the dialogue is based largely on the historical record, that I became engulfed in sadness. It was as if I was conveying long past grief which refused to be satiated. After the first performance in Rotherham, I turned nervously to a friend to see if it would 'do', and found the sadness was conveyed – she was weeping.

Glossary

Abraham Heights. A hill in Derbyshire, a beauty spot popular with socialist ramblers.

Clifford Allen. A socialist and prominent conscientious objector.

Norman Angell. A writer on peace.

Bally biz. Slang. "Bally is the equivalent of blooming; "biz" is short for business.

Barratt-Brown. A Quaker who was prominent in the No Conscription Fellowship.

Beardmore. An unpopular employer on the River Clyde.

Bleddy. Bloody; it is used by women in the Midlands as it is considered to be not quite swearing.

Boxing Day. The day after Christmas day, when people in nineteenth-century England gave presents—Christmas boxes.

British Socialist Party (BSP). Formed in 1911 by the fusion of the Social Democratic Party and a number of breakaway left-wing groups, it split during the First World War into prowar and antiwar factions; the prowar group joined the Labour Party in 1916.

Fenner Brockway. A member of the Independent Labour Party and founder of the No Conscription Fellowship who was imprisoned for his opposition to the war. He is currently a member of the House of Lords.

But and ben. A Glaswegian term for a one-room upstairs, one-room down, working-class house.

Roger Casement. Supported an unsuccessful Irish rebellion during the war and was executed by the British.

Chesterfield's tower. The Anglican church in Chesterfield, a town in the Midlands, has a leaning tower.

Clarion vans. Horse-drawn propaganda carriages in which socialists took their newspaper *The Clarion* to sell in small villages and towns.

Clarion movement. A propaganda and recreational socialist organization.

Clyde. The river near Glasgow where shipbuilding and engineering industries developed.

Clyde Workers' Committee (CWC). Formed in 1915 on the River Clyde to bring unity to workers' struggles against the conditions of wartime production, it linked together leading engineering stewards who were responsible to workshop committees.

Communist Party of Great Britain (CPGB). Founded in 1920 from several socialist groupings, it was repeatedly refused affiliation to the Labour Party and developed as a separate party.

Conchie. A conscientious objector.

James Connolly (1866–1916). Irish socialist who spent some time in the United States, where he was involved with the Socialist Labour Party and the Wobblies. Returned to Ireland and led the unsuccessful Easter Rising in 1916. Executed by the British.

Dilution. Literally, of course, "watering down," this term was used to describe the breakdown of craft skills in the First World War to enable the unskilled to do the jobs; often meant replacing skilled men with unskilled women.

Douce. Soft.

Dreadnoughts. Battleships.

"England Arise." A song written by the socialist Edward Carpenter about the hope of England becoming socialist.

Fabian Society. Founded in the late nineteenth century, its members argued for state socialism through reforms. Its most notable members were George Bernard Shaw and Sidney and Beatrice Webb.

Reuben Farrow. A Christian pacifist and member of the Derby Labour Party.

Dr. G.W. Foote. An early campaigner for birth control.

Gel. Girl, in Midlands dialect.

Lloyd George. A prominent figure in the Liberal Party who became British prime minister in 1916.

Grock, the clown. A popular entertainer.

Guild socialism. A decentralized approach to socialism based on the democratic control of industry. The movement split after the First World War on whether to seek revolution or to extend control over industry within capitalism as a means of reaching socialism. G.D.H. Cole was its most noted spokesperson.

Keir Hardie. A prominent figure in the Independent Labour Party; supported women's suffrage.

Arthur Henderson. Prominent figure in the Labour Party hated by the left for supporting the First World War.

Herald League. Formed before the First World War to sell *The Daily Herald*, many of these groups became centres of resistance to the war.

Humber. River near Hull.

Hump. Slang for in a bad mood.

Independent Labour Party (ILP). A socialist party formed in 1893. Containing ethical, reformist, and utopian elements, it looked forward to the abolition of class society and the establishment of a socialist commonwealth. Affiliated to the Labour Party, it provided many Labour MPs in the early decades of the twentieth century.

The Irish Worker. A newspaper started by James Connolly when he returned to the United States in 1910.

Irish Socialist Federation. A group started in the United States by James Connolly and Elizabeth Gurley Flynn.

Industrial Workers of the World (IWW: the Wobblies). A trade union that emphasized democratic workplace organization, the IWW attracted unskilled and many immigrant workers. Its ideas had an impact in Britain before the First World War and contributed to the syndicalist upsurge.

Ferdy Kernan. A German Jew living in Hackney, London, and member of the British Socialist Party. On the run in the First World War, he was helped to escape to the United States by Alice Wheeldon and Arthur MacManus. He was identified by having a humpback.

Davie Kirkwood. One of the militant Clydeside shop stewards; joined the Labour Party and became an MP.

Alex MacDonald. A young conscientious objector hiding at Alice Wheeldon's house.

John Maclean. A Marxist orator in Glasgow who attracted large crowds to his lectures.

Mardy. A slang word from the Midlands meaning in a bad mood.

MI5. British intelligence agency.

Ramsey McDonald (1866–1937). Founder and leader of the Labour Party; opposed Britain's fighting in the First World War and therefore associated with the left in this period.

Jack Murphy. Leader of the Sheffield shop stewards.

Lady Muck. A term for a woman putting on an upper-class style.

No Conscription Fellowship. Formed during the First World War to oppose conscription and give support to conscientious objectors, it put out a newspaper called *The Tribunal*.

Bert Parker. A conscientious objector in Derby.

Ponce. Pimp.

Robert Roberts. Author of *The Classic Slum*, an account of domestic and neighborhood life in Salford, in Lancashire.

"The Red Flag." Socialist anthem of the British Labour Party.

Ethel Snowden. Active in Labour women's organizing; wife of Philip Snowden.

Philip Snowden (1864–1937). A prominent figure in the Labour Party.

Socialist Labour Party (SLP). A small Marxist group that emphasized industrial action, but was not purely syndicalist, as it accepted the need for political action as well. Its leader, Daniel deLeon, put out a newspaper called *The Socialist*.

Special Branch. Intelligence wing of the British police.

Spiflicated. Overcome.

Summat. Northern dialect for "something."

Syndicalism. Used loosely, this term meant an approach to rank-and-file industrial organization which emphasized direct action at the workplace; it was antibureaucratic, antiparliamentarian, and antistatist. More narrowly, it referred to the groups around *The Syndicalist*, to which Guy Bowman and Tom Mann were connected.

Vesta Tilley. Popular music hall entertainer.

Trilby. A broad-brimmed soft hat worn by men.

2d. Two pennies, before British currency was decimalized.

Union of Democratic Control (UDC). Established in 1914 to try to make diplomacy more open and democratic, with the aim of preventing war.

Wanes. Scottish term for children.

John Wheatley. A Catholic socialist and member of the Glasgow Labour Party, he became an MP when Labour came to power in 1924.

Mrs. Wilkinson. A friend of Alice Wheeldon and member of the Women's Social and Political Union. A socialist, she kept a health-food shop in Derby and held advanced views on women's dress and sexual liberation.

Women's Co-operative Guild. A large organization of mainly working-class housewives that was formed in order to ensure good-quality products in co-op stores in the late nineteenth century and expanded to take on working conditions, equal pay, better maternity provision, birth control, and even abortion by the 1930s, and was involved in the peace movement between the wars.

Women's Freedom League (WFL). Split from the Pankhursts' Women's Social and Political Union because of disagreements about lack of democracy, it campaigned for peace during the war.

Women's Social and Political Union (WSPU). Grew out of the

Independent Labour Party and was formed by the Pankhursts to campaign for votes for women. It relied on militant direct action and split on issues of internal democracy and links with the labour movement. While its leaders were prowar, many local members opposed militarism. Its newspaper, *The Suffragette*, was renamed *Britannia* during the war.

Women's Suffrage Federation. Developed out of the East London Federation of the Suffragettes, the group Sylvia Pankhurst started when she was expelled from the WSPU in 1913, and put out a newspaper called *The Women's Dreadnought*.

Workers' Socialist Federation. In 1916 the Women's Suffrage Federation took this name, which expressed the broader range of action taken during the war; it changed the name of its newspaper to *The Workers' Dreadnought*.

Zepps. Zeppelins; German air balloons used for bombing.

Notes

Preface, pp. vii–xx

1. *Derby Mercury*, 31 January 1919. See also Raymond
   Challinor, *The Origins of British Bolshevism*, London: Croom
   Helm 1977, pp 144-7; Raymond Challinor, *John S. Clarke:
   Parliamentarian, Poet, Lion-Tamer*, London: Pluto Press 1977,
   pp. 42-5: F.W. Chandler, *Police Spies and Provocative Agents*,
   Sheffield: published by the author, 1936, pp. 100-12; Raymond
   Challinor, articles in *Derby Evening Telegraph*, 13 March 1976,
   and *Socialist Worker*, 10 June 1972.
2. Raymond Challinor, interview with Lester Hutchinson
   former MP for Rusholme, unpublished.
3. See, for example, *Derby Mercury*, 9 March 1917.

Rebel Networks in the First World War, pp. 5-107

Radical Politics in Derby before the First World War, pp. 5-11
1. Sylvia Pankhurst, 'The Alex Gordon Scandal', *Workers'
   Dreadnought* newspaper, 3 January 1920.
2. Raymond Challinor, interview with Lester Hutchinson,
   unpublished.
3. Pankhurst, 'The Alex Gordon Scandal', *Workers' Dreadnought*,
   3 January 1920.
4. Wheeldon Papers, Public Record Office.
5. Pankhurst, 'The Alex Gordon Scandal', *Workers' Dreadnought*,
   3 January 1920.
6. See Sheila Rowbotham, *Hidden from History*, London: Pluto
   Press 1973, for an outline of these controversies.
7. *Derby Daily Express*, 13 June 1914.
8. *Ibid.*, 8 June 1914.
9. *Ibid.*, 17 June 1914

10. Antonia Raeburn, *Militant Suffragettes*, London: New English Library 1973, pp. 238-40.
11. Sylvia Pankhurst, *The Suffragette Movement*, London: Virago 1971, p.501.
12. *Ibid.*, pp. 503-4.
13. G.D.H. Cole, *History of the Labour Party*, London: Routledge & Kegan Paul 1960, pp. 9-10.
14. Reuben Farrow, Reminiscences, unpublished, in Norah Romer's possession.
15. See Sheila Rowbotham and Jeffrey Weeks, *Socialism and the New Life: the Personal and Sexual Politics of Edward Carpenter and Havelock Ellis*, London: Pluto Press 1977.
16. Farrow, Reminiscences, unpublished.
17. G.D.H Cole, *History of the Labour Party*, p.2.
18. Pankhurst, *The Suffragette Movement*, p. 500.
19. Farrow, Reminiscences, unpublished.
20. Information from Albert Chapman, January 1980.
21. Herbert Booth, Evidence in Court, February 1917, Wheeldon Papers, Public Record Office.
22. See Bob Holton, *British Syndicalism 1900-1914*, London: Pluto Press 1976, pp. 180-3.

The Socialist Labour Party and Marxism, pp. 11-25
1. Thomas Bell, *Pioneering Days*, London: Lawrence & Wishart 1941, p. 127.
2. Branko Pribićević, *The Shop Stewards' Movement and Workers' Control, 1910-1922*, Oxford: Basil Blackwell 1959, p. 95.
3. Raymond Challinor, *John S. Clarke: Parliamentarian, Poet, Lion-Tamer*, London: Pluto Press 1977, pp. 42-3.
4. Information from Lester Hutchinson to Ray Challinor.
5. Bell, *Pioneering Days*, p. 126.
6. *Ibid*, p. 127. Another connection might have been through Winnie Mason in Southampton where one of the earlier branches of the SLP had been formed as early as 1910. (Walter Kendall, *The Revolutionary Movement in Britain 1900-1921*, London: Weidenfeld & Nicolson 1969, p. 72.)
7. Bell, *Pioneering Days*, pp. 94-5.
8. Mike Davis, 'The Stop Watch and the Wooden Shoe: Scientific

Management and the Industrial Workers of the World',
Radical America, Vol. 9, No. 1, January-February 1975,
pp. 69-95.

9. Carl Reeve and Ann Barton Reeve, *James Connolly and the
United States: The Road to 1916*, Dublin: Humanities Press
1978, pp. 63, 104, 109. See also Samuel Levenson, *James
Connolly, Socialist, Patriot and Martyr*, London: Quartet Books
1977, pp. 120-82.

10. Kendall, *The Revolutionary Movement in Britain*, pp. 63-72.

11. Bell, *Pioneering Days*, pp. 72-3.

12. Raymond Challinor, *The Origins of British Bolshevism*,
London: Croom Helm 1977, pp. 100-5; and Kendall, *The
Revolutionary Movement in Britain* 72-4; James Hinton,
The First Shop Stewards' Movement, London: George Allen
& Unwin 1973, p. 124.

13. Bell, *Pioneering Days*, p. 75.

14. Challinor, *Origins*, pp. 19-34.

15. *Ibid.*, p. 35.

16. Bell, *Pioneering Days*, pp. 38, 69.

17. William Gallacher, *Revolt on the Clyde*, London: Lawrence &
Wishart 1978 (first edition 1936), pp. 27-8.

18. Sheila Rowbotham, interview with Harry Young, February
1980.

19. William Paul, 'Compulsory Military Service: Should the
Working Class Support It?', Nottingham Socialist Labour
Party, 1912, p. 16.

20. *Ibid.*

21. *Ibid.*

22. *Ibid.*

23. *Ibid.*

24. *Ibid.*

25. William Paul, 'Labour and Empire', Socialist Labour
Party, (no date or page numbers).

26. *Ibid.*

27. William Paul, *Origin of Private Property and the State*,
Socialist Labour Party (no date).

28. Challinor, *John S. Clarke*, p. 34.

29. *Ibid.*, p. 23.

30. *Ibid.*

31. *Ibid.*, pp. 36-7.
32. Quoted in *ibid.*, p. 38.
33. Quoted in *ibid.*, p. 38.
34. *Ibid.*, pp. 37-8.
35. *Ibid.*, pp. 39-40.
36. *Ibid.*, pp. 34-5.
37. Bell, *Pioneering Days*, pp. 85-6.
38. *Ibid.*, pp. 86-92.
39. *Ibid.*, p. 92.
40. *Ibid.*
41. Jean McCrindle, interview with Jessie Findley (unpublished). See also Jean McCrindle and Sheila Rowbotham (eds), *Dutiful Daughters: Women Talk About Their Lives*, Harmondsworth: Penguin 1979, pp. 63-6.
42. Bell, *Pioneering Days*, p. 92.
43. *Ibid.*, pp. 93-4.
44. *Ibid.*, p. 97.
45. *Ibid.*, p. 94.
46. *Ibid.*, pp. 46-52. See also Samuel Levenson, *James Connolly*, p. 49; and Bernard Ransom, *Connolly's Marxism*, London: Pluto Press 1980. Connolly wrote to MacManus on 23 November 1915, regretfully refusing an invitation to speak in Glasgow at an anti-conscription meeting. His presence was required in Dublin 'in constant watchfulness'. (Connolly Archives quoted in Reeve and Reeve, *James Connolly and the United States*, p. 234.)
47. Bell, *Pioneering Days*, pp. 49-50.
48. *Ibid.*, p. 50.
49. James Connolly, 'Forward 23rd August 1913', quoted in Ransom, *Connolly's Marxism*, p.39.
50. See Kendall, *The Revolutionary Movement in Britain*, p. 162; and T.A. Jackson, *Ireland Her Own*, London: Lawrence & Wishart 1971, pp. 401-2.
51. Connolly quoted in Challinor, *The Origins*, p.111.
52. Elizabeth Gurley Flynn, *The Rebel Girl: An Autobiography* London: Masses & Mainstream 1955, revised edition 1973. pp. 29-30, 53-8, 74-6.
53. Reeve and Reeve, *James Connolly and the United States*, p. 208.
54. See Challinor, *Origins*, p. 111; Margaret Ward, *Unmanageable*

Revolutionaries: Women and Irish Nationalism, pp. 252-3; P. Berresford Ellis (ed.), *James Connolly, Selected Writings*, Harmondsworth: Penguin 1973, p. 46; and Reeve and Reeve, *James Connolly and the United States*, pp. 254-5.

55. Berresford Ellis (ed.), *James Connolly, Selected Writings*, p.195.
56. *Ibid.*
57. Bell, *Pioneering Days*, p. 96.
58. *Ibid.*
59. *Ibid.*
60. *Ibid.*, p.88.
61. Lily Gair Wilkinson, 'Revolutionary Socialism and the Women's Movement', Socialist Labour Party, c. 1910, p.9
62. Bell, *Pioneering Days*, pp. 96-7.
63. Tom Anderson, letter to *The Socialist*, April 1914.
64. See Jill Liddington, Afterword in *The Life and Times of a Respectable Rebel: Selina Cooper 1864-1946*, London: Virago 1984, pp. 450-5.
65. Suzie Fleming and Gloden Dallas, 'Jessie', in Marsha Rowe (ed.), *Spare Rib Reader*, Harmondsworth: Penguin 1982, pp. 557-8.
66. McCrindle and Rowbotham (eds), *Dutiful Daughters*, pp. 79, 83.
67. See Fleming and Dallas, 'Jessie', p. 557; and McCrindle and Rowbotham (eds), *Dutiful Daughters*, p. 79.
68. Bell, *Pioneering Days*, pp. 97-100.

Industrial Rebellion in the First World War, pp. 25-33

1. Harry McShane and Joan Smith, *Harry McShane, No Mean Fighter*, London: Pluto Press 1978, pp. 61-2.
2. *Ibid.*, p. 63.
3. Thomas Bell, *Pioneering Days*, London: Lawrence & Wishart 1941, 101-2.
4. *Ibid.*, p. 102.
5. *Ibid.*
6. Raymond Challinor, *The Origins of British Bolshevism*, London: Croom Helm 1977, p. 125.
7. Bell, *Pioneering Days*, p. 102.
8. Sylvia Pankhurst, *The Home Front*, London: Hutchinson 1932, p. 281. The evident hostility in Sylvia's attitude to

Arthur – 'Exceedingly small, almost a dwarf in stature, his
ambitions were great' – was reciprocated. Claude McKay, a
socialist from Jamaica who worked with and admired Sylvia
politically, described Arthur as gunning the hardest after her
in 1922 and calling her 'intellectually dishonest'. (Claude
McKay, *A Long Way from Home*, London: Pluto Press 1985,
p. 198. I owe this reference to Ken Weller.)

9. Bell, *Pioneering Days*, pp. 103-4.
10. Challinor, *Origins*, p. 127.
11. James Hinton, *The First Shop Stewards' Movement*, London:
George Allen & Unwin 1973, p. 106
12. Smith and McShane, *Harry McShane*, pp. 74-6.
13. William Gallacher, *Last Memoirs*, London: Lawrence &
Wishart 1966, p. 71.
14. See Challinor, *Origins*, pp. 132-3; Hinton, *The First Shop
Stewards' Movement*, pp. 113-14; and G.D.H. Cole, *Workshop
Organization*, Oxford: Clarendon Press 1973 (first edition
1923) pp. 48-65.
15. Smith and McShane, *Harry McShane*, p. 74.
16. Hinton, *The First Shop Stewards' Movement*, p. 130.
17. Gallacher, *Last Memoirs*, p. 78.
18. Hinton, *The First Shop Stewards' Movement*, p. 140-1.
19. *Ibid.*, p.141.
20. See Barbara Drake, *Women in Trade Unions*, London: Virago
1984 (first edition 1920), pp. 74-7.
21. William Gallacher, *Revolt on the Clyde*, London: Lawrence
& Wishart, 1978 (first edition 1936) pp. 91-2.
22. *Ibid.*, p. 93.
23. *Ibid.*, p. 94.
24. *Ibid.*
25. *Ibid.*, p. 98.
26. Hinton, *The First Shop Stewards' Movement*, p. 137.
27. *Ibid.*, p. 141. *The Herald*, 8 April 1916.
28. *Ibid.*, p. 159.
29. Branko Pribećević, *The Shop Stewards' Movement and
Workers Control 1910-1922*, Oxford: Basil Blackwell 1959, p. 87.
30. Gallacher, *Revolt on the Clyde*, p. 121.
31. See *ibid.*, p. 106, and David Kirkwood, *My Life of Revolt*,
London: George G. Harrap 1935, pp. 132-4.

32. Gallacher, *Last Memoirs*, p. 83.
33. Challinor, *Origins*, p. 139.
34. Kirkwood, *My Life of Revolt*, p. 134.
35. *Ibid.*, p. 139.
36. Gallacher, *Revolt on the Clyde*, p. 130.
37. *Ibid.*, pp. 108-11.
38. *Ibid.*, pp. 126-7.
39. *Ibid.*, p. 127.
40. Bell, *Pioneering Days*, p. 125.
41. *Ibid*, p. 125.
42. Challinor, *Origins*, p. 144.

Anti–War Proposals, pp. 33-40
1. Christabel Pankhurst quoted in Andre Linklater, *An Unhusbanded Life: Charlotte Despard, Suffragette, Socialist and Sinn Feiner*, London: Hutchinson 1980, p. 177.
2. Sylvia Pankhurst, *The Suffragette Movement*, London: Virago 1971, pp. 599-600.
3. Jill Liddington, 'The Women's Peace Crusade: the History of a Forgotten Campaign', in Dorothy Thompson (ed.), *Over Our Dead Bodies: Women Against the Bomb*, London: Virago 1983, pp. 188-9.
4. Raymond Challinor, *The Origins of British Bolshevism*, London: Croom Helm 1977, p. 138.
5. Fenner Brockway, 'Inside the Left', *New Leader*, 1947 (first edition 1942), pp. 26, 66-8.
6. Clifford Allen quoted in David Boulton, *Objection Overruled*, London: MacGibbon & Kee 1967, p. 101.
7. Brockway, 'Inside the Left', p. 73.
8. Boulton, *Objection Overruled*, p. 251.
9. Basil Thomson, *The Scene Changes*, London: Collins 1939, p. 222.
10. Brockway, 'Inside the Left', p. 113.
11. Boulton, *Objection Overruled*, p. 211.
12. *Ibid.*, p. 177.
13. *Ibid.*, p. 211.
14. *Ibid.*, p. 153.
15. *Ibid.*, p. 172.
16. *Ibid.*, p. 154.

17. *Ibid.*, p. 254.
18. Challinor, *Origins*, p. 142
19. Brockway, 'Inside the Left'.
20. See Sheila Rowbotham, *Dreams and Dilemmas*, London: Virago 1983, pp. 235-9.
21. Letter from a conscientious objector to Hettie Wheeldon, 9 January 1917, Wheeldon Papers, Public Record Office.
22. Information from Albert Chapman, February 1980.
23. Reuben Farrow, MSS.
24. *Ibid.*
25. *Derby Mercury*, 9 March 1917.
26. Challinor, *Origins*, p. 244.
27. Notes on the Shop Stewards' Movement, Milner Papers, Bodleian Library, Oxford, p. 10.
28. *Ibid.*, pp. 24-5.
29. *Ibid.*, p. 109.
30. Herbert Booth, Statement at the Wheeldon Trial, Wheeldon Papers, Public Record Office, p. 14.
31. Hettie Wheeldon to Winnie Mason, 14 January 1917, Wheeldon Papers, Public Record Office.
32. Winnie Mason to the Wheeldon family, 31 December 1916, Wheeldon Papers, Public Record Office.
33. *Ibid.*
34. *Derby Mercury*, 9 March 1917.
35. Letter from a conscientious objector to Hettie Wheeldon, 14 January 1917, Wheeldon Papers, Public Record Office.
36. Hettie Wheeldon to Winnie Mason, 14 January 1917, Wheeldon Papers, Public Record Office.
37. Brockway, 'Inside the Left', p. 53.

Spies and the Shop Stewards' Movement, pp. 40-48

1. James Hinton, *The First Shop Stewards' Movement*, London: Allen & Unwin 1973, p. 174.
2. *Ibid.*, p. 162.
3. *Ibid.*, p. 176. See also J.T. Murphy, *Preparing for Power*, London: Pluto Press 1972 (second edition), p. 128; Bill Moore, 'Sheffield Shop Stewards in the First World War', ed. Lionel M. Munby, *The Luddites and Other Essays*, London: Michael Katanka Books 1971, p. 246.

4. Hinton, *The First Shop Stewards' Movement*, p. 170.
5. *Ibid*, p. 170.
6. James Hinton, 'Introduction' to Murphy, *Preparing for Power* (second edition), p. 11.
7. Sheila Rowbotham and Jeff Weeks (eds), *Socialism and the New Life*, London: Pluto 1977. See also Edward Carpenter, 'Long Live Syndicalism', *The Syndicalist*, May 1912.
8. Notes on the Shop Stewards Movement, Milner Papers, pp. 62-3
9. Murphy, *Preparing for Power*, pp. 129-30.
10. *Ibid.*, p. 130.
11. Hinton, *The First Shop Stewards' Movement*, p. 176.
12. *Ibid.*, p. 177.
13. *Ibid.*, p. 210.
14. F. de Valda, *Full Measure*, London: Arthur Barker 1933, p. 218.
15. Notes on the Shop Stewards' Movement, Milner Papers, p. 53.
16. *Ibid.*, p. 64.
17. *Ibid.*, pp. 66-7.
18. *Ibid.*
19. *Ibid.*
20. *Ibid.*
21. J.T. Murphy, 'New Horizons', in R. and E. Frow and Michael Katanka, *Strikes: A Documentary History*, London: Charles Knight & Co. 1971, p. 10.
22. Notes on the Strike Movement, Milner Papers, p. 17.
23. 'Spies Report Liverpool Strike'. Notes on the Strike Movement, Milner Papers, p. 48. See also Weller, *Don't Be A Soldier, The Radical Anti-War Movement in North London, 1914-18*, London: Journeyman Press 1985, p. 51.
24. DMS, 'Spies Report Liverpool Strike', Notes on the Strike Movement, Milner Papers, p. 48.
25. *Ibid.*, pp. 47-8.
26. Unofficial Reform Committee, The Miners' Next Step, London: Pluto Press 1973. On the impact on shop stewards, see Hinton, *The First Shop Stewards' Movement*, p. 289.
27. Hinton, *The First Shop Stewards' Movement*, p. 290, and Pribićević, *The Shop Stewards' Movement and Workers' Control*, p.99.
28. Notes on the Strike Movement, Milner Papers, pp. 73-4.

29. *Ibid.*, p. 12.
30. *Ibid.*, p. 98.
31. *Ibid.*, p. 108.
32. *Ibid.*, p. 28.
33. *Ibid.*, p. 63.
34. List of individuals connected with the Labour and Peace Movements in Wales, 10 December 1916, Notes on the Strike Movement, Milner Papers, pp. 168-75; and Rough List of names and addresses of individuals connected directly or indirectly with the recent strike in Sheffield. Notes on the Strike Movement, Milner Papers, p. 81.
35. Notes on the Strike Movement, Milner Papers, p. 20.
36. *Ibid.*, p. 89.
37. *Ibid.*, p. 4.
38. *Ibid.*, pp. 106-7

The 'Poison' Plot, pp. 48-59

1. Herbert Booth, Statement at Wheeldon Trial, 5 February 1917, Wheeldon Papers, Public Record Office.
2. 'Spies Report Liverpool Strike', Notes on the Strike Movement, Milner Papers, p. 48.
3. Notes on the Strike Movement, Milner Papers, pp. 62-4.
4. Bill Ward quoted in Bill Moore, 'Sheffield Shop Stewards in the First World War', in Munby (ed.), *The Luddites and Other Essays*, London: Michael Katanka Books 1971 pp. 255-6.
5. Herbert Booth quoted in F.W. Chandler, *Police Spies and Provocative Agents*, Sheffield, 1936, p. 103.
6. Notes on the Strike Movement, Milner Papers, pp. 142-3.
7. F. de Valda, *Full Measure*, London: Arthur Barker 1933, p. 219
8. Notes on the Strike Movement, Milner Papers, pp. 142-3. 'A' to W.M.L., 9 January 1917, Wheeldon Papers, Public Record Office.
9. Weller, *Don't Be a Soldier, The Radical Anti-War Movement in North London, 1914-1918*, London: Journeyman Press 1985, p. 51.
10. de Valda, *Full Measure*, p. 219.
11. Notes on the Strike Movement, Milner Papers, p. 146.
12. Munitions in Derby, *Derby and Chesterfield Reporter*, 2 March 1919.

13. Herbert Booth, Statement at Trial, Wheeldon Papers, Public Record Office.
14. Chandler, *Police Spies and Provocative Agents*, p. 107.
15. *Ibid.*, p. 103.
16. Booth Statement, Wheeldon Papers, Public Record Office.
17. *Ibid.*
18. Chandler, *Police Spies and Provocative Agents*, p. 107.
19. de Valda, *Full Measure*, p. 270.
20. Chandler, *Police Spies and Provocative Agents*, p. 107.
21. *Ibid.*
22. de Valda, *Full Measure*, p. 221.
23. *Ibid.*
24. Chandler, *Police Spies and Provocative Agents*, p. 104.
25. Booth Statement, Wheeldon Papers, Public Record Office.
26. *Ibid.*
27. Chandler, *Police Spies and Provocative Agents*, p. 107.
28. *The Times*, 8 March 1917, quoted in Chandler, *Police Spies and Provocative Agents*, p. 108.
29. William Melville Lee, report of Second General Conference of the Rank and File Movement, 3 and 4 March 1917. Notes on the Strike Movement, Milner Papers.
30. Derby Mercury, 9 March 1917.
31. Herbert Booth, Statement at the Wheeldon Trial, Public Record Office; and Chandler, *Police Spies and Provocative Agents*, p. 109.
32. Winnie Mason to Alice Wheeldon, 29 January 1917, Wheeldon Papers, Public Record Office.
33. Hettie Wheeldon to Winnie Mason, 14 January 1917, Wheeldon Papers, Public Record Office.
34. *Ibid.*
35. Chandler, *Police Spies and Provocative Agents*, p. 106.
36. *Derby Mercury*, 9 March 1917.
37. Chandler, *Police Spies and Provocative Agents*, p. 105.
38. *Derby Mercury*, 16 March 1917.
39. *Ibid.*
40. *Ibid.*, 9 March 1917.
41. Winnie Mason to Alice Wheeldon, 7 January 1917, Wheeldon Papers, Public Record Office.
42. Wheeldon Papers, Public Record Office.

43. Winnie Mason to Alice Wheeldon, January 1917, Wheeldon Papers, Public Record Office.
44. Wheeldon Papers, Public Record Office.
45. Winnie Mason to Alice Wheeldon, 7 January 1917, Wheeldon Papers, Public Record Office.
46. *Derby Mercury*, 16 March 1917.

Divisions in the State, pp. 59-67

1. Bentley B. Gilbert, *British Social Policy 1914-1939*, London: B.T. Batsford 1970, p. 3.
2. *Frederick Edwin, Earl of Birkenhead*, by his son, London: Thornton Butterworth 1935, p. 5.
3. Pankhurst, *The Home Front*, London: Hutchinson 1932, p. 185.
4. See Sheila Lewenhak, *Women and Trade Unions*, London: Ernest Benn 1977, pp. 144-63.
5. Pankhurst, *The Home Front*, p. 186.
6. *Ibid*.
7. Lewis Minkin, *The Labour Party Conference*, Manchester: Manchester University Press 1980, p. 382.
8. Alan Clarke (ed.), *A Good Innings, The Private Papers of Viscount Lee of Fareham*, London: John Murray 1974, p. 142 (first limited edition 1939). See also *Who's Who*, 1926.
9. Interview with the Right Honourable Christopher Addison in the United States, *The Manufacture of Munitions*, London: James Truscott 1916, p. 2.
10. James Hinton, 'The Clyde Workers' Committee and the Dilution Struggle', in Asa Briggs and John Saville (eds), *Essays in Labour History, 1886-1923*, London: Macmillan 1971, p. 154.
11. David Lloyd George, *War Memoirs*, Vol. 1, London: Odhams Press 1938, p. 147.
12. Hinton, 'The Clyde Workers' Committee and the Dilution Struggle', in Briggs and Saville (eds), *Essays in Labour History, 1886-1923*, p. 155.
13. Frederick Edwin, Earl of Birkenhead, by his son, pp. 50-1.
14. See Tony Bunyan, *The History and Practice of the Political Police in Britain*, London: Quartet 1977, pp.10-11.
15. Frederick Edwin, Earl of Birkenhead, by his son, p. 58.

16. Lloyd George, *War Memoirs*, Vol. 1, p. 82.
17. Constantine Fitzgibbon, *Out of the Lion's Paw*, London: Macdonald Library of the Twentieth Century 1969, pp. 56-62, 83-5.
18. William Camp, *The Glittering Prizes*, London: MacGibbon & Kee 1960, p. 112.
19. *Ibid.*, p. 45.
20. *Ibid.*, p. 62.
21. Bunyan, *Political Police in Britain*, pp. 35-6.
22. T.A. Jackson, *Ireland Her Own*, London: Lawrence & Wishart 1971, pp. 392-76.
23. Camp, *The Glittering Prizes*, p. 60.
24. *Ibid.*, p. 127.
25. See *ibid.*, pp. 46, 60, 99, and Frederick Edwin, Earl of Birkenhead, by his son, p. 31.
26. Camp, *The Glittering Prizes*, p. 62.
27. *Ibid.*, p. 44.
28. R.J. Minney, *Viscount Addison, Leader of the Lords*, London: Odhams Press 1958.
29. Clarke (ed.), *A Good Innings*, p. 148; Lloyd George, *War Memoirs*, p. 556.
30. See Sylvia Pankhurst, *The Home Front*, p. 420. See also Lloyd George, *War Memoirs*, Vol. 1, p. 550.
31. Lloyd George, *War Memoirs*, p. 581.
32. Quoted in Christopher Sykes, *Nancy, The Life of Lady Astor*, London: Panther 1979, p. 194.
33. Clarke (ed.), *A Good Innings*, p. 151.
34. *Ibid.*, p. 165.
35. *Ibid.*, p. 163.
36. *Ibid.*, pp. 8-72.
37. Gilbert, *British Social Policy*, p. 6.
38. Camp, *The Glittering Prizes*, p. 105.
39. *Frederick Edwin, Earl of Birkenhead*, by his son, p. 83.
40. Bunyan, *Political Police in Britain*, p. 116 (footnote).

Rival Intelligence Agencies, pp. 67-80

1. F. de Valda, *Full Measure*, London: Arthur Barker 1933, pp. 19-129.
2. Letter from E.R. Hardcastle to Raymond Challinor, 13

August 1978. (I am grateful to Ray Challinor for this reference.)

3. Booth Statement, Wheeldon Papers, Public Record Office.
4. *Ibid*.
5. Smith, *Famous Trials of History*, p. 221.
6. Lester Hutchinson, interview with Raymond Challinor, unpublished.
7. Booth Statement, *Wheeldon Papers*, Public Record Office.
8. *Derby Mercury*, 9 March 1917.
9. *Ibid*.
10. E.R. Hardcastle, letter to Raymond Challinor, 13 August 1978.
11. Thomas Bell, *Pioneering Days*, London: Lawrence & Wishart 1941, p. 177.
12. *Daily Herald*, 27 December 1919.
13. *Workers' Dreadnought*, 3 January 1920.
14. *Daily Herald*, 27 December 1919.
15. Colonel Labouchere, Addison Papers, Late 1916–early 1917, Bodleian Library, Oxford. (I owe this reference to Guff Putowsky.)
16. *Daily Herald*, 27 December 1919.
17. *Ibid*.
18. *Ibid*.
19. *Ibid*.
20. 'Spies report Liverpool Strike', Notes on the Strike Movement, Milner Papers, pp. 47-9.
21. 'Memoranda of Statement 13/12/16', Notes on the Strike Movement, Milner Papers, pp. 97-8.
22. Notes on the Strike Movement, Milner Papers, pp. 108-9.
23. *Daily Herald*, 27 December 1919.
24. *Derby Mercury*, 9 March 1917.
25. Notes on the Wheeldon Case, Milner Papers, p. 142.
26. *Ibid*., p. 142.
27. *Ibid*.
28. *Ibid*., p. 144.
29. *Ibid*., p. 145.
30. *Ibid*.
31. de Valda, *Full Measure*, p. 218.
32. Basil Thomson, *Queer People*, London: Hodder & Stoughton 1922, p. 266.

33. Tony Bunyan, *The History and Practice of the Political Police in Britain*, London: Quartet 1977, p. 111.
34. *Ibid.*, p. 113.
35. *Ibid.*, pp. 154-5.
36. Nigel West, *MI5*, London: Bodley Head 1981, p. 49.
37. *Ibid.*, pp. 46-9.
38. Thomson, *Queer People*, p. 266.
39. *Ibid.*, p. 266.
40. *Ibid.*, p. 270.
41. Basil Thomson, *The Scene Changes*, London: Collins 1939 pp. 273, 275, 284.
42. Thomson, *Queer People*, p. 320.
43. *Ibid.*, p. 270.
44. Basil Thomson, *The Story of Scotland Yard*, London: Grayson & Grayson 1935, pp. 235-8.
45. *Ibid.*, p. 238.
46. Thomson, *Queer People*, p. 274.
47. Thomson, *The Story of Scotland Yard*, pp. 238-9.
48. *Ibid.*, p. 240.
49. *Ibid.*
50. See R.J. Minney, *Viscount Addison, Leader of the Lords*, London: Odhams Press 1958, pp. 109-37.
51. See Christopher Addison, *Four and a Half Years*, Vol 1, London: Hutchinson 1934, pp. 135-42, 187.
52. *Ibid.*, p. 235.
53. *Ibid.*, Vol. 2, p. 324.
54. Memo by Kellaway to Minister, 9 February 1917, Addison Papers.
55. Addison to Kellaway, February 1917, Addison Papers. (I owe these references to Guff Putowsky.)
56. Notes on the Strike Movement, Milner Papers, p. 123.
57. Umberto Woolf to Kellaway, 12 February 1917, Addison Papers. (I owe this reference to Guff Putowsky.)
58. Raymond Challinor, *The Origins of British Bolshevism*, London: Croom Helm 1977, p. 147.
59. Unnamed informer, Notes on the Wheeldon Case, Milner Papers, p. 146.
60. Bell, *Pioneering Days*, p. 125.
61. Thomson, *Queer People*, p. 274.

62. *Manchester Guardian*, 6 August 1919.
63. Notes on the Strike Movement, Milner Papers, pp. 143-4.
64. Walter Hill was a friend of Carpenter and put Gordon up for the night.
65. Unnamed informer, 10 March 1917, Notes on the Strike Movement, Milner Papers, p. 146.
66. Notes on the Wheeldon Case, Milner Papers, p. 144.
67. F.W. de Valda, *Adventure Is My Business*, London: Herbert Jenkins 1941 pp. 129-30.
68. John Buchan was Press Liaison Officer for MI5 in 1917, West, *MI5*, p. 47.
69. See West, *MI5*.
70. de Valda, *Full Measure*, p. 222.

Prison and its Aftermath, pp. 80-83
1. F.W. Chandler, *Police Spies and Provocative Agents*, Sheffield: 1936, p. 101.
2. Anne Marrecco, *The Rebel Countess: The Life and Times of Constance Markiewicz*, London: Corgi 1969, p. 219.
3. *Ibid.*
4. *Ibid.*
5. *Ibid.*, p. 220.
6. *Derby and Chesterfield Reporter*, 28 February 1919; *Derby Daily Express*, 22 February 1919. See also Bell, *Pioneering Days*, London: Lawrence & Wishart 1941, p. 126.
7. Reuben Farrow, letters.
8. Sylvia Pankhurst, *Workers' Dreadnought*, 3 January 1920.
9. *Ibid.*
10. *Ibid.*
11. *Derby Daily Express*, 22 February 1919.
12. *Derby Mercury*, 28 February 1919, 7 March 1919.
13. *Ibid.*, 28 February 1919.
14. *Ibid.*
15. *Ibid.*
16. *The Socialist*, 6 March 1919.
17. *Ibid.*
18. Raymond Challinor, *The Origins of British Bolshevism*, London: Croom Helm 1977, p. 145.
19. *Derby Daily Express*, 22 February 1919.

20. Sylvia Pankhurst, *Workers' Dreadnought*, 3 January 1920.
21. Challinor, *Origins*, p. 146.
22. W. Mellor, *Daily Herald*, 20 December 1919. Thomson had become 'Director of Intelligence' in May 1919. But he fell from grace in 1921. The reasons for his dismissal are not clear. William Camp says he was convicted of a sexual offence (Camp, *The Glittering Prizes*, London: MacGibbon & Kee 1960, p. 112). Tony Bunyan says Lloyd George decided to take seriously an incident in which four young Irishmen painted 'Up the Sinn Fein' on his summer house, which Thomson had decided to treat as a prank, but that there was probably pressure from both the War Office, which wanted to boost MI5, and from the Metropolitan Police who disliked Thomson's autonomy (Tony Bunyan, *The Political Police in Britain*, London: Quartet 1977, p. 118).

Bearing the Burden, pp. 83-97
1. *The Socialist*, 6 March 1919.
2. Jill Liddington, 'The Women's Peace Crusade', in Dorothy Thompson (ed.), *Over Our Dead Bodies*, pp. 192-5.
3. Suzie Fleming and Gloden Dallas, 'Jessie', in Marsha Rowe (ed.), *Spare Rib Reader*, Harmondsworth: Penguin 1982, p. 133.
4. Derby Monthly Reports, Women's Guild, October 1919.
5. *The Socialist*, 6 March 1919.
6. *Ibid.*, 20 November 1919.
7. *Ibid.*, 27 November 1919.
8. Liddington, 'The Women's Peace Crusade', in Dorothy Thompson (ed.), *Over Our Dead Bodies*, p. 193.
9. *The Socialist*, 20 November 1919.
10. *Ibid.*, 21 August 1919.
11. *Ibid.*
12. *Ibid.*
13. *Ibid.*
14. *Ibid.*, 11 December 1919.
15. Doris Alison, letter to Sheila Rowbotham, February 1980.
16. Harry Young, interview with Sheila Rowbotham, February 1980.
17. Smith, *Famous Trials*, p. 223.

18. *The Socialist*, 13 February 1919.
19. *The Socialist*, 21 August 1919.
20. Information from Albert Chapman.
21. Harry Young, interview with Sheila Rowbotham, February 1980.
22. Thomas Bell, *Pioneering Days*, London: Lawrence & Wishart 1941, p. 128.
23. Rough List of names and addresses of individuals connected directly or indirectly with the recent strike at Sheffield, Milner Papers, p. 79.
24. Notes on the Strike Movement, Milner Papers, p. 177.
25. James Hinton, *The First Shop Stewards' Movement*, London: Allen & Unwin 1973, pp. 216-20.
26. *Ibid.*, p. 215.
27. J.T. Murphy, *The Workers' Committee: An Outline of its Principles and Structure*, London: Pluto Press 1972 (first edition 1917), p. 18. See also Sylvia Pankhurst, *The Home Front*, London: Hutchinson 1932, p. 162, on the issue of equal pay. On the organization of women workers and the emergence of the demand for equal pay, see Barbara Drake, *Women in Trade Unions*, London: Virago 1984, pp. 68-110.
28. Hinton, *The First Shop Stewards' Movement*, p. 237.
29. *The Socialist*, 14 February 1920.
30. Hinton, *The First Shop Stewards' Movement*, pp. 196-212.
31. Ken Coates, Introduction, *British Labour and the Russian Revolution*, London: Spokesman (no date), p. 114. Challinor, *The Origins of British Bolshevism*, London: Croom Helm 1977, p. 213.
32. Bell, *Pioneering Days*, p. 125. Raymond
33. Bell, *Pioneering Days*, p. 149. See also *British Labour and the Russian Revolution*.
34. Coates, *British Labour and the Russian Revolution*, p. 14.
35. William Gallacher, *Revolt on the Clyde*, London: Lawrence & Wishart 1978, p. 144.
36. *Ibid.*, pp. 177-8.
37. Bell, *Pioneering Days*, pp. 150-1.
38. *Ibid.*
39. *The Socialist*, 1 December 1918.
40. *Ibid.*

41. Bell, *Pioneering Days*, pp. 158-9.
42. *The Socialist*, 1 December 1918.
43. Walter Kendall, *The Revolutionary Movement in Britain 1900-1921*, London: Weidenfeld & Nicolson 1969, p. 386.
44. Bell, *Pioneering Days*, p. 159.
45. Challinor, *Origins*, p. 192.
46. *Ibid.*, pp. 199-200.
47. *The Socialist*, 6 March 1919.
48. *Ibid.*, 30 January 1919.
49. *Ibid.*, 14 February 1920.
50. *Ibid.*
51. J.T. Murphy, *Preparing for Power*, London: Pluto Press 1972.
52. See Murphy, *The Workers' Committee*, pp. 14-15. In MacManus's case this was to shift towards the conviction that a leadership could not reliably emerge from specific struggles. Those who had been working to create the crisis had to provide the lead. In 1925, he claimed that this was Connolly's position, though, in my view, the scattered notes on Anabaptism and other early movements of social protest do not justify such an interpretation. See Arthur MacManus's Foreword to 'James Connolly: the Beginnings of Communism', *Communist Review*, July 1925, p. 119.
53. Bell, *Pioneering Days*, p. 180.
54. Kendall, *The Revolutionary Movement in Britain*, pp. 199-211.
55. *Ibid.*, p. 217.
56. *Ibid.*, p. 231.
57. *Ibid.*, p. 229.
58. Challinor, *Origins*, p. 232.
59. L.J. Macfarlane *The British Communist Party*, London: MacGibbon & Kee 1966, p. 95.
60. Bell, *Pioneering Days*, p. 193.
61. Cathy Porter, *Alexandra Kollontai*, London: Virago 1980, p. 388.
62. Harry Young, Interview with Sheila Rowbotham, February 1980.
63. Claude McKay, *A Long Way From Home*, London: Pluto Press 1985, pp. 200-21.
64. Macfarlane, *The British Communist Party*, pp. 84, 286.
65. Nigel West, *MI5*, London: Bodley Head 1981, pp. 78-9.

66. Tony Bunyan, *The History and Practice of the Political Police in Britain*, London: Quartet 1977, pp. 158-61.
67. West, *MI5*, p. 79.
68. Kendall, *The Revolutionary Movement*, p. 339.
69. *Ibid.*, p. 326.
70. *Ibid.*, p. 390.
71. See Raymond Challinor, *John S. Clarke: Parliamentarian, Poet, Lion-Tamer*, London: Pluto Press 1977, p. 61.
72. *Ibid.*, pp. 57-85.

Preparing for Power, pp. 97-107
 1. J.T Murphy, *The Workers' Committee: An Outline of its Principles and Structure*, London: Pluto Press 1972.
 2. Stuart Hall, 'The State: Socialism's Old Caretaker', *Marxism Today*, November 1984.
 3. E.P. Thompson, Postscript 1976 to *William Morris, Romantic to Revolutionary*, London: Merlin 1977, p. 792; and E.P. Thompson, 'The Soviet Union: Detente and Dissent', in *The Heavy Dancers*, London: Merlin Press 1985, p. 129.
 4. E.P. Thompson, Postscript, p. 792.
 5. F.M. Atkinson, 'Syndicalism', *Daily Herald*, 20 June 1912.
 6. *Ibid.*
 7. Ken Weller, *Don't Be a Soldier, The Radical Anti-War Movement in North London, 1914-1918*, London: Journeyman Press 1985, p. 6.
 8. Bertrand Russell, *The Ploughshare*, August 1916, quoted in Raymond Challinor, *The Origins of British Bolshevism*, London: Croom Helm 1977, p. 137.
 9. See Sheila Rowbotham, *A New World for Women, Stella Browne, Socialist Feminist*, London: Pluto Press 1977.
10. Jean Gaffia and David Thoms, *Caring and Sharing: The Centenary History of the Co-operative Women's Guild*, Manchester: Co-operative Union 1983.
11. Noreen Branson, *Popularism 1919-1925, George Lansbury and Councillors' Revolt*, London: Lawrence & Wishart 1979.

Friends of Alice Wheeldon, Foreword pp. 111-121

1. See Richard Pankhurst, Introduction to E. Sylvia Pankhurst, *The Suffragette Movement*, London: Virago 1977 (first edition 1931), pp. 500-19.
2. See C.L. Mowat, 'Ramsay MacDonald and the Labour Party', in Asa Briggs and John Saville (eds), *Essays in Labour History 1886-1923*, London: Macmillan 1971, pp. 139-40.
3. Leonard Hall, 'My Version of "Syndicalism"', *The Syndicalist*, May 1912.
4. Ken Weller, *Don't be a Soldier: The Radical Anti-War Movement in North London, 1914-1918*, London: Journeyman Press 1985, p. 10. On the Wobblies and offshoots in Britain, see *ibid.*, pp. 63-9. On the Socialist Labour Party see Raymond Challinor, *The Origins of British Bolshevism*, London: Croom Helm 1977; and Walter Kendall, *Revolutionary Movements in Britain, 1900-1921*, London: Weidenfeld & Nicolson 1969. On syndicalism see Bob Holton, *British Syndicalism 1900-1914*, London: Pluto Press 1976; and Geoff Brown, 'Introduction' in *The Syndicalist*, Nottingham: Spokesman Books 1975. On links with anarchism see John Quaill, *The Slow Burning Fuse*, London: Quartet 1978.
5. *The Syndicalist*, July 1912, November 1912, December 1912, February 1913. The syndicalists were also active among teachers: *The Syndicalist*, January 1914.
6. Geoff Brown, 'Introduction' in *The Syndicalist*, p. viii.
7. Holton, *British Syndicalism*, p. 186.
8. Papers found at 12 Peartree Road in December 1916. Wheeldon Papers, Public Record Office.
9. Challinor, *Origins*, p. 144. Debate G.G. Coulton MA National Service League *v*. William Paul, 'Compulsory Military Service: Should the Working Class Support It?', Nottingham Socialist Labour Party, 1912.
10. James Hinton, 'Introduction' in J.T. Murphy, *The Workers' Committee: An Outline of its Principles and Structure*, London: Pluto Press 1972 (first edition 1917), p. 3.
11. Alastair Hatchett, 'Introduction', in William Gallacher and J.R. Campbell, *Direct Action: An Outline of Workshop and Social Organization*, London: Pluto Press 1972 (first edition

1919), p. 13. See also Richard Hyman, 'Foreword', in Carter
L. Goodrich, *The Frontier of Control*, London: Pluto Press
1975 (first edition 1920), pp. vii-xix.

12. See, for example, William Gallacher, *Last Memoirs*, London:
Lawrence & Wishart 1966, and *Revolt on the Clyde* (1936),
London: Lawrence & Wishart 1978; David Kirkwood, *My
Life of Revolt*, London: George C. Harrap 1935.

13. See, for example, Branko Pribićević, *The Shop Stewards'
Movement and Workers' Control, 1910-1922*, Oxford: Basil
Blackwell 1959; Holton, *British Syndicalism;* James Hinton,
The First Shop Stewards' Movement, London: George Allen &
Unwin 1973. For recent correctives to this approach, see Ken
Weller, *Don't be a Soldier: The Anti-War Struggle in North
London 1914-1918*, London: Journeyman Press 1985; and
Joan Smith, 'Liverpool and Glasgow Labour Tradition',
History Workshop Journal, No. 17, Spring 1984.

14. For a discussion of these biases in feminist historiography, see
Jill Liddington, *The Life and Times of a Respectable Rebel:
Selina Cooper 1864-1946*, London: Virago 1984, pp. 450-5; Jill
Liddington, 'Rediscovering Suffrage History' *History
Workshop Journal*, No.4, Autumn 1977, pp. 192-203; Jill
Liddington and Jill Norris, *One Hand Tied Behind Us: The Rise
of the Women's Suffrage Movement*, London: Virago 1978;
Geoffrey Mitchell, Hannah Mitchell (eds), *The Hard Way Up*,
London: Virago 1977; Ada Nield Chew, *The Life and Writings
of a Working Woman*, presented by Doris Nield Chew,
London: Virago 1982. On links with Irish nationalism see
Margaret Ward, *Unmanageable Revolutionaries: Women and
Irish Nationalism*, London: Pluto Press 1983; Andre Linklater,
*An Unhusbanded Life: Charlotte Despard, Suffragette, Socialist
and Sinn Feiner*, London: Hutchinson 1980.

15. See Sheila Rowbotham, *Hidden from History*, London: Pluto
Press 1973.

16. See Hall, 'My Version of "Syndicalism"'; F.J. Pinnell Dalson,
letter to Guy Bowman: 'Personally, I am a Socialist who believes
in direct action, and like yourself in a new morality, but we have
a long way to go yet, for to my mind neither Syndicalism nor
Socialism, as taught today will do; but both combined.
Syndicalism alone would lead to the re-enacting of the history

of the Guilds; Socialism alone, to State capitalism and officialism.' *The Syndicalist*, July 1912.

On Edward Carpenter's synthesis of socialism, syndicalism and feminism, see Chushichi Tsuzuki, *Edward Carpenter 1844-1929: Prophet of Human Fellowship*, Cambridge: Cambridge University Press 1980, pp. 157-63. For American echoes of similar debates see Philip S. Foner, *Women and the American Labor Movement: The Wobblies and the Women Worker*, New York: Free Press 1979, pp. 184-204: and Bruce Dancis, 'Socialism and Women in the United States, 1900-1917', *Socialist Revolution*, No. 27, Vol. 6, No. 1, January-March 1976, p.120.

17. See David Coates, *The Labour Party and the Struggle for Socialism*, Cambridge: Cambridge University Press 1975. p. 12.

18. See, for example, Rowbotham, *Hidden from History*; Liddington and Norris, *One Hand Tied Behind Us*; Geoffrey Mitchell, Hannah Mitchell (eds), *The Hard Way Up*; Chew, *The Life and Writings of a Working Woman*; Linklater, *An Unhusbanded Life*; Suzie Fleming and Gloden Dallas, 'Jessie', in Marsha Rowe (ed.), *Spare Rib Reader*, Harmondsworth: Penguin 1982, pp. 553-61; Liddington, *Selina Cooper*; Pankhurst, *The Suffragette Movement*; Jill Liddington, 'Looking for Mrs Cooper' and Angela Tuckett, 'Enid Stacey and Linda Grant: Women's Work and Trade Unionism in Liverpool, 1890-1914', in 'Women and the Labour Movement', *Northwest Labour History Society Bulletin*, 1980-81; Jean Gaffin and David Thoms, *Caring and Sparing: The Centenary History of the Co-operative Women's Guild*, Manchester: Co-operative Union 1983.

19. See Stephen Yeo, 'A New Life: The Religion of Socialism in Britain 1883-1896', *History Workshop Journal*, No. 4, Autumn 1977, pp. 5-57; Stanley Pierson, *Marxism and the Origins of British Socialism: The Struggle for a New Consciousness*, Ithaca and London: Cornell University Press 1973; Sheila Rowbotham and Jeffrey Weeks, *Socialism and the New Life: the Personal and Sexual Politics of Edward Carpenter and Havelock Ellis*, London: Pluto Press 1977; Sheila Rowbotham, 'In Search of Carpenter', in *Dreams and Dilemmas*, London: Virago, 1983 pp. 234-56

20. See Pankhurst, *The Suffragette Movement* and *The Home Front*, London: Hutchinson 1932; Challinor, *Origins*; Fenner Brockway, 'Inside the Left', *New Leader*, 1947, pp. 43-119; David Boulton, *Objection Overruled*, London: MacGibbon & Kee 1967; Weller, *Don't Be a Soldier*; Sheila Rowbotham, 'She Lived Her Politics, Lilian Wolfe', in *Dreams and Dilemmas*, pp. 235-9; and Sheila Rowbotham, 'Florence Exten-Hann, Socialist and Feminist', *Dreams and Dilemmas*, pp. 223-8.
21. Robert Barltrop, *The Monument: The Story of the Socialist Party of Great Britain*, London: Pluto Press 1975, p. 57.
22. Notes on the Wheeldon Case, Milner Papers, p. 143.
23. *Ibid.*
24. Jill Liddington, 'The Women's Peace Crusade, The History of a Forgotten Campaign', in Dorothy Thompson (ed.), *Over Our Dead Bodies: Women Against the Bomb*, London: Virago 1983, pp. 180-98.
25. *Ibid.*, p.192.
26. See F.W. Chandler, *Police Spies and Provocative Agents*, Sheffield 1936, pp. 101-2, and Challinor, *Orgins*, pp. 124-30.
27. Barltrop, *The Monument*, p. 56.
28. See Boulton, *Objection Overruled*, pp. 133, 154, 172-3, 211-18.
29. Bentley E. Gilbert, *British Social Policy, 1914-1939*, London: Batsford 1970, pp. 2-25.
30. See Barbara Drake, *Women in Trade Unions* (1920), London: Virago 1984, pp. 68-110; and Sheila Lewenhak, *Women and Trade Unions: An Outline History of Women in the British Trade Union Movement*, London: Ernest Benn 1977, pp. 144-63.
31. Mowat, 'Ramsay MacDonald and the Labour Party', p. 145.
32. Tony Bunyan, *The Political Police in Britain*, London: Quartet 1977, p. 161.
33. Stuart Hall, 'The State: Socialism's Old Caretaker', *Marxism Today*, Vol. 28, No. 11, November 1984, p. 25.
34. See Gaffin and Thoms, *Caring and Sharing*, pp. 16, 68-73; also Rowbotham, *Hidden from History*; Sheila Rowbotham, *A New World for Women: Stella Browne, Socialist Feminist*, London: Pluto Press 1977; Dora Russell, *The Tamarisk Tree: My Quest for Liberty and Love*, London: Elek/Pemberton 1975, pp. 169-89.
35. Annie Davison in McCrindle and Rowbotham (eds), *Dutiful*

Daughters, Women Talk About Their Lives, Harmondsworth:
Penguin 1979, pp. 65-6.

Friends of Alice Wheeldon, Afterword, pp. 200-205

1. Raymond Challinor, *The Origins of British Bolshevism*,
   London: Croom Helm 1977, p. 144.
2. Thomas Bell, *Pioneering Days*, London: Lawrence & Wishart
   1941, pp. 85-6.
3. See Linda Gordon, *Woman's Body, Woman's Right*,
   New York: Grossman 1976, pp. 186-245; Bruce Dancis,
   'Socialism and Women in the United States 1900-1917',
   Socialist Revolution, No. 27, Vol. 6, No. 1, January-March
   1976, pp. 96-7; Mari Jo Buhle, *Women and American Socialism,
   1870-1920*, London and Urbana: University of Illinois Press
   1983, pp. 268-80.
4. Suzie Fleming and Gloden Dallas, 'Jessie', in Marsha Rowe
   (ed.), *Spare Rib Reader*, Harmondsworth: Penguin 1982,
   pp. 553-61.
5. *Ibid.*, pp. 553-7.
6. Jean McCrindle, interview with Jessie Findley, unpublished;
   Annie Davison, in Jean McCrindle and Sheila Rowbotham
   (eds), *Dutiful Daughters: Women Talk about Their Lives*,
   Harmondsworth: Penguin 1979, pp. 62-6; William Gallacher,
   Last Memoirs, London: Lawrence & Wishart 1966,
   pp. 71, 102; William Gallacher, *Revolt on the Clyde* (1936),
   London: Lawrence & Wishart 1978.
7. Sarah Clarke is mentioned in Raymond Challinor, *John S.
   Clarke, Parliamentarian, Poet, Lion-Tamer*, London: Pluto
   Press 1977, p. 42. Annie Davison expresses comparable
   reservations in her reflections on the Glasgow anarchist-
   feminist Annie Gordon in McCrindle and Rowbotham (eds),
   Dutiful Daughters, p. 83.
8. Fleming and Dallas, 'Jessie', pp. 558-9'; Sylvia Pankhurst;
   The Home Front, London: Hutchinson 1932, p. 372. There
   were links with J.T. Murphy, one of the leaders of the
   Sheffield shop stewards, and with F.W. Chandler, then a
   prominent figure in the Sheffield Socialist Labour Party.
9. I am grateful to Albert Chapman for this information.

10. DMS report on the Liverpool strike, p. 48, and AG report, p. 62. Notes on the Strike Movement Now Developing in the North and West of England, Milner Papers.
11. Tony Bunyan, *The History and Practice of the Political Police in Britain*, London: Quartet 1977, pp. 111-17; and Nigel West, *MI5*, London: Bodley Head 1981, p. 49.
12. On John S. Clarke see Challinor, *John S. Clarke*.
13. Bell, *Pioneering Days*, pp. 94-7.
14. *Ibid.*, pp. 125-7.

Index